EL DORADO COUNTY LIBRARY

3 1738 00366 2473

D0426779

EL DORADO COUNTY FREE LIBRARY
345 FAIR LANE
PLACERVILLE, CALIFORNIA 95667

DISCARD

They Also Served

OTHER BOOKS BY
OLGA GRUHZIT-HOYT

Lust for Blood, 1984
Exorcism, 1978
Demons, Devils, and Djinn, 1974
American Indians Today, 1972
Aborigines of Australia, 1969
The Bedouins, 1969
Witches, 1969
If You Want a Horse, 1965

with Edwin P. Hoyt:
Freedom in the News Media, 1973
Censorship in America, 1970

They Also Served

American Women in World War II

Olga Gruhzit-Hoyt

A Birch Lane Press Book
Published by Carol Publishing Group

EL DORADO COUNTY FREE LIBRARY
345 FAIR LANE
PLACERVILLE, CALIFORNIA 95667

DISCARD

Copyright © 1995 by Olga Gruhzit-Hoyt

All rights reserved. No part of this book may be reproduced in any form, except by a newspaper or magazine reviewer who wishes to quote brief passages in connection with a review.

A Birch Lane Press Book
Published by Carol Publishing Group
Birch Lane Press is a registered trademark of Carol Communications, Inc.
Editorial Offices: 600 Madison Avenue, New York, N.Y. 10022
Sales and Distribution Offices: 120 Enterprise Avenue, Secaucus, N.J. 07094
In Canada: Canadian Manda Group, One Atlantic Avenue, Suite 105, Toronto, Ontario M6K 3E7
Queries regarding rights and permissions should be addressed to Carol Publishing Group, 600 Madison Avenue, New York, N.Y. 10022

Carol Publishing Group books are available at special discounts for bulk purchases, sales promotions, fund raising, or educational purposes. Special editions can be created to specifications. For details, contact Special Sales Department, Carol Publishing Group, 120 Enterprise Avenue, Secaucus, N.J. 07094

Manufactured in the United States of America
10 9 8 7 6 5 4 3 2 1

Library of Congress Cataloging-in-Publication Data
Gruhzit-Hoyt, Olga, 1922-
    They also served : American women in World War II / by Olga Gruhzit-Hoyt.
        p. cm.
    "A Birch Lane book."
    ISBN 1-55972-280-0
    1. World War, 1939-1945—Women—United States.   2. World War, 1939-1945—Participation, Female.   3. Women—United States—History—20th century.   I. Title.
    D810.W7G67   1995
    940.54'1373'082—dc20   94-43921
                                                                      CIP

For all the American women
who served in World War II

CONTENTS

PREFACE

I had been involved with military history for quite some years, and I had developed the nagging thought that I seldom read about the exploits of the women who served in World War II. There were hundreds of books by and about men recounting wartime experiences, but few from the thousands of women who had joined the military or civilian agencies to serve their country.

I thought it was time that these women should have some kind of public recognition. I began collecting material for a book based on their firsthand accounts. I never realized that it would be such a vast project. I wrote to the military department headquarters, which all generously supplied me with suggestions on how to contact the women. I wrote to service magazines, veterans associations, official departments of history—and every likely source I could think of.

It took some months for my requests for women to contact me to be published in military newsletters, various bulletins, newspapers, and magazines. At first I heard from only a few women; as time went on I heard from more and more. Suddenly the flood gates opened and scores of inquiries and firsthand accounts came in. I went from despair over receiving enough material to despair over handling such a bulk of painstakingly remembered experiences of the war. I was constantly amazed at the fabulous memory for detail that so many women had after fifty years (although some factual errors did creep in), and I was struck by their eagerness to tell their tales. After the war most had slipped back into domestic duties, or pursued civilian careers. Their wartime service had never been widely recognized, except by their peers in their various veterans groups.

Some of the women had served in dangerous situations, exposed to bombings or snipers. Others held boring routine jobs, but even these women felt that their service had been good. The experience was new, their horizons were broadened as they met women from all parts of the country. They learned to get along with others, and many made friendships that have lasted to this day. The women all learned discipline—and some loved it. Almost every account closed with the remark "I was proud to have served."

I made many friendships in the course of writing this book, most by voluminous correspondence, some by long telephone conversations. I also found a new realization of the immensely supportive role these women had played in the war.

The women who served in World War II had volunteered. They accepted the scrubbing of garbage pails, the marching, marching, marching, the coding and the decoding, the horrors of war, and the heartbreak, and they served gladly. Now, with their older wisdom, they can only hope that their children and their grandchildren will never see the need for wartime service. I thank them all.

This book was written to express appreciation and give recognition to those dedicated women of fifty years ago, no matter whether they served as military or civilian personnel. They did, indeed, serve honorably and well.

Delhi, New York
August 1994

ACKNOWLEDGMENTS

I am most grateful to the following for help in locating the women who served during World War II:

Iris J. West, Army Nurse Corps Historian, Center of Military History, Department of the Army; Jake Jones; Margaret Salm, WAC; Jan T. Macauley, SPAR; Florene Miller Watson, WASP; Beatrice Falk Haydu, WASP; Deborah Shavers and Linda DuMoulin of Women Military Aviators, Inc.; Charity Adams Earley, WAC; Women in Military Service for America Memorial Foundation, Inc.; *Leatherneck*, Marine Corps Association; Celin V. Schoen, Executive Director, Delaware County Chapter, American Red Cross; Yvonne C. Pateman, WASP; Ethel Finley, president, WASP; Bernard F. Cavalcante, Head, Operational Archives Branch, Naval Historical Center, Department of the Navy; Mary Stewart, Retired Nurses Association; Constance Miller, associate editor of *Carry On*, Women's Overseas Service League; Danny J. Crawford, Head, Reference Section, History and Museums Division, Marine Corps Historical Center; Women Marines Association, Quantico, Virginia; Maggie M. White, director of the Women Marines Association, Area L; Mary L. Stremlow, Deputy Director, Division of Veterans' Affairs, State of New York; Fern Farrington, president of Coast Guard Cutters Unit Ninety-two;

WAVES National; Jeanne Gleason, SPAR; M. A. Ewen, *The Connection*, Retired Army Nurse Corps; the *New York Times Book Review*; Alliance of Women Veterans, Santa Ana, California; Virginia Allred, editor of *'Nouncements*, Women Marines Association; *American Legion Magazine*, Women's Army Corps Veterans Association, Fort McClellan; Veterans of Foreign Wars; Willard J. Webb, Chief, Historical Office, Joint Staff, Washington, D.C.; Ivan Molotsky of the Washington bureau of the *New York Times*; Dr. Judith Bellafaire, Center of Military History, Department of the Army (Field and International Division); Walt Grudzinskas, Historical Services Branch, Center for Air Force History, Department of the Air Force, Bolling Air Force Base; Phyllis E. Phipps-Barnes, Director of Education, Fiftieth Anniversary of World War II Commemoration Committee, Department of the Army; Geoffrey M. T. Jones, president of the Veterans of OSS; Mrs. John L. Undercoffer, *The Oversea'r*, American Red Cross Overseas Association; Luayne R. Kendrick, Alabama State Director, WAVES National; Elsa Cooke, editor of the *Gazette-Journal*, Gloucester, Virginia; Will Molineaux, book editor of the *Daily Press*, Newport News, Virginia; the *Daily Star*, Oneonta, New York; R. M. Browning, Jr., Historian, U.S. Coast Guard Public Affairs Staff, Washington, D.C.; Richard W. Peuser of the Military Reference Branch, Textual Reference Division, National Archives, Washington, D.C.; Barbara Pathe, Coordinator of Historical Resources, National Headquarters, American Red Cross; Mary Beth Straight, Notebook Editor of *Proceedings*, U.S. Naval Institute; Patrick Gibbs at the National Headquarters, American Red Cross; Cannon Free Library, Delhi, New York; Dan Eades; Benton Arnovitz; Lucia Staniels.

And, of course, this book could not have been written without the help of the women who served during World War II. Literally hundreds of women wrote in to inquire about the project and to offer their stories. Nearly one hundred actually wrote up long accounts for me; alas, space does not permit the use of so many. But I am grateful to all these women, who re-created the events of fifty years ago for me.

I must also give thanks to Andree Christman, who kept her computer spinning for me, to my grandsons Nathaniel, Sam, and Zach Berliner for their generous clerical help, to my agent, Henry Shaw, for his moral support, and to my editor, Hillel Black, for thoughtful guidance.

INTRODUCTION

When World War II began, the traditional concept that a woman's place was in the home was still prevalent in American society. The pattern of schooling, a stint in the workplace, then marriage was considered the ideal by most people, including women; the model of family life had long been established. It was "mom and pop and apple pie" and raising the children. Pop went to work and mom stayed home, with few exceptions.

Marriages were generally consummated with the idea of lasting "'til death do you part." The word *homosexual* was unspoken in polite gatherings. AIDS was unheard of, and teenage pregnancy was a "hushed up" affair. Family television did not exist, let alone a computer internet.

The change in the status of women, and, as a matter of fact, in the whole fabric of society in America over the past half century has been remarkable.

As far as women are concerned, certainly their position has improved and the possibilities for outstanding achievements have been greatly broadened.

Today's society is alien to that world of fifty years ago, and vice versa. In the milieu of the forties it was no wonder that many women were subject to parental disapproval, or at least apprehension, when they decided to enlist in the military or seek opportunity, adventure, and experience in overseas posts during the war. Many parents felt that it just wasn't "proper"; their daughters belonged at home. Of course, many parents were proud of their daughters for wanting to enlist. People felt ambivalent. "Nice girls" didn't join the military. It should have been no surprise that the men scoffed at the "broad-ass marines," or that attempted date rape occurred. Society's opinion of women who joined the military was often far from favorable, and many who enlisted were subject to undeserved criticism and disrespect.

The official U.S. Army history of the WACs in World War II cites incident after incident of the slander campaign against the WACs. These women were not alone. There were the men who joked that they had "joined the navy to ride the WAVES." Obscenities directed at many military women were common.

However, in some of the services the women were not denigrated or harassed. Treatment was generally best for women employed in traditional roles—for example, the nurses of the army and navy and the women of the Red Cross, or women in specialty groups such as the Office of Strategic Services, where the level of education was universally high and in the WASP, whose pilots often had far more hours in the air than the men they encountered.

It was only gradually that the women in some of the services received the respect they deserved. When the men saw the dedication and capabilities of the women, they were often surprised and impressed, and a measure of dignity was accorded to them. One officer who had claimed he wanted no women in his command soon asked for more to be sent. They were willing, they worked hard, and they had learned military discipline.

One cannot truly claim that the women who served in World War II were pioneers. Women had served with the military during World War I, and even long before that. Witness the case of Clara Barton who had worked with the wounded in the wars of the nineteenth century and had founded the American Red Cross.

The great contribution of the women who served in World

War II was that so many served, and served in so many fields that previously had been the prerogatives of men. They served in greater numbers than in any period in the past and they performed in job categories that were traditionally filled by men. Not only were they file clerks, office workers, cooks, and bakers; they also worked as auto mechanics, truck drivers, and pilots, radio operators and cryptographers. They quickly became proficient in the occupations held by men, thus freeing the men for combat duty, fulfilling one of the primary goals of their enlistment.

It was only logical that after the war many women would not go back to "hearth and home." The nurses who had to make life and death decisions on their own on flight evacuation duty were not likely in the future to be satisfied with being handmaidens to doctors. In all fields, the women learned a sense of self-esteem and an independence that would help push the so-called women's liberation movement into overt action. By no means did all the women who served want to pursue careers; many of them married and happily raised families. And, perhaps surprisingly, many have celebrated fiftieth anniversaries of their wartime marriages. But many women, having had new vistas open to them, wanted to become more equal with men in a career world they now found widely expanded.

The positive impact of the women in the military in World War II brought about a significant change in the discriminatory attitudes of the male military. As a result, many nontraditional military specialties have been opened to women. From 1973 to 1976, all of the services decided to train women as noncombat pilots. Years of debate on the role of women in the military followed, and the highly visible presence of women during Operation Desert Storm spotlighted the issue. About forty-one thousand female troops served in the Middle East at that time; with the new technological advances of warfare, the line between combat and noncombat zones became blurred.

Beginning in the 1970s many women in the military began to achieve positions of major responsibility. An army nurse became the first woman to wear the star of a general officer (1970); an air force woman became the first female major general in the

U.S. armed forces (1973). An army woman became the first female helicopter pilot (1974) and the first female aviation battalion commander (1991). A Coast Guard woman became the first woman to command a military vessel, a Coast Guard cutter (1979); an Air National Guard woman became the first woman qualified as a fighter pilot in the ANG (1994) and the first woman pilot to graduate from the Air Force Test Pilot School (1989). Shelia E. Widnall was a groundbreaker, becoming secretary of the air force, the first woman service secretary in the Department of Defense. All these women were truly pioneers.

In 1993, Congress repealed the combat exclusion law, which opened warships to women. In March 1994 the navy ordered women to report to duty aboard the aircraft carrier *Eisenhower*, which became the first navy combat ship to have women permanently assigned to the crew. By fall 1994, the number of warships open to women had increased sharply.

Laws prohibiting women serving as combat pilots have been repealed. In 1993, the secretary of defense, Les Aspin, ordered the services to begin training women for these jobs. In January 1994 Mr. Aspin moved to open more group-combat jobs to women by lifting the Pentagon's so-called risk rule, which barred women from certain military jobs simply because those jobs were dangerous. Secretary Aspin came forth with a new definition of ground combat, with the result that women are now barred only from units that engage the enemy on the ground with weapons and are exposed to hostile fire and have a "high probability of direct physical contact with personnel of a hostile force."

By midsummer 1994 the army was planning to open more than thirty-two thousand combat positions that had been previously closed to women. For example, women can now fly Cobra and Apache helicopters as cover for tanks on the battlefield. But even with the new rules, women are still barred from 27 percent of the army's jobs. They will not be allowed to fly choppers for stealthy special operations units or operate the Multiple Launch Rocket System, a key field artillery weapon.

Most jobs in the navy and air force are now open to women. The Marine Corps plans to open thirty-three previously closed fields, but will keep women out of infantry, armor, and field artillery units. There will be more changes, and more advancement and participation by women in the military in the future. Much discussion today hinges on what is, and what is not, combat service.

But think back to World War II. The WACs who followed the armies through western Europe into Germany were already serving in combat areas. They were exposed to snipers and enemy bombings. The same was true of the Red Cross women whose clubmobiles were attached to army forces. Army nurses in Manila endured the Japanese bombings, and some were taken prisoner for the duration of the war. One army flight evacuation nurse in Europe was shot down by the Germans and held captive. In the United States, the WASP flew every type of military plane from manufacturer to air base destination, through foul weather, sometimes in faulty planes. They were not in combat zones, but they risked their lives, and some women pilots were killed in the line of duty.

There is no doubt that military women today owe much of their advancement in the services to those women who served in World War II. By virtue of their vast numbers and their display of proficiency in the many and varied areas in which they served, they proved that women could and should participate in the defense of their country.

They Also Served

PART ONE

Army Nurse Corps

American nurses began serving in the military as early as the Revolutionary War, working on a contract basis with the Continental Army. They continued serving during the Civil War, nursing for both the Union and Confederate armies.

During the Spanish-American War contract nurses, though few in number, served so effectively that in 1901, under an army reorganization act, they were appointed in the Regular Army, although not actually commissioned as officers.

In July 1918, during World War I, the Nurse Corps was redesignated the Army Nurse Corps by another reorganization act. During that war the corps consisted of over twenty thousand nurses, over half of whom served overseas.

During World War II, the Army Nurse Corps reached a peak of fifty-seven thousand nurses and functioned in the United States and in the European and Pacific theaters of war. They served wherever they were needed to care for American soldiers—on hospital ships, in flight evacuation crews, on the beachheads, and in hospitals at home and overseas.

Army nurses were already stationed overseas when the Japanese attacked on December 7, 1941. Some were working at Tripler General Hospital on Oahu when the Japanese swooped down on Pearl Harbor. The same day, as Manila was attacked, other army nurses were on duty at Sternberg General Hospital in the city. The two hospitals had been considered plum assignments until the day the casualties came flooding in.

Many American women rushed to enlist in the corps when war was declared; others waited until they could meet age and training requirements. Some received army training before going overseas, some did not.

Army nurses were sent to the Middle East, to Cairo, to Palestine, to the Persian Gulf Command. Nurses served in Algeria during the North African battles and followed the army as it struggled up the boot of Italy.

Many nurses served in England first, amidst the ruins of the Battle of Britain and the oncoming buzz bombs. As the tempo of the war increased in 1944, the nurses moved into France, landing on Omaha and Utah beaches in Normandy after the June 6 D-Day assault. They proceeded eastward following the Allied drive to Germany, moving ever closer to the fighting front through the rubble and debris left from Hitler's occupation of western Europe. Sometimes they nursed the wounded in buildings, sometimes they made do in hastily erected tent cities. As the men slogged through the winter snow and suffered from the heat, so did the army nurses.

In the Pacific theater the nurses turned yellow from the antimalarial Atabrine they were ordered to take. They suffered the mud, the monsoons, the cold, the malaria and dysentery.

Army nurses cared for the wounded, the victims of land mines and shrapnel. They saw men with their intestines hanging out of their bodies, with legs so maimed they required amputation. The life was rough and hard, but the nurses worked around the clock to take care of and heal—as best as they could—the American soldiers.

During World War II, 201 army nurses died, 16 as a direct result of enemy action. One nurse was shot down and taken prisoner by the Germans. Others were captured and interned by the

Japanese. More than 1,600 nurses were decorated for "meritorious service and bravery under fire."

In April 1947, by an act of Congress, the Army Nurse Corps became a part of the Regular Army of the United States.

1

Death in Minutes

Harriet Holmes had enlisted in the Army Nurse Corps on May 30, 1936, when she was twenty-seven years old. By the end of 1941 she was on duty in Hawaii.

It was early morning on December 7 when Harriet and the other nurses at Tripler General Hospital, near Honolulu, saw the smoke and the rising sun emblem on the planes overhead. There was shock and disbelief. The Japanese had bombed!

The ambulances streaked onto the hospital grounds, one after another, the crews bringing in the casualties. The surgical room was soon full; new arrivals were taken to makeshift operating rooms on the terraces.

Harriet Holmes was assigned a bed, and in the beginning as soon as a man was placed there, he died of his wounds. Her first four patients died within minutes.

"We just tried to get one cleaned up, then we'd find that he had died. Somebody would remove the body, and bring another. We couldn't even change the sheets."

The nurses gave the wounded intravenous fluids and sought help for the severely burned men. Those with head injuries and

multiple fractures lay on the beds until the surgeons could tend
to them. Harriet and the other nurses worked hour after hour.
She was told at 5:00 P.M. to go off duty and get some rest.

"I was absolutely numb. I remember we worked like machines.
When I went to get a few hours sleep before going back for
night duty, I was so shocked by what I had seen and what had
been going on at the hospital that there was no way I could have
gone to sleep."

Harriet reported back at 7:00 P.M. for duty on the temporary
wards that had been set up. She worked like a robot.

"I continued. I don't know how. With nursing once you get
back on duty, you get back into the old routine and your training comes to the forefront. This keeps you from thinking too
seriously about what you've seen. You just take care of your
patients and do what you're supposed to do."

The hospital staff had put curtains over the windows for a
makeshift blackout. All lights were doused in the wards, except
for one small corner where the nurses could prepare their medications and injections.

The nurses listened to all kinds of rumors. They heard that
the Japanese would probably be back that night—in full force.
They could see fires in the hills above, and they were told they
were signals for the Japanese to follow on a return bombing.

It was a hard and anxious night.

"Everyone was absolutely in a state of shock. Shock was the
only spirit. I couldn't say morale was high because we never
even thought about it. It was just this look of utter amazement
on everyone's face. We were completely unprepared for it.
There was no excitement or hysteria. It was simply shock and
utter disbelief."

By the end of the day, and the first night, the hospital staff
had achieved a semblance of order; however, Harriet recalled
one incident that was the direct result of confusion and haste.
The hospital used the theater in the compound for a morgue.
Sentries guarded the theater, and about midnight one of the
young men thought he heard a sound inside. He reported this
observation to the officer of the day. The soldiers entered the
morgue and found a man still alive.

"He was brought out and revived. He never knew that he had been rescued from the morgue. We guarded that secret from him so that he would never find out."

Going off duty that morning, Harriet found it hard to realize that the previous night she had been dancing at the Officers' Club without a care in the world.

2

The Pearl of the Orient

Edith Shacklette enlisted in the Army Nurse Corps and was assigned to the Sternberg General Hospital in Manila, the Philippines.

Edith had always considered Manila the most coveted assignment in the Army Nurse Corps. It was known as the Pearl of the Orient—duty was good and the scenery spectacular.

All that suddenly changed in December 1941. Pearl Harbor and the Philippines were bombed the very same day. Casualties came flooding into Sternberg Hospital, which was soon filled to capacity.

The nurses, along with a few enlisted men and doctors, were sent out in groups all over Manila to set up little hospitals in schools or any suitable buildings they could find to take care of the overflow of patients from Sternberg. They worked hard and hastily. The bombing continued. The nurses knew they would have to leave Manila soon.

Edith was working to set up a new hospital when word came that they would evacuate that evening. It was Christmas Day, 1941.

The nurses had Christmas dinner at the mess hall, each taking some extra food with her. As dark closed in they were bused
down to the docks to wait for a boat for Bataan. While they waited they could see the ammunition being blown up across the
bay at Cavite. It was the first of many "fireworks" they would see.

Finally the harbor boat came, and they boarded and the ship
crossed Manila Bay, about twenty or twenty-five miles, to Lamay
on Bataan. It was early morning by the time they disembarked
and were taken to what became known as Hospital Number
Two. It was an open-air hospital, with no buildings except for
one little one, which they put canvas over to make into an operating room. "Everything else was out under the stars, under the
trees, in the jungle."

The patients came from the front, by truck and any type of
ambulance that could be found. More and more casualties
arrived, and the nurses worked longer and harder.

"You didn't have hours. You just got up at daylight and
worked till dark, after dark."

The nurses quickly set up new wards under the trees as the
old ones filled up. Edith was there from the day after Christmas
until early February, when she was promoted to first lieutenant
and sent a few miles to the rear to Hospital Number One at Little Baguio to be chief nurse.

When Edith arrived at Little Baguio she was running a high
fever. She learned she had malaria. She was miserable for four
days until the quinine broke the fever and stopped the chills.
She went back to nursing long hours.

The Japanese bombing of Bataan Peninsula continued. Medi-
cines were in limited supply. It was difficult to keep instruments
sterile as more and more operations were performed. There
were rumors that they would somehow be helped. The fleet was
outside Corregidor, and everyone at the hospital hoped the
ships were coming their way. General Douglas MacArthur had
gone to Australia, and General Jonathan Wainwright was on
Corregidor, defending the island.

One night in April 1942, Edith was summoned to army headquarters in her capacity as chief nurse at Little Baguio. It was

just about dusk when Colonel Duckworth, the commanding officer, called her.

Edith recalled that he said, "The word is Bataan will surrender tomorrow and we're going to get the nurses over to Corregidor. We don't want to have women around when the Japanese soldiers come in. You go tell everybody to stop what they're doing, take what possessions they can and the bus will be down here in about thirty minutes."

They got away about 9:00 P.M.

"When we were loaded, ready to go, of course there was crying. We hated to leave our patients—hated to leave our group. But the bus had already started and Colonel Duckworth stopped it and made me roll down the window. He handed me the American flag. We had not flown the flag, but we flew it inside on the wall all that time. So he told me when I got over to Corregidor to take it to the commanding officer, which I did the next day. And I'm always sorry that had I not given it away, I'd maybe have kept it and brought it back to America. But, of course, we didn't know at that time what was going to happen."

The nurses went by bus down to the boat, and they waited for some time. It was four miles across to Corregidor, and they finally arrived at 3:00 A.M. Bataan fell to the Japanese six hours later.

After General Wainwright had moved to Corregidor for the defense of the Philippines, the Japanese had increased their heavy artillery fire and bombardment. The fifteen-thousand-strong American garrison had concentrated its forces around what was known as the Malinta Tunnel.

When the nurses arrived on Corregidor, they were taken directly to the tunnel.

It was, according to Edith, "a great big long tunnel underground. I don't know the dimensions anymore, but forty or fifty feet tall, with laterals running off each side. That was where much of the equipment and ammunition and everything else was stored out there. There was one lateral that was a hospital. We had bunk beds, three tiers high, that we and the patients were in."

The nurses had no field equipment when the war started.

Edith finally got some GI shoes and some coveralls, which was her uniform while she worked in the tunnel, from April 9 until May 6.

The nurses all did duty or worked in the operating room, wherever they were assigned. The hours were not long, as the whole group shared the work, but "it was bad because the vibration of that bombing was horrible."

"It would make your head ache. It would be dusty. But at nighttime it would die down and we would make the best we could of our living. We had adequate food. We never were hungry."

The Japanese continued their bombardment of Corregidor; on May 4, they fired over sixteen thousand shells during the night to cover the landing of two thousand Japanese troops with tank support the following evening. The American defenses in the Malinta Tunnel area were broken, and the Japanese demanded surrender of Wainwright's forces.

"Prior to our fall, [May 6] we heard that at twelve o'clock General Wainwright would surrender. At ten it looked like twelve would never come to me. The pounding was terrific. It really was.

"I saw the first Japanese about two o'clock in the afternoon after we had surrendered at twelve. He came and looked down the tunnel and went ahead. That was the first Jap I had seen.

"They kept the nurses in the medical tunnel for about three weeks. For some reason, they moved us into another tunnel by ourselves. I think the Japanese didn't have nurses like we had and they couldn't think that we were really part of the military. So they moved us out, but we still took care of the patients.

"Then after a little while, they moved us back up into the bombed-out hospital. We had great big holes in the wall, great big holes in the floor. And we were up there for, I would say, two or three weeks. Then word came that the nurses were being taken to Manila. And that's when they took us away from the military.

"They did have a harbor boat come and get us. They took us into what was known as Santa Catalina Girls School. It was a Catholic girls' school and it was right across the street from

Santo Tomas University. Seemingly, from what we were told, they didn't know what to do with us. They didn't want us to be part of the military, but we weren't exactly civilians. So they kept us in that school for six weeks until they claimed they got orders from Tokyo about what to do with us. Then they turned us into Santo Tomas, the civilian internment camp."

Edith Shacklette (Haynes) was a "guest" of the Japanese at Santo Tomas from the summer of 1942 until liberation in February 1945.

3

Palestine, Persia, and POWs

Susan Eaton came from a poor immigrant Hungarian family. She milked the cows on their small Massachusetts farm before school and on Saturdays "hired out" for two dollars a day to earn money for nursing school. She was working as a floor nurse at a nearby hospital when the Japanese attacked Pearl Harbor. The next day, December 8, 1941, she enlisted in the Army Nurse Corps.

Susan had been somewhat surprised when she had talked to the other nurses at the hospital. There was little enthusiasm to join up. Most of them either said "I'm too scared" or "I'm afraid they'll send me far away."

Susan, however, had "a zeal to be part of our country's defense." Shortly after enlisting, she received orders to report to Fort Devens, Massachusetts, the closest training facility.

"I arrived there on April 29, 1942, as a second lieutenant. I was twenty-three years old. I almost thought I was one of God's angels!"

Training was the usual army training: line up for everything, receive shot after shot, fingerprinting, clothing issue, including a gas mask—and a forty-dollar a month allotment.

By 1942 Susan had tired of sloshing around during training in the late New England snow, so she was grateful to receive orders for temporary duty with the Twenty-fourth Station Hospital at Fort Bragg, North Carolina. At least she was going south, where it was warmer.

Susan lived with the other nurses in a barracks without screens, right beside the mule pens. The nurses still trained, and sometimes filled in at one of the general hospitals nearby. By September Susan was on her way to Indiantown Gap Military Reservation, where there were no patients to tend to. Her days seemed to be spent completely "in a learning state." The nurses had gas mask drills, hiked with them, and climbed up and down rope ladders.

After three months, Susan was sent back to the Twenty-fourth Station Hospital. But this trip was different: "orders said 'Per secret orders.' We were going to a port of embarkation."

On December 19, 1942, Susan, along with other nurses, boarded the SS *Mariposa,* a converted luxury liner, at Hampton Roads, Virginia. The *Mariposa* was now a troopship, accommodating three thousand soldiers and forty-seven nurses.

Life aboard ship was routine, until "one day, suddenly out of the blue, someone had to go to sick bay. The dreaded diagnosis—measles! So we were now quarantined. Funny, where could we go anyhow?"

The nurses were on call for duty for the duration of the forty-day trip. While the *Mariposa* zigzagged to keep from being tracked by enemy subs, the troops and nurses continued their routine fire drills, wearing their Mae Wests. They crossed the equator, and the weather grew hotter and hotter. The *Mariposa* skirted the Cape of Good Hope, Africa, headed through the Straits of Madagascar, and on February 1, glided into the Middle East port of Suez.

The nurses gathered their gear and disembarked. They were billeted in a makeshift building in Port Said, still not knowing their destination. Their first stop was a villa on the outskirts of Cairo on the way to Tel Let Winski, Palestine.

"February and March were very, very cold months, and the building of our future hospital proceeded at a snail's pace, for the customs were all different: the Jews didn't work on Saturday, the Moslems didn't work on Friday, and the Christians didn't work on Sunday."

Since the hospital was not ready, the nurses indulged themselves with magnificent sightseeing: Jerusalem, Jericho, Bethlehem, the hills of Judea. They swam in the Dead Sea. They crossed a bridge over the Jordan River, where Susan filled a bottle with water, which she later took home to the United States.

Again the nurses were given new shots and a new assignment—the Persian Gulf Command, with headquarters in Teheran. It was a three-day trip involving a mountain-climbing train to Beirut, then a large, tired yellow bus across the shifting sands of the desert to Baghdad, then a temporary station for a few days in Ahwaz, Iran, while Abadan Island across the river prepared to receive them. Finally on May 11, 1943, they went aboard a small amphibious army vehicle, which crawled up on the shore of Abadan Island.

"When we arrived we saw unspeakable filth and unsanitary conditions at the small Iranian hospital there. We tried to help out temporarily. Dirty floor mats, loved ones crouched beside the patient. One sheet, no pillowcase, and droves of flies. We could only extend a caring hand and heart at the moment."

The nurses were assigned to the army's 256th Station Hospital.

"We learned that our hospital was a left-over Douglas Aircraft building. The boards and other materials for construction had come from the crates containing the aircraft parts, which had been sent here from the States to the assembly plant manned by civilians, army personnel, and natives. A Quonset hut was snuggled up against one side to provide protection from sandstorms. This was to be our barracks. We were right next to a triple airfield—American, British, and Russian—where the assembled planes were tested, then given to the Russians under a U.S. lend-lease program.

"It certainly was a help to have the small hospital intact to start our patient care. Our Russian patients proved the most difficult to care for. We tried to learn a little Russian so that we could be friendlier caregivers. All in all, we tried to conquer

their arrogance, but it was doubly hard when they would throw
the whole untouched tray right on the floor! Now and then they
would attempt a bit of friendliness. The soft smile of a woman
left them in finer spirits; on their discharge there were many
offers of bottles of vodka.

"We were always sympathetic to the Iranian natives. Our small
hospital clinic was open to them twice a week. Since we could
do so little—it was hard not to do more. Their biggest health
problem stemmed from an unclean environment. (Chickens
and goats wandered through their tents anytime they felt like
visiting.) The disease was leishmaniasis, the result of some kind
of an insect bite that caused an ugly infection and open sores,
and was extremely contagious. Of course since they had no concept of disinfectants or bandages just about everybody had it.
Also I had it. (I still have a couple of small scars on my legs.)

"We had a nurse with us who was really beautiful. Sadly, somehow she contracted leishmaniasis, especially on her face. She
had to be sent home with huge, ugly pockmarks covering her
face. She was almost unrecognizable.

"We tried to teach the children how to brush their teeth. I
thought they were going to be perfect examples of learning
good oral hygiene until they all stuck the brushes in their pockets and continued to gulp down the tube of toothpaste.

"We did surgery, to a minimum: appendectomies and repair
of injuries. On the medical side we were kept busy with widespread malaria. At that time, it took the lives of quite a few soldiers.

"Recreation was also at a bare minimum. The British, who had
been at the airfield for some time, had a club down in their area
called Gymkhana, just a few miles from us. We were delighted
when they asked us to come down to their dances. Ecstasy was
the word, to dig in the bottom of the footlocker for that old,
faded lavender evening gown! Many of the officers had their
families with them, and brought us out of our 'sand-shells' back
into reality. To know there were other humans here enduring
120-degree weather besides us.

"While at the 256th Station I guess we were pitied a bit. Along
the way we were 'detached,' or sent up to army hospitals in

northern cooler mountainous areas, for a change. We were temporarily attached to stations on the Russian border, in Teheran, and even made it back to Tel Aviv."

In January 1945 the nurses received secret orders. "We were leaving the Persian Gulf Command for sure. Usually we could sense a change ahead of time, especially when it was 'sleeve up' and 'turn around' time. After that came different clothing exchanges for a different climate. On January 25, 1945, we departed Abadan for the European theater of operations. February 11 we saw land. It proved to be the harbor of Marseilles, France. What a sight! We had slowed, almost to a stop, and had to move with extreme care. The whole harbor looked like Satan's junkyard. Huge ships were half under water, lying in every imaginable way; some belly-up, some on their sides, and a couple with their bows high in the air. Not a word was heard; we thought we were seeing the ultimate wasteful carnage of our whole journey. It took quite some time to maneuver through without damaging our ship or hitting an unexploded mine. The Germans must have strutted their stuff after this bombing. We didn't stay there too long, as the Germans were still bombing, especially at night.

"As we were debarking from our ship, our GI's were really ticked off, and with good reason. Wearily, they marched off, passing a bunch of fresh recruits who had served for about a month, hollering loudly, 'Hey, here comes our replacements.' After being in Iran two years, there were plenty of 'unmentionable thoughts' on our boys' part, but they didn't start a riot.

"We were to be quartered next in a very famous private French girls' school with a lovely view, high on a hill over the harbor. For two weeks we made do with another empty building. At least there were cots to sleep on, and some bedrolls. The surroundings weren't very peaceful. At night the bombs came out—still. We were always ready to cut loose and go out for a walk, until we heard how unsafe it was. A small child was killed the day before we arrived in an innocent-looking empty field outside our window. It was profusely mined.

"Night after night the harbor was bombed. The Germans weren't leaving any of those pitiful ships above water.

"March 7, 1945, we were billeted in Dijon, France. It was such a pretty little city, but here again, it was another school.

"A few days later, after sitting on a train siding, under possible fire, we journeyed on to Nancy, France.

"On April 26 we arrived at Rhineau, Germany. If the harbor in France distressed us, this was equal to that. Ernie Pyle, who had covered the news, had had a bridge named for him upon his death. His famous bridge was now lying prostrate in the Rhine River. The city of Mannheim was without a skyline. Nothing over four feet or so high, nothing but piles and piles of rubble. Beautiful buildings and churches had stood proudly on this ground.

"We questioned the decision of our driver as he stopped in a nice family neighborhood, in front of sturdy brick homes. Surely this was not for us. But it was.

"The German families who had previously called it home were now living straight across the street in shacks, like chicken coops. A sturdy barbed-wire fence encircled them (or us). The little children, barely dressed for the cold, hung on the fence, probably wondering why we were in their house.

"One time after being there about a week a poor haggard woman came to the door (on our colonel's orders) to get a few necessary pots and pans to use for the home delivery of her unborn child. Some people made caustic remarks that we were helping the enemy, but most of them accepted the humanitarian act.

"A path, about a quarter of a mile in length, led from our front door over to the large SS school. It was all enclosed in barbed wire, so we were ordered to wear our helmets coming and going to the school. It was nothing like our schools in the States. In full view high up near the ceiling were giant figures of German soldiers showing how to subdue the enemy. They had swords, and axes raised, while one foot was on the neck of their enemy. This was apparently the beginning of little tots' education of German supremacy—depiction of the SS troops.

"Our plan was to renovate the school into a hospital to receive our soldiers back from the death camps of captivity.

"At least we were now able to help. The ambulances would

drive up, loaded with released prisoners of war. Their gaunt faces told all. They smiled faint smiles of everlasting gratitude. They were so thin—tall, once-sturdy athletes with paper-thin skin pulled over their bones. Actually they had to be handled like cherished newborn babies.

"Of course we had to feed them (very small amounts) of a special diet at first. Light, bland food, because their stomachs were so shrunken a piece of bread would fill them up. I became fully aware of what they had gone through while I was on night duty. At all hours they would be beside my desk begging for just a crust of bread. On making the beds in the morning we often found little cherished pieces hidden in their pillows.

"The silent contrast of the physique of the Germans, carrying the almost weightless stretchers of our men and openly deriding our men, said everything.

"Finally, it was time for a little R and R. In May 1945, a few of us got to go to the United Kingdom for seven days. In London on V-E Day we sat lining the curb near Westminster Abbey and watched a sight we would likely never see again. The queen, in all her pomp and finery, rode slowly past in her heavily decorated carriage.

"On our return to Germany, we were happy to get our bronze star from the Rhineland and central Europe campaign, on June 7, 1945.

"We were still in the Twenty-sixth Field Hospital, APO 758. We turned in a bunch of supplies again on September 13. It was good to get rid of some heavy stuff such as our belt and pistol, the bedroll, leggings, and helmet also. That helmet was my fondest and closest companion all that time. Not on my head especially, but to hold that precious helmet full of water for the day's ration.

"We did go traveling. On October 10 we arrived at Pas-de-Lanciers, France, at another hospital staging area. Day by day our load was getting lighter and lighter. I had one precious little lovable ball of fur left, Ancie (ANC, Army Nurse Corps), my little grey schnauzer. She was loved and fondled by all. She wasn't quite alone, as there mysteriously appeared other little pets hoping to go to the United States on a free visa.

"That staging area didn't seem to be close enough, so we moved again on October 22 and were reassigned to the Twenty-first General Hospital at the Calais staging area. Ancie's excellent training to ride in my musette bag, so silently, with just a little black nose and one eye visible, paid off.

"But very sadly, while she was tied to a tent stake, a two-ton truck rambled by, swerved, and sent her to heaven. The nurses gave her a very loving and mournful service (without the body). True to the rumors, on boarding the SS *Hermitage* on October 27, any small animals were confiscated.

"Needing a spiritual lift, I had to laugh at the next entry of orders. We were considered 'shipment #RE7358, dated 13th, Oct. Shipment.'

"The *Hermitage* was quite similar to the *Mariposa*. In fact, she had slightly better accommodations. I guess the absence of hourly threats of danger on the high seas, measles, and forty days on board accounted for that. Inside, though, were many 'locked-up' memories being shared; the foreboding feeling we would not see each other again persisted. Late one afternoon, we saw land! It was November 6, 1945.

"I felt great exhilaration and patriotism as we sailed into New York Harbor. Our beloved Statue of Liberty, arm held high with the Torch of Peace, for me—for us. Seemingly the band saying, 'We've missed you,' completing the feeling of 'mom and apple pie.' This, followed by a nonchalant but poignantly strong hug to friends—'So long, see ya.'

"The umbilical cord of World War II was severed for us forever."

Susan Eaton married Jim Fox in 1946, whom she had met during the war while on R and R in Cannes. They had three sons, who were all baptized with the water Susan had taken from the River Jordan during her stint in Palestine. After thirty-four years of marriage, Jim Fox died. For the last twenty years Susan has been enjoying her three grandsons, golf, watercolor artistry, and trying to keep in touch with her many friends.

4

A Warm Body for France

Jeanne Kahn Paul grew up in what she considered a nice sub-
urban town. She was an only child, living with her grandparents.
In her teens she moved to New York City, where she began
studying to be an advertising artist. But by the time she graduated she had a "gut feeling" that she would never make it in the
art world. This was in 1937, and the options open to Jeanne
seemed limited: either teaching or nursing. Jeanne decided on
nursing.

As Jeanne put it, she "survived" Beth Israel Hospital School of
Nursing.

"In those days, like all nursing schools, it represented a very
structured and strictured introduction to the real world. After
graduation and a couple of years of in-hospital duty, I started
looking for a little more excitement. I even considered taking a
job with a copper corporation in Peru, but when my father and
I read the contract very carefully, we both decided that three
years in a mountain mining camp was not really the key to a glorious future.

"So on September 1, 1942, when I was twenty-four, I joined

Army nurse Jeanne Kahn Paul (right) relaxing outside tent quarters, Lauterbach, Germany, in sunsuit handmade from captured German tablecloths.

the Army Nurse Corps as a second lieutenant on limited service status because I am quite nearsighted. This meant I'd be limited to service on the eastern seaboard, without much chance of overseas duty. This changed, either because the army was tired of my nagging them for overseas duty or because it was becoming desperate for warm bodies."

A month and a half after arriving in England, Jeanne and her fellow nurses embarked near Southampton and landed in France on July 18, 1944.

"My most vivid memory is that of climbing down rope ladders into little boats that took us ashore on Utah Beach. Ashore was some mess—littered with debris, bodies, abandoned German pillboxes. We were put on trucks and driven past St. Lô and other heavily damaged areas to our first tent city.

"When we got to that compound, which had been erected in a hurry, our main problem, besides the rain and mud, was coping with the makeshift latrine, which kept blowing down—but after a while that became a minor problem—as long as the latrine existed at all.

"In France our 106th Evacuation Hospital was usually located in a cow pasture, not always cleared. The enlisted men preceded us and set up our quarters, which were pyramidal tents heated by potbellied stoves. They would set up the hospital tents and we'd get to work on the casualties. An evac hospital receives wounded from aid stations and field hospitals. Some of the guys were in pretty bad shape, lots of young kids full of shell fragments, which our surgeons had to remove. Apparently the Germans used shells that were full of all sorts of metal fragments, and they were pretty nasty.

"I worked in the operating room, usually a twelve-hour shift. There were only forty nurses in the unit, and about the same number of officers, not all of whom were doctors. Enlisted men also assisted in the OR and they were fantastically skilled. Guys with no previous training learned on the job, working with orthopedists, brain surgeons, maxillofacial surgeons—and they were compassionate and efficient.

"Most of the surgery was done either under local or very short-term general anesthesia—time was of the essence. I think our recovery rate was probably pretty good, for our patients were young, healthy, and in the early days of the war were not too exhausted.

"The German POW patients were the most frightened supermen I've ever seen—they were sure the American doctors would kill them or at least amputate something. We really didn't discriminate except in terms of priorities—they were patients, too!"

The nurses worked their way across France. At Thionville on the Moselle River near the German border they were finally housed in a real building, a very nice school. They remained there through Christmas 1944 and the Battle of the Bulge, which continued into January 1945.

"Our next encampment was within Germany, also in a building, but it was so dirty that we would have preferred our tents. We started seeing more POWs in pretty bad shape—some with gas gangrene because they had been left out on the fields. We also sensed that the civilian population did not really love us. They worked for us, accepted our food and cigarettes, but when we walked down the village streets, windows were shuttered. The next month, while on a routine reconnaissance to search for another location to set up the hospital, one of the surgeons was killed, and the two men with him were taken prisoner."

The nurses moved on to Austria, then were sent to Marien-bad, Czechoslovakia, early in the summer of 1945. All this time Jeanne had been in touch with her fiancé, who, was, as she was, part of Patton's Third Army. The war in Europe had ended in May; now the "powers that be" decided that Jeanne's unit would be suitable for duty in the Pacific theater. Jeanne and her fiancé decided to get married—a reasonable excuse for sending her home.

"That was not easy. It took weeks of protocol and reams of paper before the okay came through from army headquarters. Finally, in Regensburg, Bavaria, we found an army rabbi who tore himself away from a baseball game to perform the ceremony.

"I now received orders to go home. We had filled a very important role, and whether because women were in short sup-ply in the European theater, or because of the work we did, we were treated very well.

"All I can say is that nothing in the aseptic environment of Beth Israel Hospital prepared me for tent ORs where a nurse and doctor would simply change gloves and dash to another adjacent table. We learned the value of antibiotics, liberally sprinkled on wounds. In other words, we got down to basics. It was definitely no-frills surgery.

"Sometime in September 1945, I received orders to Le Havre, where a passel of other nurses, also married, were awaiting trans-portation home.

"When we returned stateside, as we rode from Boston toward Fort Dix, it looked as though New England had just been paint-ed clean and white for our benefit. That view of our untouched countryside will always remain with me."

After the war, Jeanne Kahn Paul went back to nursing until she and her husband adopted a daughter in 1950. They had three children in the following years. When the children were older, Jeanne went back to work in a proctologist's office and worked there until she retired five years ago. Currently she works in the family wholesale art materials business and hopes to keep working forever. Throughout the years she has become "a permanent student to keep from getting really moldy," picking up credits toward "a degree I may never achieve."

5

Land Mines and Learning Compassion

Emma Porteus grew up on a dairy farm in a valley near the foothills of the Catskill Mountains in New York. She trained as a nurse and secured a hospital job in the state, then joined the Army Nurse Corps in October 1942, when she was twenty-seven years old.

Emma was first stationed at Pine Camp, now known as Camp Drum, in upstate New York, not far from the Canadian border. A half year later she was transferred to Torney General Hospital near Palm Springs, California, where she spent six months on the wards before she was transferred to the operating room to train as an anesthetist.

She studied and progressed from minor operations to major surgery. She was an accomplished anesthetist by 1944, when she arrived at the 170th General Hospital, a tent hospital outside Le Mans, France, southwest of Paris.

In September, when there were enough nurses at the hospital so that she could be released from the wards, Emma was

assigned to the operating
room to administer anesthesia. While working there an
incident occurred that made
"an important change of attitude" in Emma's life.

"After seeing and hearing
the stiff goose step of the German army earlier, I somehow
developed a hateful attitude
toward any Germans (men).
A POW was brought by
stretcher into the x-ray tent
with a left lower fractured
tibia. I went over to x-ray to
check his chart because he
would come to the OR to
set his tibia and put a walking cast on. When, as I
approached him in my OR

Army nurse Emma Porteus outside her tent
at Le Mans, France, 1944.

suit inside the lab coat, he looked at me, his pupils suddenly
dilated, and he fainted. His chart informed me that he was seventeen years old, understood the English language, and his
name was Karl. As soon as he recovered, I asked Karl why he
fainted suddenly. He told me that his chief officer had told him
that if he ever landed in an American army hospital his left leg
would be cut off. No wonder Karl fainted when I approached
him.

"The procedure to be used for his injury was explained and
he understood. A statement of principles of the Red Cross Nurses (Humanity, Impartiality, and Neutrality) was given him to
read, which he understood. He no longer had any fear of us.
Karl came out of the operation and hospital in good shape and
spirits. Later he told us that many of his classmates and friends
who did not want to join the army had suddenly disappeared,
never to be seen again. They were told what to do, could never
make a choice themselves.

"This made me realize the freedom of choice we have in

Army nurse Emma Porteus with other nurses waiting for jeeps to pick them up in France, 1944.

America; also it was not the common people of Germany who were waging this war, just Hitler and his gang. My hateful attitude changed to compassion for those caught in this situation: Fight or die by the leaders of their own country. What would I do in this situation? After this experience it was much easier to care for any wounded soldier, thus developing a more real cosmopolitan attitude. This made me a better and more caring individual."

Emma found that the most difficult cases were the results of land-mine explosions, which often caused soldiers to lose an arm or leg. "All this was rough for each patient, but each one came through this ordeal quite well and later returned back home using the artificial limb. For these men, it was great to be alive and be back home with family."

Then on May 8, 1945, came V-E Day. There was, of course, much celebrating. The U.S. Army had a huge parade through the streets of Paris, and Emma and the other nurses of the 170th joined in the festivities. They were pleased that the day was sunny and warm. They had lunch and a glass of wine at a sidewalk cafe, then it was back to the hospital routine. The patients began talking about going home.

The war in the Pacific ended in August, and by Christmas 1945 the workload at the tent hospital was much lighter. The nurses worked eight-hour shifts now, instead of the usual twelve. Soon Emma, along with three of her tentmates, received orders to return home.

They packed quickly and rushed to board the *Westpoint*, which would take over nine hundred military personnel back to the United States.

The ship docked at Boston Harbor and the nurses reported to Fort Devens, Massachusetts. Two days later Emma received her last thirty-day leave, plus discharge papers, separating her from the army, but in reserve status. She was home on December 28, 1945.

"All the old deep tiredness and anxiety began to wane gradually as the days went by, making it possible to not look back but to concentrate on the future."

After the war Emma continued nursing as a career. She intensified her study of anesthesiology and secured a good job at Johns Hopkins Hospital in Baltimore. The Korean War began in June 1950; in December, four days after Christmas, Emma received military orders to report to Fort Devens, Massachusetts, in January.

At Fort Devens Emma again was assigned to administer anesthesia in the operating room. In February 1952 she received orders to go to Korea, but she was seriously ill with pneumonia, so the orders were rescinded.

Emma Porteus received her full army discharge on June 14, 1952. She packed her army bags for the last time.

"I put my military experience behind to look toward a new normal life in our free country, with more understanding and concern for my fellow human beings."

In the fall of 1952 Emma Porteus became a nurse anesthetist on the staff in the operating room at the Wilson Memorial Hospital in Johnson City, New York, where she worked until her retirement in the fall of 1976. Since that time she has been a volunteer with the American Red Cross bloodmobiles and the blood pressure clinics in her New York hometown of Oneonta. She is a member of the American Legion Post.

6

So Far From Anywhere

As long as she could remember, Signe Skott Cooper had wanted to be a nurse. She was still in nursing school at the University of Wisconsin on December 7, 1941. She well recalls the next day, when eleven o'clock classes were canceled so that the students could hear President Franklin D. Roosevelt's declaration of war.

"As student nurses, we became very much aware of the war. We worked long hours on the hospital wards, as more and more of the hospital's nurses left for military service. Shortages of equipment and supplies, such as rubber goods, especially intravenous tubing, then made of rubber instead of plastic, were common. One of the interns was of Japanese origin, and I recall a patient saying when he came into her room, 'Get that dirty Jap out of here!'

"Before I completed the nursing program in February 1943, several of my classmates and I had joined the Red Cross junior reserve, as a prelude to joining the Army Nurse Corps. I was sworn in on May 19, 1943, when I was twenty-two, after having passed the physical exam at Truax Field in Madison. My orders read to report to Fort Belvoir, Virginia.

"I didn't really have any basic training, nor any orientation to the hospital, except what little was given me by the head nurse on the first ward I was assigned. Occasionally we did some drilling after our work day was over, and we had occasional training sessions that consisted of news reels and propaganda films. Mostly, the nurses learned from one another.

"The army was segregated in 1943, and there were three battalions of black soldiers at Fort Belvoir. But the hospital was not segregated, so we had both black and white patients, and some of the corpsmen ('ward boys' they were then called) were black. Some of the corpsmen were very good, others were mediocre, a few were inadequate, and most of them had little training for their responsibilities.

"My work was on the medical wards, and my first assignment was on an isolation unit, where patients were recovering from spinal meningitis, after a small epidemic on the post. Patients with mumps were also admitted to this unit, and occasionally one with scarlet fever.

"Here I saw my first patient with malaria, a returnee from the South Pacific. I nearly dropped the thermometer I had used for taking his temperature when he walked in to the unit to be admitted; it registered 105 degrees. When I asked him how he felt, he said, 'I have a headache.' The teeth-rattling, bed-shaking chill soon followed.

"Later I was transferred to a ward of patients with pneumonia and upper respiratory infections. Penicillin was just coming into use, and the policy was that the doctors had to mix the penicillin powder with sterile distilled water (as if we couldn't read the directions!), but the nurses could administer it. At that time nurses did not generally give intramuscular injections and I had never been taught the procedure, but I soon learned. After the advent of penicillin IMs rapidly became an accepted nursing procedure—initially [an injection] had to be given every three hours to maintain the necessary blood levels; and doctors did not want to get up at night to administer it.

"I was critical of the chief nurse and her assistant because of their lack of clinical knowledge, which I could have tolerated, except they were always giving us incorrect information (nobody knows as much as a new graduate!) But a few of my peers were also lacking in what I considered essential nursing knowledge; I was surprised when the nurse on the ward next to mine asked me to show her how to figure insulin dosage after one of her patients went into insulin shock three days running."

Signe was sent overseas in September 1944, along with several other nurses from Fort Belvoir. None of them knew they were going to the China-Burma-India theater (CBI) until they were airborne. This flight from New York in a C-47 with bucket seats was Signe's first airplane ride. On the way to the Far East they had a day stopover in Casablanca, Morocco, where the nurses experienced their first "culture shock": child beggars everywhere, an obvious lack of sanitation, and great contrasts of filth and squalor with a splendid glittering palace.

They stopped briefly in Cairo, refueled in Abadan, and flew on to Karachi, which was then in India.

Karachi offered more culture shock: "the naked, pot-bellied children, beggars everywhere, constantly coming up to us and crying, 'baksheesh', the ramshackle homes, people with physical deformities of every description, men wandering around the streets with huge snakes entwined around themselves, the sacred cows wandering wherever they pleased, and crowds of people wherever we were."

In Karachi, Signe volunteered to special a patient with polio one night; he died the next day. She felt quite sad that her patient went off to war and died of polio. (This was, of course, before the polio vaccine was developed.)

From Karachi the nurses flew to Chabua in the province of Assam. "It was from here that U.S. planes flew 'the Hump' (the Himalayas) to our allies in China. We went by truck to our new home, the Twentieth General Hospital. A University of Pennsylvania unit, it was the largest army hospital overseas; half of its two thousand beds were for Chinese patients. The hospital unit had been in India since March 1943, and we were sent over as replacements for the nurses who had been there since then.

"The hospital was at the beginning of the Ledo Road (later renamed the Stilwell Road), and all we could write of our location in our letters was 'somewhere along the Ledo Road.'

Designed to be a route to China, it was then still being built, a slow process of hacking it out of the mountains."

At the hospital compound the nurses lived in *bashas* made of bamboo, with concrete floors and corrugated iron roofs covered with thatching to keep them cool. They had electricity—one electric bulb hanging from the center of the room—and kerosene lanterns in case the electricity went off. They had showers nearby and a latrine a half block away.

Signe and her roommate had two paid native servants—a sweeper, who cleaned their floors, and a bearer, who ran errands, such as buying bananas at the bazaar, hung their clothes out to air daily to prevent mold, and cleaned and polished their shoes.

Signe started work on the general medical wards, then was transferred to the scrub typhus (tsutsugamushi fever) ward. "I recalled that when we came to this disease in our communicable disease class in nursing school the teacher said, 'We can skip this one—you'll never see it.' Caused by a jungle mite, it is a very debilitating disease, and our casualty rate was high: we averaged a death a day while I was working there. The patients were acutely ill, and caring for them took all the nursing skills we possessed. Some patients recovered and were sent back to their units, but many of these I saw later in the psychiatric units.

"There wasn't much in the line of treatment for patients with scrub typhus. Patients were given PABA (para-aminobenzoic acid), now used as a basis for sunscreens. Many required oxygen, given by mask, and moving the heavy tanks around was a nuisance to someone used to oxygen piped to patients' rooms. Most patients were given IVs and special high-caloric diets. Never had I worked as hard, nor felt the work more satisfying.

"But the work was depressing, and after a month or so when I was moved to the psychiatric unit, I was not too unhappy about it. The psychiatric unit consisted of five wards, including two locked ones, where I worked most of the time. Here we occasionally had psychotic Chinese patients, since there were no locked wards in the Chinese part of the hospital. Our patients were very ill, and most of them were sent home. One, who was admitted to an open ward, was found hanging by his bathrobe belt in the latrine, but was rescued in time to save his life.

"One of my patients was a nurse from a station hospital up the road from us. She was quite ill, and after a couple of weeks was sent home. All psychiatric patients were sent home by sea rather than by air, for reasons I do not know. I heard afterward that she jumped overboard on the way home, but do not know if this was really true, and I like to believe that it wasn't.

"A number of patients were diagnosed 'psychosis—probably due to Atabrine.' I believe that army did not want to admit that Atabrine really caused the problem, because everyone was required to take it as a malaria preventive. We were expected to take it, and I did, except on my days off.

"We had one episode where two patients acted very 'high' at intervals and it took some time for the staff to figure out that their buddies were slipping them hashish (potent Indian marijuana) through the door whenever they came to visit. Patients in locked wards were rarely allowed visitors, but could talk to them through the barred door, and this is how the patients got their 'fix.'

"Selected patients were given insulin and later electric shock therapy. I often worked in the rooms where these treatments were given."

Leisure activity was limited. Signe wrote letters, knitted, or read. "The 'pony editions' of magazines, such as *Time, Newsweek*, and *The New Yorker* were available to us (through the Red Cross, I think) and were lifesavers to me, as were the small paperback books printed in overseas editions. I enrolled in a correspondence course in psychology, which I enjoyed, but the mails were slow and the time gap between lessons was a bit frustrating.

"For recreation, we played cards, mostly pinochle. One of the nurses in our *basha* bought a hand-cranked phonograph; it cost three hundred rupees (one hundred dollars at that time), and at first all she had was one record, with 'Manhattan Serenade' on one side, and Ravel's 'Bolero' on the other. I had an overwhelming feeling of sadness and homesickness whenever it was played. By Christmastime, she had secured a record of 'White

Christmas,' which she played over and over; the song certainly reflected our sentiments.

"The men had baseball teams, so we occasionally watched the games. Movies were shown frequently. We carried our bamboo stools to sit on, and the only entrance requirement was to smear the oily, vile-smelling mosquito repellent on one's hands and face. And of course there were no matinees, as the 'theater' was outdoors and we had to wait until it was dark enough to show the movies.

"We were so far from anywhere that there wasn't anyplace to go. People who dated often went to the one restaurant in Ledo that wasn't 'off-limits'; restaurants were inspected by army personnel for their sanitation. Parties and dances were held occasionally at the Officers' Club.

"Life in that part of India was quite monotonous—essentially the same duties, the same people, the uninteresting food. The part of the world we were in is said to have the highest annual rainfall. The constant rain during the summer monsoon was not only monotonous, it was irritating, as it caused our shoes and clothing to mold. On sunny days our bearer would hang the clothes out on the line and carry our shoes to the front porch to dry out.

"But the shorter winter monsoon was worse, for cold weather came with it. I wore my pajamas under my slacks when I went to work, but we had only a kerosene heater that didn't give much warmth. And we did not have warm clothes with us. When the monsoon was at its worst and the paths their muddiest, we wore our brown ankle-high 'L'il Abner' shoes or leather boots which we had made in the bazaar.

"I don't recall much about Christmas overseas—I probably worked nights both Christmas Eve and Christmas Day. I do remember accompanying patients to the chapel for midnight mass, and I recall our feeble attempts at decorating. We made a long garland of green tea leaves and hung it in front of the locked psych unit; it was really quite impressive. I also recall that one of the nurses in my *basha* received a huge fruitcake after Christmas, with mold on it about an inch thick.

"My health was good while I was in India, but on a routine

check on all the hospital personnel, I was identified as a carrier of amoebic dysentery, so was hospitalized to take the 'cure.' For me, the treatment was worse than the disease, since I had never had any symptoms. It consisted of a daily injection of emetine, along with oral carbarsone. As its name suggests, emetine is an emetic, and causes dreadful nausea and vomiting. We would lie on our beds all morning, fighting the nausea and suffering from the accompanying dizziness and weakness. Six or seven of us nurses were on treatment, so we commiserated together on the nurses' ward. And even after we were discharged our treatment continued, as we were on diodoquin for a month after completing the other drugs.

"After we had been in India about a year, my roommate, Berenice, our next-door neighbor, Anne Dorsey, and I were sent to rest camp in Darjeeling. It wasn't a camp—we stayed at the rather elegant Mount Everest Hotel. Darjeeling, famous for its tea, is in the foothills of the Himalayan Mountains, and is noted for its cool climate.

"We went by train, in our private car. It was bare, except for three benches that we sat or slept on. There was no way of going from one car to another, as in American passenger trains. We carried our own food (C rations), since eating on the way was problematic. Because India had no system of standard railway gauges, every time we came to another province, we would have to leave our car, go to another track, and look for our car, always labeled in chalk '3 Army nurses.'

"The most unusual part of this trip was the ride up the mountains into Darjeeling. At one point all the passengers had to leave the train and walk about half a mile while the engineer slowly eased the train around a curve where heavy rains had washed out much of the area surrounding the tracks.

"Shortly after we returned from Darjeeling, Berenice was married to Arthur Germain, who was with the Corps of Engineers. They were married in the chapel, followed by a reception in the Officers' Club.

"We heard the news about President Roosevelt's death and V-E Day—I do not remember the circumstances in either instance. But when V-J Day finally came, we didn't believe it, because we had heard rumors of it for several days, and we assumed this was just another rumor.

"Shortly after V-J Day I was transferred to the Eighteenth General Hospital in Myitkyina, Burma. Here the hospital wards were tents, and I shared a (leaky) tent with another nurse. I worked on a medical ward for six weeks or so, then was sent back to the Twentieth General for a stop on my way home.

"The day we departed from Karachi we stood in line for what seemed like hours waiting to board the *General Richardson,* as a loudspeaker blared the music of 'Sentimental Journey' over and over. At least the music seemed appropriate.

"We passed through the Suez Canal, stopped in the middle for the exchange of gold in payment for our use of the canal, and slipped into the green waters of the Mediterranean Sea, then into the Atlantic Ocean.

"Somewhere in the Atlantic we hit a November storm, and the seas were so rough that when we went to eat, the dishes kept sliding off the tables. We survived the storm and docked in New York Harbor at night. The lighted Statue of Liberty was truly a sight to behold.

"From New York we went by bus to Fort Dix, New Jersey. My biggest impression of Fort Dix was going to breakfast the next morning and seeing what people were eating: chocolate malteds, ice cream sundaes, bacon, lettuce, and tomato sandwiches, big glasses of milk—all things we had not had in India.

"My experience in the Army Nurse Corps was a good one. I had a variety of professional experience, saw medical conditions (dengue fever, scrub typhus, leprosy) I would never have seen in this country, and met some interesting people. This is not to say that it was easy—I really would not want to live through it again—but it's an experience I am glad to have had.

"I was discharged from the army on February 10, 1946, but I had accumulated a lot of terminal leave. I was back in Madison, working at Wisconsin General Hospital, shortly after January 1.

"I was young when I joined the army, with very little professional experience, but I learned quickly. The nurses had a very good support system, as it would be called today; we helped each other through the rough times; we encouraged each other;

we shared the good times and provided solace in the tragic ones, as when one of the nurses who lived in my *basha* received word that her sister, a chief nurse in New Guinea, had died there.

"Nursing was never the same after World War II. We had carried a lot of responsibility during the war, and we were not going back to the 'physician's handmaiden' role. We had learned to be assertive, to demand recognition for our abilities and skills. And many of us took advantage of the GI Bill of Rights to further our educations. For most of us, the experience of the war benefited us both personally and professionally."

After Signe Skott Cooper was discharged from the Army Nurse Corps, she returned to Wisconsin to work at a Madison hospital as a nurse. She secured her bachelor's and master's degrees and in 1948 was appointed to the faculty of the University of Wisconsin School of Nursing. In 1955 she began a joint appointment with the School of Nursing and University Extension, directing a statewide continuing education program in nursing until her retirement in 1983.

She now volunteers at the local historical museum and at the university arboretum and writes biographies of Wisconsin nurses for a nursing publication.

7

Capture

Reba Zitella Whittle was the only American nurse captured and imprisoned by the Germans during World War II.

She joined the Army Nurse Corps in June 1941, when she was twenty-one years old. She served at an air base in New Mexico and at army station hospitals there and in California for twenty-seven months before she applied for the Army Air Forces School of Air Evacuation. She volunteered, as did all the other applicants.

She received intensive training, so that she would be largely self-sufficient on the flights the C-47s would make on evacuation duty. The C-47s had dual duties. They would carry cargo and troops to the battlefronts and, after unloading, would evacuate the wounded and return to base.

Reba learned to use the equipment and medical supplies on the plane for treatment to relieve pain, to prevent hemorrhage, to treat shock, to give oxygen—in other words, to handle any emergency by herself, for only on rare occasions did a surgeon accompany a patient on a flight.

Reba was rated as a flight nurse on January 22, 1944, and went to England, where she was stationed at various bases. Between then and September, she flew over forty missions, with a total of five hundred hours of flying time. She made flights to Scotland, Ireland, Belgium, and France.

On September 27, 1944, Lieutenant Whittle left on a routine mission to return casualties. Excerpts from her unedited diary best tell the story:

Wednesday, Sept. 27, 1944, I left England with big intentions of returning as to go to London on my day off starting Thursday, Sept. 28. [The plane was headed to France to pick up twenty-four patients on litters. It is believed the pilot ran off course into enemy territory.]

Was sleeping quite soundly in the back of our hospital plane until suddenly awakened by terrific sounds of guns and crack-lings of the plane as if it had gone into bits. For a few moments I hardly knew what to think. Suddenly looked at my Surgical Tech opposite me with blood flowing from his left leg. The noise by this time seemed to be much worse. But to see the left engine blazing away—is simply more than I can express—But never thought I would land on the ground in one peace [sic]. My prayers were used and quick.

Started to scream and cry as most women would—but Sgt. Hill consoled me and assured it wouldn't help—at that time I realized he had been injured and should be the one crying. About that time he was hit in the left arm as I had my head on his left shoulder.

Suddenly we hit the ground splash—myself landing in the navigator's compartment head first. The ship was nearly blazing and holes every place—some large enough to crawl through back in the fuselage. Noticed the others crawling out the top hatch—so immediately went zooming out—3 out before I—the pilot last—who fell as if he had been badly wounded. One never came out. [Lieutenant Whittle suffered a concussion and a severe laceration of the forehead. Later that day, she developed back pain, head pain, and dizziness.]

Immediately we saw soldiers not many yards away. At first we thought they were British soldiers. Second glance we recognized they were German GIs. This feeling is one never dreamed of having. But thought—we've had it chum. The first thought in my mind—my boyfriend, and he would be waiting back at my quarters that evening. But how thankful and grateful to be alive.

They took a glance with their guns pointing and immediately one took out a bandage and put it around my head as it was bleeding. The surprised look on their faces when they saw a woman was amazing. But they bandaged us and away we marched, our ship still burning. The firing was terrific, the sounds terrific.

They took us to a small village rather a couple of old houses and there we sat on the ground until an officer came and suppose they had a discussion of some sort by the sounds of the conversation—not understanding German couldn't say.

After awhile sitting there some guards march us to a small town about 3/4 or 1 mile where we went into a dank dungeon cellar which really looked very spooky and smelled very bad. There a Dr. came in—had small candles for light and looked each of us over. Only one was really wounded. That being my Sgt. They gave him some M.S. [morphine sulfate, a common, potent analgesic] so we thought and they rebandaged the 3 of us who had slight wounds and accidently cut part of my hair when cutting bandage.

Here they took our personal belongings such as passes and money—rank and name.

The name of the village—sign Achen 4 Kil.—have no idea but it had been practically evacuated, saw only a couple of civilians and occasionally an army vehicle and soldiers running around. Naturally all glaring at us—babbling something which none of us knew what they were saying.

Off again—naturally walking—which had to be very slow on the account of Sgt. Hill's wounded leg. As we walked along the street of the village a German soldier came up and yanked my Air Corps patch off my shoulder and threw it down saying something. For why I don't know unless it was hanging loose as I was the only one he took it off.

Think it took us about an hr and considered it about 2 or 3

miles—that I couldn't be sure but it seemed like miles. Here we came to a neat brick house which at first seemed nice to be at as the firing still whistled.

Marched us in where 4 or 5 German officers sat in this office. There we stood like dummies and them giving us terrific glares. They showed us immediately into another room where the guard gave the Sgt. a glass of wine. Before he had time to complete his wine they pushed us outside.

We arrived at a huge-looking place surrounded by very high metal fence and a guard at the gate to let us in. All seeming very suspicious to me. Did as ordered out and up those dark steps, naturally our guards still with us and into an office where German officers were sitting. Very little said as no one could speak English. In came a huge container of cold stewed potatoes which they sat in front of us. These potatoes just wouldn't go down. Naturally we knew not what next—but they motioned for us to follow again. Up more stairs into a dirty room, they pointed to a straw mattress on the floor, then to me. Joining room was 2 double-deck beds for the 4 fellows. Out they went and locked the outside door.

Was so scared and the thoughts of being in the 1st room alone next to the outside door was worse. So got my mattress and pulled it into the others room. There the 5 of us attempted to sleep but little was done. First comes the interpreter asking casual questions. The air raid alarm came and he said, "Well too bad—you know you might be bombed by your own people." And out he went. This night was the longest I ever spent. A continuous tapping went on all night—each time I dozed this would awaken me. Then the horrors of what next went on and on.

Next A.M. [September 28] they came in and gave us cold black German coffee, black bread and margarine. We ate what we could as we were hungry and knew not when we might eat again. After this we sat in this room for a long time, a guard with us. The fellows drew a circle and pitched coins to pass the time and we gazed out the window. Time went very slowly.

At eleven we left again this time in an old truck on top of wood chips. Seems we went such queer ways and so slow. But the truck ran on wood chips as we were carrying so I found out later. So that explained the slowest and the driver was always killing his engine.

Stopped in several villages for why I don't know. Once an old man well dressed came up and asked "Americans?" and spoke very good English. He talked to us about 10 minutes. But each time he saw a German officer he would pretend he was leaving. He also wished us good luck. People all gaped at us as they do all POWs but took another glance when they saw a woman. Guess many have wondered just what I was.

Next stop was a German hospital where they unloaded the wood. A German officer takes us in. Where more questions asked. And just what I was—a Dr. came in and looked all over and asked me questions of being a nurse. Shook his head saying, "Too bad having a woman as you are the first one and no one knows exactly what to do."

Sisters brought us in a bowl of hot sauerkraut of a mixture and slim slices of black bread. Which tasted very good as it was hot and very clean. As soon as we had completed out in the yard to wait for the truck to be finished of unloading. People were looking from all windows and every place at us. The sisters got me a chair and I was shivering—so was everyone else. A sister came with a tray of coffee and soups. Was good and help the shivering. They also brought me an old overcoat which felt wonderful.

Soon we were off again—plus a few German soldiers and an officer—this time to Köln. Seems it took us a very long time as they had loaded empty crates on. Then they stopped at a fruit orchard where they loaded the crates and bags with apples and pears. Wasn't bad as we certainly ate enough of them. They left them off different places. Seems we went in circles in the city before getting to the air field. The city was very badly damaged. Could hardly see a house or building that wasn't torn up or windows in it. Something was still burning as a raid had been just a few hours before we arrived.

At Köln they gave me a room alone—called me out first. Naturally I didn't know what was going on and I definitely didn't want to be alone. This is when I really first let down and cried.

They couldn't figure out what was wrong with me. So I asked for my Surg. Tech to be put in there with me. Felt much better when he came in but couldn't stop crying for quite awhile.

Later a Dr. came in and looked each and every one over. No one really needed anything except Sgt. Hill. But the Dr. was very good to all and put fresh dressings on.

Went to bed—all we took off was shoes and I neatly slept after I finally got to sleep between air raid alarms. Naturally every move the guard made seem to awaken me—but did rest. Next morning as usual cold coffee and black bread, more alarms and etc. [September 29].

About 10 A.M. they came after me first where I was taken about a block and a half into one office then into another where about 6–8 officers were. They all rose and greeted me. Again many questions asked me. They also saying what a pity for them to have an American nurse and tried to assure me I would be back very shortly. The shock and everything had me very upset and tears were hard to hold back—a few started down my cheek and they thought someone must have been brutal to me so they asked that. Then they asked if I had had enough of it. So I said yes enough black bread and cold coffee.

Then he takes me into another office where I sat down and he offered me a cigarette—took it as I had none. When I stopped crying he brought the others of the crew into this office and asked them a few questions. Was beyond me why they took me before all the other officers and not them.

Here is where they took everything from us such as pictures, pencils and what had already been taken and we signed for it. Told us we would leave evening sometime by train for Frankfurt. First start of any POW. Also said the reason of night travel was it was safer.

That day at noon they gave us a very good and hot meal. Nothing like home, but good in comparison. During our stay another American officer was there too. They wouldn't let him talk to us until we all left for the train and he came too.

About 5:30 or 6 late evening, we walked with the officer who escorted us to a trolley, then to the train. Fortunately the train was in so we got in as the officer said, "Out of the cold."

The station seemed rather beaten up. The guard pointed out the huge castle to me and it looked very beautiful of what I could see in the darkness. Traveled at night.

At app. 2 A.M. we stopped to change trains and had a 2 or 3 hour wait. So he takes us down into cellar-looking place at the station where about 8 or 10 more American boys and a British boy were. Was very dirty and dingy looking, but was warm and out of the cold. Some of these boys had been at a hospital so they had Red Cross parcels. So we had a bite to eat which was thoroughly enjoyed. The best of all was the cig.

At app. 5 A.M. the entire group of us went up to get on our train. Never saw them again until we got to our destination which was Frankfurt. There we got off and got on a trolley which went very near the Stalag, or POW camp. They marched us all up to the camp where we stood outside in sort of formation.

Immediately they took the 6 of us in. Only a few minutes after we were inside they asked me to go with one of them. In which I naturally did—not knowing what would happen. Those were sad moments as I left the only people I knew and knew quite well I would never see them—but that was that. Took me to a room about 8 x 8 ft, motioned for me to enter and closed the door. Well that was a cell and I was locked in proper. Extremely depressing. The more I thought of being in a cell and wondering what [would] happen next I became terrified and started crying. Felt more like screaming and a perfect wonder I didn't.

Actually I didn't start crying until a guard opened the door and slammed a black sandwich on the table which really sounded like a chunk of wood. Felt just like a child and wanted to throw it back and do wish I could have.

The place was dirty but at least the warmest place we had been and was so tired and filthy myself.

Two German officers came in and just to look at them made me cry more.

Took my name and said how sorry they were to have a nurse as a POW as they had no facilities at all. Asked some questions and said I would go to a hospital nearby and they had a few of our boys there. A guard and an officer went with me. They gave me a blanket to wrap around me as it was very cool. Had to walk about 15 min. and seemed way up in the woods.

Arrived through locked gates of course and into a large area which was very beautiful—nice lawn, flowers and very nice looking buildings under those huge trees—HoheM [Hohemark Hospital]. All Germans—Sat me in a small hall, gave me coffee, black bread as usual and butter. It did taste good.

A German Sister was getting my room ready and one glance said I could have a bath first if I desired. Naturally that did sound wonderful, but for some reason tears would keep coming. When they took me into the room I felt more or less lost. No clothes except what I had on and had had on since I left 4 days past. Guess I felt sorry for myself.

In came a gentleman first I thought an American but was British with an American R.C. capture kit. In it was a men's shorts, socks and what have you—cig., gum. All looked good as that was all the clothes available. Then he brought me a pair of men's trousers.

He left and a German orderly locked my door, then I suddenly got hysterical. A German Sister came in to try and console me, but couldn't speak a bit of English. She was such a sweet old soul. After my cry had calmed—the Ger. Dr. had been in—went to take my bath still crying. Asked for a wash cloth in my motion language and the maid who was mopping thought I was afraid the tub wasn't clean and got some disinfectant and started letting the H_2O out of the tub. Then the Sister came with the wash rag. Now it seems funny, but certainly not then.

My room was very comfortable with a large down comforter, curtains and spotless overlooking a big garden. The Sisters brought me flowers, fruit and gave me 6 bobby pins.

I ate with a Capt. Stuffan and W.O. Stanley who worked there. They took me for walks in the area morning and evening.

The surprised looks of some of our boys to see me was amazing. Anyway they all treated me swell.

The morning of Oct. 6, 1944, left with a G. officer for Obermassfeld—left at 9 A.M. and arrived about 7:15 P.M. Had a box lunch along. Naturally everyone would gaze to see a woman

POW with a guard. But that didn't bother me much—was wondering what would happen to me. Felt sure I was going to find news on me returning home.

This was a British and American hospital run by British Drs. Maj. Sherman and SBO [senior British officer] met me and was extremely nice to me. But he was extremely overworked and overcrowded and his problem was a place to even put me up to sleep as they had all men. So he placed me in an examination room to sleep.

Helped the Maj. with some diphtheria shots in his dispensary and he also started me on my shots.

Next A.M. are in their so-called mess combination living quarters for some of the Drs. Later the Maj. takes me for a tour over the hospital. All the boys seeming very glad to see an American nurse plus being greatly surprised and all anxious to hear how I was taken. [By now it was October.]

Shall never forget one of our boys by the name of Davis from Dallas who had lost his right arm. His kind words and hospitality was really appreciated. Then to see how he made himself so useful after having an arm off was remarkable.

All the hospital staff were very good, but I especially liked Maj. Sherman as he dealt with me more and acted CO and can never express my full thanks to him. About noon he came and told me I would go to Meiningen as they had several bus loads of pts. going. So left for my new place again. By this time I was wondering if I would even stay there [Meiningen Stalag Nine C]. But nevertheless obeyed as they definitely had no place for a girl there.

With the load of pts. arrived at this place about 4:30 P.M. A very large building which used to be an old concert hall. A few barracks scattered in the yard behind the barbed wire. Many fellows out in the yard.

A room was being made ready for me. [It] was on the 4th floor and I was the only person on that floor. They put little scanty curtains and fixed my room up as nice as possible which was very comfortable. Their orderly took care of me as well and awakened me each morning and brought my washing H_2O.

Sunday Oct 8—my first walk in the mountains. They were

allowed walks with a guard so many hours a week. Thoroughly enjoyed this but not being used to walking was extremely tiring. The country was perfectly beautiful.

Capt. Laurie took me around the entire hospital to see all the boys. Was greeted cordially by all but naturally I felt very out of place being among over 500 men.

That night the boys had a concert which they had to alter considerably in order to have a woman present and thoroughly appreciated them making the arrangements. The show was very good—had different skits, song. Was very hard to understand the British and Scottish boys and usually all our boys would yell out translation.

Monday Oct 9—I started to work in the Massage room. Mainly on burn cases by supervision of Lt. Sinclair, a Scottishman, who was one of my favorites later on. This helped pass my time and gave me something to do each day. Had my own patients and enjoyed talking to them. As most were USAs which pleased me.

This hospital was one where patients came after so long as very sick ones to get legs and PT—it was called a rehabilitation center. The work was perfectly marvelous these 2 Scottish men did—leg joints all movable and teaching the boys with artificial legs to walk. They had a big gym. Capt. Laurie gave all his exercises to these boys in casts with legs off.

All his machines and exercise apparatus had been made with British materials. No help from the Germans.

They had a leg shop where 3 boys worked every day making legs which were certainly excellent to be made out of what they could get. And to think these boys had never done this in civilian life.

Several occasions the officers invited me to their private messes to have evening tea. They would save until they had sufficient ingredients and made cake or a sort of pie—which were very good. Food wasn't much as a rule, but we never went hungry.

The German rations to POWs were very little, but again the Red Cross comes in. The American, British and Canadian all sent R.C. food parcels which actually saved many from going hungry. At first full parcels but shortly after I arrived everyone went on half which made it a little less. But most foods were CHO starch so no one lost much weight.

Never got over my feeling out of place and I stuck to my room most of the time especially after I moved one floor down to a very long room with a stove in it.

Capt. Laurie had 3 pictures framed for me, curtains were made, had a bedside table, a table and a tiny cupboard in my room. Only room to get around—but found it quite comfortable. Capt. Laurie also had me an easy chair made.

They all actually were too good to me. Always trying to get or make me something to be more comfortable and make me happy.

One fellow gave me a small bag with an old white shirt and some hankies in it.

A South African gave me a lovely bottle of perfume which he had carried through Sicily and Italy and had been a POW for 4 years. He was very timid and shy as he gave it to Maj. Evans, the A. Supply officer to give it to me.

Some of the boys made little what nots for me. [English fliers gave her the silk lining from their flying boots, with which she made her underthings.] Some sending them up and wouldn't give their names. Usually found out later and thanked them as I certainly appreciated each and every one.

After about 4 weeks of no lipstick, one day Maj. Sherman sent me some over—again this was stuff from home sent to the boys in the dramatic supply. Wasn't what I would buy back home, but think I was more proud of it than any expensive brand I would buy, as this was my only thing to be feminine. Was too bad I didn't get out of the plane with my jacket as I even had nail polish in the pocket.

The German officer in charge got his wife to get me a few more bobbie pins and curlers. So I took great pride in my hair.

Was allowed a bath once a week and that day was always enjoyed. Then the problem was of it being warm. Was much luckier than the boys as the orderly brought me a pitcher of warm H_2O night and mornings so I had a sponge bath twice a day in my room.

Did my own washing in my room of my towels and pajamas—

only had 2 of each. But this always passed time. Therefore, more or less enjoyed doing it.

Passing time was the great problem. My mornings were OK as I worked, afternoons and evenings sometimes seemed like days. Tried reading as they had a fair size library but my mind just couldn't stay on a book. Tried drawing, painting, embroidery, knitting, making little animals.

During my stay the Swiss Board came by to see boys who were to be repatriated. All amputations automatically would and others went before the board. I didn't see this board, but about 4 weeks later the Swiss Welfare Commission came by and they were to see me.

Was so in hopes they would have some news on me. They were very nice to talk to but knowing little about my case and said it was so unique. Naturally I was quite disappointed. Not being able to gather anything new of what would be done. They said it all was held up on my government to reply [with] a decision of what they wanted to do.

Promised to gather all information available from our embassy when they returned to Swiss. Also see what the G. government had to say in Berlin.

One of my surprises was on Nov 23 when I had a message from an old friend who I had known back in San Antonio when he was a cadet and I a student nurse. Many people around who I had not known previous. Therefore it really cheered me up.

The message was sent by another officer who thought my name slightly familiar. When he saw me he remembered we came to England on the same boat—had even played cards and seen a show together. He had run around on the boat with a good friend of mine and knew many of the girls from my squadron. Therefore I thoroughly enjoyed talking with him and he also said the same. After 2 months of seeing so many of our boys and never one you had known previous.

Reba Whittle stopped writing in her diary at the end of November 1944, but she was not repatriated until the end of January 1945. She was told she was being exchanged for German prisoners of war and left her stalag on the evening of January 25, 1945, accompanied by members of the German Red Cross. She was put in a boxcar, along with a number of other prisoners, the majority of whom were ill.

She first went to Switzerland, where a Swiss couple took her to their home and she had her first truly hot bath in months. The next day she was repatriated with 109 other American prisoners of war.

The month after that she signed a certificate stating that she would reveal none of her experiences, except to chosen military officials. It was only after the war ended that much was known about her capture by the Germans.

On August 3, 1945, Reba Whittle married Lieut. Col. Stanley W. Tobiason, who had been a pilot stationed in England at the time her plane was shot down. Reba died of breast cancer in 1981, and was buried in the National Cemetery at Presidio, California. She had been a courageous woman.

8

A Bombing Mission

Elise Berger had grown up in Springfield, Illinois. When she was twenty-one she enlisted in the Army Nurse Corps. It was December 1944. Less than a year later she, along with forty-four other nurses, arrived on Tinian, a small island in the central Pacific. Tinian had been important to the Allies since it had three large air bases from which the B-29 bombers could take off to bomb the Japanese mainland.

In July 1944 the U.S. Marines had taken nearby Saipan in bloody battles with the Japanese, and it was from Saipan that they assaulted Tinian, which was secured by August.

In 1945 when the nurses arrived for duty with the 309th General Hospital, they were housed in Quonset huts, which were fenced in and highly protected by guards since, as Elise wrote home, there were still "plenty of Japs" in the area. Shortly before Elise had arrived, two nurses and two male army officers had been murdered by the Japanese and had been found hanging from trees in the jungle. It was common knowledge that some Japanese were still living in coral caves on the island.

Each day was full for the nurses, beginning in the early morn-

ing, when they were awak-
ened by the roar of bombers'
motors. Their quarters were
located between two big airfields on the island, and the
pilots' flight plans for their
daily missions took them
directly overhead.

One day was especially
memorable for the nurses:
August 6, 1945.

"It was a very clear moonlit
night when the plane took
off. The stars were spectacular. I wish I had been at the
field for takeoff but we were
not allowed out at that hour.
Our gates were closed and a
guard was at the gate. That

Elise Berger, right, relaxes with other army nurses on Yellow Beach, Tinian, 1945.

afternoon we begged off our assignments at the station hospital
to see the crew of the *Enola Gay* land at the field. The area was
packed with officers and men on the taxiways, all cheering with
cameras clicking and tape recorders rolling. The crew lined up
in front of the plane for an air force general. Tibbets, the pilot,
received the Distinguished Service Cross on his coveralls, and
Parsons the Silver Star."

The first atomic bomb had been dropped on Hiroshima.

On August 8, Elise and a group of other nurses were invited
to the Air Force Club to socialize, as they often did, with the
crews who had been on missions. "Their objective during the
day was to shoot down as many Japanese planes as possible and
to have many missions to their credit. They needed the little
relaxation at the club. Sometimes, a tentative date never came
to pass, for that very day the pilot would have been shot down."

That evening, Elise was sitting next to a pilot at a long table
with the other nurses and officers of the wing.

"He seemed somewhat nervous and frequently looked at his
watch as he sipped at his one beer—the quota for air force per-

sonnel assigned to a mission. He said, 'I have a big assignment tomorrow. I'm going to do something spectacular.'

"We were used to that kind of talk and the pilots got to be called 'glamour boys' because of their bragging. My response was 'Oh, you guys, always are bragging—what about the army, navy, marines, engineers, Seabees, and medical staff on this island—don't you think we do anything worthwhile?'

"Then he said in a low voice so no one else could hear, 'Mark my words. I'm going to go down in history books.'"

Very early on the morning of August 9, a B-29, the *Bock's Car*, roared down the runway and took off from Tinian. A little over seven hours later, at 11:01 that day, it dropped the second atomic bomb, called the Fat Man, over Nagasaki. The pilot was Elise's confidant of the previous evening. He *did* have a special mission.

Elise and the other nurses had had no idea about the operations of the 509th Bomb Group, because the men lived by themselves in a compound on another part of the island. The nurses knew they had been selected to do "something special." They learned about this "special" event after Colonel Tibbets and his crew dropped the first atomic bomb.

On V-J Day the men happily drank up their ration of beer, and a few days later the chaplain of the island held a solemn high mass of thanksgiving for the end of the war. The general

Breakfast on Tinian, after a high mass of thanksgiving on V-J Day. The planes that dropped the atomic bombs on Japan took off from the island.

of the island also spoke at the mass, and it was then that Elise learned that her hospital unit would be sent to Japan.

Elise stayed on for a time at Tinian. In the middle of October, she received her orders to go to Sasebo, Japan. The nurses boarded the APA *Gage 168* and after they docked in Sasebo, went by train to Fukuoka and then to their hospital, which was located about two miles from the city.

Elise found that nursing in Japan meant using primitive and makeshift equipment: empty beer cans served as thermometer holders and specimen jars; instruments

Army nurses on Tinian drinking their ration of beer in celebration of V-J Day.

were sterilized with a match. She used sheets from her footlocker to make dressings for the injured. The marines had not left them much. Elise was assigned to a recovery ward. She wrote home:

"Jeep accidents rate first over here, and then casualties from the Philippines en route to the States. The majority of cases are severe burns, malaria, dysentery, and jungle rot. We have no washcloths. We have to heat the water for baths in a bucket upon a potbelly stove. The patients have to be fed out of a mess kit for their C rations, and they have to drink from a granite bowl; we have no cups. The patients that have come up from the Philippines deserve better than that."

Daily life in Japan was varied. Events ranged from the horror of seeing a Japanese rummage in crumpled ruins and "knock himself to eternity by picking up an unexploded hand grenade" to receiving a beautiful obi.

Conditions improved for the nurses, but Elise was upset at much of what she saw in Japan. "Most of them here had their homes destroyed and carts are continually going by on the

Army nurses wearing gas masks during basic training at Camp McCoy, Wisconsin, 1944.

streets containing salvaged possessions. It sure looks pitiful. They eat anything they can find.

"The other day I went out for my laundry at the prison. It sure was gruesome, moldy and cold. The prison hospital was horrible, there were over 200 people lying on the cold cement waiting for death. There were five sick ones with a blanket over them and shivering because they were stark naked. The mean old Jap attendants laughed at their sick moaning and crying from pain. Oh, I wanted to go in and help them so badly even if they were Japs, but the attendant would not let me get farther than the door."

It took until February 1946 for Elise's hospital unit to be declared surplus, and soon after she boarded the USS *Pope* at Yokohama for the voyage home to America. In April, at Eastertime, she received an honorable discharge from the United States Army. She had, she wrote, been proud to be a part of service to her country.

Elise Berger married in 1946, and during the Korean War traveled throughout Europe as a dependent of army personnel. Returning to Springfield, she resumed nursing and received her bachelor of science degree.

She retired in 1988. She has three children and eight grandchildren. She volunteers at a local hospital and is active in church work. She is a member of the Women's Overseas Service League and in 1994 hosted a lecture series at the Illinois State Museum in connection with a traveling exhibit about Americans in World War II.

PART TWO

Navy Nurse Corps

In May 1908, Congress passed a bill establishing the Nurse Corps as an integral part of the United States Navy. The women of the corps were the only women in the navy. While they were considered military personnel, not civilians, they did not have official status as either officers or enlisted personnel. They were under navy regulations but did not receive any retirement benefits.

The first members of the corps—only twenty women—were stationed at the naval hospital in Washington, D.C. By 1910, navy nurses were permitted to serve overseas, and by 1920 they were on duty on hospital ships.

During World War I, 1,835 navy nurses served, but after the armistice, their numbers slowly dwindled. Enlistment continued to decline until 1938, when there were rumblings of the coming war. The Naval Reserve Act was passed, enabling qualified nurses to be recruited for the Nurse Corps Reserve. When the United States declared war in 1941, the number of nurses joining the corps rapidly increased as women rushed to join the services.

The nurses of the Regular Navy and the naval reserve served

in hospitals at home and overseas; they worked on air evacuation planes and hospital ships. At the time of peak enrollment
in 1945, there were 11,086 nurses on duty with the corps.

The navy nurses provided essential support in the battle
against the Japanese in the Pacific theater. Hospitals all over the
United States received the living casualties of the war that had
intensified as the Allied forces sought to reverse the first flush
of Japanese victories. The surprise attack on Pearl Harbor had
been only the beginning.

During the early years of the war, Americans fought bitterly
for New Guinea, for Guadalcanal, in the Solomons,
Bougainville, and the many other islands overrun by the Japanese. Navy nurses looked after the patients sent home from these
battles who needed surgical, orthopedic, and long-term care.

As the war accelerated, the nurses were shipped overseas in
greater numbers, to fleet hospitals, to Brisbane, to New Guinea.
Whether the fighting men were wounded or suffering from "jungle rot" or mental exhaustion and anxiety, the nurses were
there, enduring the long hours and miserable conditions to try
to make the men whole again.

In 1944, after the Allies had turned the tide of battle on the
ground, sea, and in the air, the Japanese became desperate and
started the training of the kamikazes—the suicide pilots. They
launched them against the Allies in the invasion of Leyte,
against the U.S. fleets at Okinawa, against Allied ships wherever
they could find them. The kamikaze became a terrifying
weapon, causing horrendous casualties, many of whom were
cared for by the navy nurses.

Wherever they were stationed, the navy nurses endured long
hours and often miserable conditions. They proved that they
had the training, the will, the heart, and the stamina to help the
fighting men of their country in their time of need.

*After the defeat of the Japanese, a grateful nation welcomed the navy
nurses home. In 1947, in recognition of their service, the Navy Nurse
Corps was made a full, permanent, commissioned staff corps of the U.S.
Navy.*

9

And the Kamikazes Came

Kathryn Lichty grew up on a Illinois farm during the Depression. She had always wanted to be a nurse, and in 1935 she managed to persuade her father to let her enter nurses' training at St. Francis Hospital in Freeport, Illinois. After Kathryn graduated from nursing school, she secured a job at St. Francis, and then proceeded up the financial scale with new jobs in Chicago and later in Santa Maria, California, where she fell in love with the state and its palm trees, flowering oranges, and wonderful climate. "I felt," she wrote, "as though I had died and gone to heaven."

Then came December 7. Kathryn wanted to join the Navy Nurse Corps, but she had just begun her postgraduate work. She called her parents and asked what she should do. Her mother advised her to finish her schooling and then apply for the navy. That's exactly what she did.

She was ordered to Long Island's St. Albans Naval Hospital on October 12, 1943. She was twenty-six years old.

"I had no indoctrination, and the shock of going directly from being a civilian to navy regulations was something else, but I

Navy nurse Kathryn Lichty (first right) with other nurses at Patuxent River, Maryland.

found I liked it—the discipline and all that was done in the 'navy way.'"

Life at St. Albans was very pleasant for Kathryn. She worked in routine surgery, and when not busy there worked in Central Supply. The nurses at the hospital "felt like queens" when they took advantage of the free beauty treatments offered to service-women by Helena Rubinstein and Elizabeth Arden.

After a few months at St. Albans, Kathryn was ordered to Patuxent River, Maryland, as surgery supervisor and anesthetist.

"We did everything. Fortunately, I had first choice for my corpsmen and WAVES—and what wonderful young men and women they were. One of the cases I vividly remember is a cae-sarian section that had to be done on a lieutenant commander's wife, after a very hard and prolonged labor. No one but me had ever seen a section done. I explained to the fellows what to expect, and as I told them, 'I'll be busy with the anesthetic, so

Navy nurses on the town at El Morocco in New York City. Kathryn Lichty is third from right.

you'll be on your own.'" Fortunately all went well, and the executive officer gave them all a "job well done" commendation.

Early in 1945, Kathryn, along with several other nurses, was ordered to Oak Knoll Naval Hospital in Oakland, California. It was here, in the midst of the area's natural beauty, that Kathryn felt the impact of the horrors of war.

The naval hospital was a huge complex, built on a series of hills, with many walking bridges and temporary buildings of stained redwood. At its peak, the hospital had eight thousand patients, three thousand corpsmen, five hundred nurses, and five different surgeries. Kathryn was assigned to bone and brain.

"I remember well a young enlisted man who had seen much action in the Pacific theater. He had been rotated home and sent to Oak Knoll for a physical—had never been wounded, not even a scratch. His complaint at sick call was 'Doc, I can't keep up with my buddies the way I used to.' The findings were a brain tumor. I gave the anesthetic for the eight-hour surgery—and in those years it was N_2O and ether. All of us were devastated at the prognosis. We lost him a week later."

Then the Japanese kamikaze attacks began in earnest.

"The most horrible cases of burns and injuries I have ever

seen before or since. It was not uncommon to have more than
nine hundred cases admitted over a period of twenty-four hours.
Everyone had to take turns to care for the casualties.

"I felt rage at the Japanese government for these horrible
attacks, knowing they were using last-minute tactics; rage at seeing our men suffer—totally helpless in that there was nothing to
do for some of the victims except adjust the pillows under their
heads, listen to them, hold their hands, promise to send a letter
to someone. I had to wonder many, many times, When will the
men who send our sons, husbands, brothers into battle ever
learn? Most of the cases, of course, were horrible burns, fractures, debridements, and so on. Working around the clock, of
course, was tiring, but no one complained. We were the lucky
ones, we still had our bodies intact. A job had to be done."

Three weeks before V-J Day, forty-three of the nurses were
ordered to Okinawa, but before they could be shipped out, the
Japanese surrendered. With the end of the war, the navy nurses
were shunted off to San Francisco to face a commanding officer
who asked them, "Where did you come from?" He sent them
out to find a hotel, and after some weeks they were ordered
back to Oak Knoll.

It was February 1946 before Kathryn Lichty was discharged
from the service to pick up the threads of her civilian life.

*Following her service, Kathryn Lichty married, was widowed, and
remarried. She had one son and now has one grandson. Kathryn and
her husband just celebrated their forty-fifth year of marriage.*

*Kathryn Lichty Piaskowski continued as a nurse anesthetist until she
retired in the 1970s. She now does volunteer work for senior health
screening programs.*

PART THREE

Women's Army Corps

On May 15, 1942, President Franklin D. Roosevelt signed the bill authorizing the formation of the Women's Auxiliary Army Corps, which would function with the U.S. Army, but not be a part of it. The purpose of the WAAC was to utilize women's talents and abilities in the war effort and to provide women to serve as army support staff, freeing men for combat duty. It was the first military service during World War II to enlist women, and the only one to offer overseas duty.

At the time the WAAC was established, the Axis powers had scored victory after victory over the Allies. In June 1941, Hitler had invaded the USSR. The Japanese had bombarded Midway, invaded the Gilbert Islands, seized Guam, Rabaul, New Britain, and Tulagi, and attacked Burma. The Japanese were launching massive air attacks on Darwin, Australia. Maj. Gen. Jonathan Wainwright had surrendered the Philippines to the Japanese.

With the announcement of the formation of the WAAC, women flocked to enlist, eager to serve in any capacity, at any place. Training began at Fort Des Moines, Iowa, in July 1942, with 440 women enrolled in the newly created six-week officer candidate school. At the same time some 125 enlisted women took a four-week basic training course.

As more and more women enlisted, the WAAC expanded. They established a second WAAC training center in Daytona Beach, Florida, and later opened training centers at Fort Oglethorpe, Georgia; Fort Devens, Massachusetts; and Camp Ruston, Louisiana. Some of the first class of WAAC officers served at the training centers, indoctrinating new recruits in the army way.

After training, the women were detailed to almost every branch of the army. They were cooks, typists, postal workers, and telephone operators, cryptographic technicians, teletypists, clerks, and radio intelligence officers. One group even tested chemically impregnated clothing.

The first detachment of WAACs sent to an overseas post arrived in North Africa in January 1943 to be part of Gen. Dwight D. Eisenhower's staff. The following September, President Roosevelt established the Women's Army Corps (WAC) to replace the auxiliary organization, thus giving the women full military status. By this time, some sixty thousand women had enlisted to serve in the army.

In January 1944, Eisenhower became supreme commander of the Allied forces in Europe. The first U.S. air raid was made on Berlin that spring; in June, D-Day began the great assault on the Continent. Thousands of WACs had been serving in England, and many of them followed the Allied forces as they drove into France, liberated Paris, and pushed through Belgium and Luxembourg toward Germany itself. Eisenhower's "little carrier pigeon" WAC messenger was on duty in the war room in Rheims, France, when the Germans signed the official declaration of surrender.

Thousands of WACs also served in the Middle East, in the Far East, and in Pacific areas. There they worked in all kinds of jobs, as coders in message centers, as radar specialists, photolaboratory and medical technicians, as clerical workers, telephone operators, translators, drivers, in intelligence—in jobs that needed to be done.

They worked in Egypt, India, China, Australia, New Guinea, and in the Philippines. As these women served in foreign areas, the Allies turned the tide of the war as they drove the Japanese from the islands captured in the flush of early victories. Some battles were fiercely fought, and there were many American casualties before the Japanese surrendered.

Some of the WACS who served in combat areas also were casualties. During the war, 181 WACs died, and 16 were awarded the Purple Heart. Sixty-six WACs became prisoners of the Japanese. By their service in the United States, in Europe, and in the Pacific the women of the WAC were valuable assets. They were needed and they served their country well.

After the war, on June 12, 1948, a law was passed making the Women's Army Corps a permanent organization to provide a nucleus for expansion in case of emergency.

10

Discrimination

Charity Adams was one of the first black women to be accepted for the first officer candidate class at the first WAAC Training Center at Fort Des Moines, Iowa. She had grown up in a segregated South and enlisted into an army corps that, she soon discovered, was similarly segregated.

When the black women in her group arrived at the fort's reception center, their first instruction, given by a young red-haired male second lieutenant, was: "Will the colored girls move over on this side."

Charity Adams Earley wrote in her book many years later, "There was a moment of stunned silence, for even in the United States of the forties it did not occur to us that this could happen."

It did happen.

I sent in my application to join the Women's Army Auxiliary Corps on the recommendation of the dean of women of my alma mater. Although I had no idea what being in the army would mean it did seem to promise more excitement than my

Charity Adams sports the WAAC summer uniform, 1942.

teaching job. My parents' approval came in the form of a "if that's what you want to do."

After the most complete examination, physical, mental, and psychological, I have ever had, followed by an interview in which I assured the interviewers that I was the best qualified candidate they had, I left Fort Hayes in Columbus, Ohio, four pounds lighter.

Three days later I received notice that I had been selected for the WAAC. At this point, I had three choices. I could refuse to join, I could be sworn into the corps on July 13, 1942, and be put on leave until the eighteenth, or I could report on July 18, prepared to travel, and be sworn into the corps. By the thirteenth, I was eager to go, so I reported and was sworn into the corps. I was twenty-three years old.

On the morning of July 18, 1942, I reported to the headquarters of the Seventh Service Command at Fort Hayes, packed and ready to leave. Immediately, we climbed onto our first truck to be driven to the railroad station, where we marched in twos to the coach to which we were assigned, not realizing how inappropriate our high heels, our smart suits and picture hats would be in a few hours. The trip to Iowa was filled with getting acquainted, the loss of air conditioning with a change of coach, and finally arrival at the Des Moines railroad station, where it was raining and murky. We marched by two to the truck for our second ride, this one to Fort Des Moines, the site of the first WAAC Training Center.

We had been integrated with all the activities at Fort Hayes and on the trip to Fort Des Moines. When we were assigned to our quarters, suddenly the Negro women were in separate quarters, where we remained during our training.

We were part of the first group of women to join the WAAC. There were four hundred white women and, per the conditions of the times, 10 percent of the number of white women meant there was an allotment of forty Negro women.

The training for the first class of officer candidates began on July 20, even though members of the class continued to arrive. There were four training companies and our group of Negro women were assigned to First Company, Third Platoon. Although we marched as the third part of the first company, we had separate classes, except for physical training, which was held for all classes on the parade grounds. Over the six weeks of our training "the Third Platoon" became an affectionate term to its members.

Our trainers, officers and enlisted personnel, were all white men. They were indeed carefully picked and trained. They were all polite and helpful, although there were a few instances when they did not know how to talk to women. After all, they were accustomed to training men. Gradually, as women officers were available, the men all transferred out, the enlisted men first, then the officers as women took their assignments. Most of the male officers with whom I worked showed the least amount of racial prejudice. Some of them became friends whose help I still appreciate.

The first class of officers graduated on August 29, 1942. Traditionally, class members graduate in alphabetical order. My name was Adams, and I was the first name on my company roster. Using the traditional system I would have been the first WAAC officer to be commissioned. Since I am a Negro, that could not be. Our class graduated by platoon: I was the first black officer to be commissioned from the Third Platoon. There were four Negro candidates whose last names began with the letter *A*.

Immediately following graduation, we moved out of the training barracks into other quarters. Eleven of us from the Third Platoon moved into Quarters Number One, the first house among quarters for officers at the other end of the post. The rest of our group all moved to other quarters. We also began interviews to ascertain the types of job assignments we would have. The man who interviewed me never raised his eyes from the papers before him but he did tell me as he dismissed me, "I don't know what you young women can do. You are too young to handle people." I thanked him and left. The interview was on Saturday afternoon, and on Monday morning I was assigned as a company commander of a basic training company.

The company to which I was assigned was Company Twelve, Third Training Regiment, a company that existed mostly on paper since only a small number of Negro women were joining the WAAC. The company was located in Boomtown, a newly developed part of the army post. All of us assigned to Company Twelve went out to locate our buildings and prepare them for the troops we knew would come. And they did, at first in such small numbers that we had as many officers as trainees.

In a short time there was a realignment of company designations. Our Company Twelve became Company Fourteen for several weeks. Eventually, our company was designated Company Eight, and it was with this number that the company became the showplace of the training center. Many commanders in the field would not accept Negro personnel unless there existed a segregated assignment for them. For that reason my officers and noncommissioned officers were not sent into the field as rapidly as white personnel, so we learned to use training materials and methods over and over again.

All of the commissioned officers were titled third officer at graduation. Upon promotion the next title would be second officer, and the next would be first officer. These titles were the equivalents to second lieutenant, first lieutenant, and captain. We were addressed with the army titles but used the WAAC titles for official signatures.

The Training Center had continued to graduate third officers as they trained enlisted personnel to serve at various army posts and medical installations. On December 23, 1942, the entire first officer class was promoted, most to second officer, while twenty-four of us were promoted to first officer (captain) so that the corps could have some command structure. I was one of those promoted to first officer.

All this time I was still the commanding officer of a basic training company where we made newly arrived civilians into women soldiers. Well into the spring of 1943, I remained with Company Eight. As a captain, I was very senior since most officers only had a few months of company duty before they were shipped out to some base for duty. I had become sort of advisor to company commanders new on the job or with less experience than I had. Somehow the noncommissioned officers of Company Eight also remained with the organization.

In May of 1943, I turned the company over to Lt. Alma Berry when I was reassigned to the Training Center headquarters as a training supervisor. We watched over the training activities and, when needed, created and scheduled new programs. Over the months, I gradually acquired additional assignments such as station control officer, forms control officer, and work simplification officer.

On September 1, 1943, all members of the WAAC who chose to remain in the corps were sworn into the U.S. Army, Women's Army Corps, after being dismissed from the WAAC the day before.

On a very hot day that same month, I received word to report to Colonel McCoskrie, the Training Center commandant, at the reviewing stand on the parade grounds. When I arrived at the reviewing stand, Maj. Harriet West, from WAC headquarters in Washington, was with the colonel. The three of us moved into position to review the troops. Suddenly, Colonel Mac and Major West reached up and pinned major's leaves on my shoulders. I think that was the only real surprise I received during my military service.

The Women's Army Corps had grown so much that two additional training centers had been opened. Thousands of women had been out on assignments to replace men to be sent to the front, which had been the original plan. Unexpected specialist jobs developed and many officers were needed for administration of WAC organizations. At one point, there was a surplus of people waiting for assignments while male unit commanders were being persuaded that women could do jobs in the military.

In many cases, Negro WACs were sent out for specific jobs but were used in very demeaning jobs and assigned to inappropriate quarters. There were many cases of mistreatment of Negro women, and in many cases the women had to be reassigned because the officers in charge were unwilling to use them in the jobs for which they were trained.

White women were being sent overseas for duty with American troops. Most of us had given thought to and had wanted to go overseas. However, no Negro women were being sent, and the reason given was that the presence of Negro women would cause trouble, the nature of which we were unable to imagine.

When I moved into Quarters Number One in August of 1942 I had assumed that it was a short-term housing assignment. I lived in that house more than two years while all the other housemates changed. I settled in, did a bit of decorating of the quarters. I even had a vegetable garden behind the house. I think I used my vegetables two or three times at the house but I was happy to give them to our mess hall.

In addition to my many assignments from the training office I went on War Bond drives to cities in Iowa. I also was the accompanying officer for troop movements to other army installations, where I was happy to visit with officers formerly stationed at Fort Des Moines. I had two temporary duty assignments at WAC headquarters in the Pentagon Building.

One day I asked my commanding officer why I did not get an assignment away from Fort Des Moines. He said that there had been several requests for me but he had refused to let me go unless there was at least the opportunity for promotion. Soon after that my orders were issued for overseas duty.

The organization of the 6888th Central Postal Directory Battalion was the result of the strenuous efforts of the Negro press and the national civil rights organizations. Commanding officers of units in the European theater of operations were reluctant to accept Negro WACs for assignment, although white WACs had been in the ETO for almost two years.

When the unit was finally authorized, prospective members were assembled at Fort Oglethorpe, Georgia, for training and final clearance. The women, both officer and enlisted, came from units all over the country. At Fort Oglethorpe, the unit had to be reduced in size. Some of the reasons for elimination were health conditions, fear of going overseas, insubordination, and lack of cooperation.

As well as supervising the trainees, the officers received much of the same training received by the troops. The unit was temporarily organized into four companies.

After a week of training, Captain Abbie N. Campbell and I received orders to proceed to Washington, D.C., carrying sufficient equipment and supplies to live for three months. We had to find our own quarters—fortunately I had close friends who accommodated us.

For two days we reported to various offices, finally receiving orders, with Priority II clearance, for departure to Paris. Per our instructions, we opened our orders after one hour in flight and discovered that we were en route to London.

We reported to the WAC director for the ETO, who helped us get our quarters and mess hall assignment. Immediately, we began reporting to various departments and were received in Paris by several generals, including the first African-American general, Brig. Gen. B. O. Davis, whom I had known in college. We also reported to Lt. Gen. John C. H. Lee, commanding general, communications zone, European theater of operations, who invited us to dinner at his suite.

During the course of the dinner, General Lee turned to me and asked, "Adams, can your troops march?"

This man was my boss, so there was only one answer. "Yes, sir. They are the best marching troops you will ever see."

General Lee then asked when our outfit would be in Birmingham.

"They will arrive on the twelfth, sir, and be in quarters on the thirteenth."

"Good. I will be in Birmingham on the fifteenth to review the troops."

Captain Campbell was not very happy about my confidence in the marching ability of our troops. We met the troops in Glasgow, Scotland, on February 12, 1945, as they came down the gangplank of the *Ile de France*. They had been eleven days at sea, being chased by German U-boats. Because of the seasickness, the salt spray, and the limited personal conveniences, the group was a very unhappy group. Many declared that they would never go back home until a bridge was built over the Atlantic.

Because of my promise to General Lee, we concentrated on getting the troops in quarters and seeing that the uniforms were in decent condition. Every officer gave 100 percent to get done all the things needed. The troops wondered what all the rush was about; they wanted to rest.

General Lee and his entourage arrived three minutes before the appointed hour, and the 6888th passed in review for the first time, successfully.

We were immediately aware of the citizens of Birmingham as they were of us. They referred to us in terms that were not in use in 1945, some of which we had never heard. "Black" came into use some years later, and we had never heard the term "Negress". They followed if we were on the streets and passed, in great numbers, by our facility. White soldiers, who had been in Birmingham long before we arrived, had supplied the populus with unbelievable tales about Negroes—and the Birminghamites believed them. They kept trying to see evidence of the tales they had heard.

I was in command of a battalion, as ordered, and we were attached to the headquarters, First Base Post Office, and referred to as the battalion. We were organized into five companies: Companies A, B, C, and D were the postal service companies, while Headquarters Company was the administrative and support unit for the battalion.

We kept waiting for the written orders for what we were now doing: the directory service was operating. Finally on March 2, 1945, I issued General Order One in which I assumed command of the 6888th Central Postal Directory Battalion. On March 21, Maj. Charity E. Adams and Capt. Abbie N. Campbell were relieved from assignment to the First Base Post Office.

A postal directory unit is responsible for the redirection of mail that has had one attempted delivery. In war zones personnel move frequently and the postal service attempts delivery for thirty days, using the change of address card filed with the directory. The total of U.S. personnel was estimated to be about 7 million (only the War Department knew the exact number). At one point we knew we had at least seventy-five hundred Robert Smiths.

The members of the 6888th fought World War II on many fronts:

1. the prejudice of males against females
2. the prejudice of whites against blacks
3. the prejudice of natives against foreigners
4. organizational prejudices brought from home
5. the common enemy we all fought.

One of the two recreational hotels maintained by the American Red Cross was used by WAC enlisted personnel. The women of the 6888th used the facility for about a month before the Red Cross decided to establish a segregated hotel for them. I was invited to see the hotel when it was acquired and when it was furnished. On my first visit I urged them not to furnish the hotel since none of the women, black or white, had complained about sharing the same building. On the second visit I assured them that no members of the 6888th would spend one night in their new hotel.

In the meantime, my staff and I had planned what we would offer the women in order to avoid being assigned to a segregated hotel on their London visits. These were adult women who could make their own choices and we took a chance on our plans. However, when the entire group was called together and the situation was explained, the women agreed to our terms. We had to stand together for the cause.

Because all the enlisted women lived in the same building I decided I wanted a Quonset hut so the NCOs would have a place to relax away from the troops. My first three requests went up the channels and came back marked "Request denied." After the fourth request I received a telephone call from a high-level supply officer who asked, "Adams, what the hell do you want with a Quonset hut?"

When I explained he said, "You are supposed to move to the Continent soon."

"I was told that in January when I arrived, sir, and it's three months later. Besides, the hut can be taken down and moved when we move."

"Well, I'll see." One week later a platoon of engineers arrived with two Quonset huts. One was set up immediately for the non-coms. Several weeks later the second hut was put up as an officers' club. Sure enough, as soon as we dedicated the officers' club with a party, we received our orders to move to Rouen, France.

Overseas calls from the USA to London were routed through the Birmingham telephone exchange. Operators of the 6888th soon made friends with the city operators via the telephones. During the early morning of April 12, the telephone rang in our quarters. The call was for me from our chief operator.

"Major Adams," the operator said. "I just got a call from one of the Birmingham overseas operators with whom I have a telephone friendship. She is in the process of putting through a call to the prime minister at 10 Downing Street, but she paused long enough to signal that the president is dead. President Roosevelt is dead."

We were all shocked and really feared for our treatment when President Truman took office. As we worried we participated in over thirty memorial services; every service wanted representatives of the American forces. I personally attended five services as, to my surprise, I was the highest-ranking American officer in the immediate area.

On V-E Day I was en route to Paris from where I would go on to Rouen to prepare for the arrival of the 6888th. France was celebrating and Paris was one great party with Allied personnel as the guests of honor. For souvenirs, the citizens of Paris tore insignias and epaulets off and took gear and shoes, offered wines to all. I saw five men tear a jeep apart and pass out large pieces for souvenirs. I had to take refuge in a male transit officers' hotel.

Two days later I managed to get to Rouen, where things were going well in preparation for the troops, except for one problem. Bunk beds for 887 people had been lost somewhere in the south of France. And the troops were en route. Regular army cots could not be used because they would need twice the space of bunk beds. One of the German prisoners of war made a suggestion to solve our problem. Hence, the 6888th became the only army unit with double-decked army cots. Several weeks after the troops were in these quarters, some soldiers liberated the exact number of mattresses needed to make the cots comfortable.

Our jobs remained the same but there were other interesting aspects of our service. The fighting was over and the troops were moving back from the front. It seemed that most of them came through Rouen. One day about a week after we started working in Rouen, as I was walking across our small army post, a non-com said to me, "Major, there are seven hundred and twenty-five enlisted men for each enlisted woman and thirty-one officers for each female officer.

"You mean in the ETO, I suppose."

"No, ma'am. I mean outside our gates."

I immediately went to a window overlooking the gates. The number was not exact, but it was close. Shortly after that day, as a result of a conference with a committee of enlisted women who met with me, the post was declared off-limits to men on Monday, except those who worked there, so that the women had at least one day to themselves.

We had a medical officer assigned to the unit. As the men were reassigned from the battle zones, we were assigned a second medical officer. He asked for a conference with me right away. He said he had been an obstetrician but hoped he would not be called to use those skills after his years at the front. I assured him that he could take care of cuts and bruises since we had rare need of his specialty.

The U.S. government had a contract with the French government to employ a number of civilians. As a result we had two hundred civilian workers, who were assigned to the postal directory, for whom we provided the noon meal. The first few days on which we provided that meal many of our contract workers collapsed. Our well-trained mess officer recognized that their wartime diets made their systems unable to handle the amount and types of food served in one meal. The problem was solved by serving two meals from one ration.

Soon after V-E Day things began to change for the 6888th. Our workload began to shrink slowly. Personnel who had earned sufficient points returned to the States. We had a few marriages and husband and wife reunions when the men came from the front.

In October we moved the unit to Paris, where we lived in hotels: enlisted personnel had an entire hotel, including a mess hall, while the officers were quartered in rooms in the smaller Hotel Etats-Unis. This time the workplace was some distance away and required transportation.

By December, the unit was small enough for me to return to the States. I did stay long enough to see "Yankee, Go Home" signs go up on the walls of the buildings in Paris right under the older signs that read "Kilroy Was Here."

After spending the entire war gossiping about why the women were in the service, the public was now interested in hearing our stories. I was, and am, very proud of my time in the military and accepted a number of invitations to speak to various groups.

Most of all I am proud to have had the opportunity to serve with such a fine group of women soldiers and to have been their commanding officer. Almost fifty years later, collectively and individually we have pleasant recall of the 6888th, of the common battles we fought and special friendships, which last till now.

Charity Adams went back to school after the war for a master's degree. She worked briefly as manager of a music school, then returned to the field of education as Dean of Student Personnel Services at Tennessee A & I College (now University) and Dean of Students at Georgia State College (now Savannah State College).

She married in August 1949 and moved to Zurich, where her husband was a medical student at the University. They returned to the United States and settled in Dayton, Ohio. They had two children, and Charity Adams Earley became active in community affairs, hoping to have, by her service, "smoothed the way to some degree for the next generation."

11

Mosquitoes and Mud

Gertrude Morris had just married her college sweetheart, a newly commissioned second lieutenant in the United States Army, and they had settled happily and comfortably in an apartment near Fort Bragg, North Carolina. They "naively assumed" they would spend the rest of the war years there, but within two months Lieutenant Morris was on his way to join the North Africa invasion. Gertrude Morris was now a "forlorn bride" and returned to the family farm in rural New Jersey.

But there was no doubt in Gertrude's mind as to how she would spend the rest of the war. It was November 1942, and she was twenty-three years old. She enlisted in the WAAC and was sent to Fort Des Moines, Iowa, for her basic training. She remembers quite vividly the cold at the newly-established base; the corps was so new that proper women's uniforms had not yet been manufactured.

"... falling out for reveille at 6:00 A.M. in dark, below-zero weather in deep snow ... the oversized man's GI overcoat, which I wore over a thin fatigue dress ... a typical sad sack GI shivering with a coat dragging in the snow."

After basic training and a few months of clerical work, Gertrude went to Fort Oglethorpe, Georgia, for reassignment. She was sent to Kansas City, Missouri, where she attended radio operator's school for three months and dreamed about becoming a radio operator on an airplane—an impossible dream for a WAAC.

Next, it was on to Blackland Army Airfield in Waco, Texas, a pilot training base.

"The army, having trained me in Morse code, in its great wisdom now placed me as a control tower operator, where all communication was by voice."

In the control tower she helped direct the training flights and all other incoming and outgoing traffic. It was "the most exciting job" she had ever had. Gertrude can still remember their call letters "MF81."

Then, in another of the army's mysterious ways, for no discernible reason Gertrude was again transferred, this time to Ellington Field in Houston, Texas, a training base for flight navigators, where she was assigned to a dull typing job.

"Fortunately my boredom lasted only a few months. Back I went to Fort Oglethorpe, which was then a staging area for overseas assignment. My excitement was intense—not only was I to go overseas, but perhaps I would by some fantastic stroke of luck cross paths with my husband, who was by then in Germany with the Ninth Infantry Division. This was the fall of 1944; he had participated in the North Africa invasion, followed by Sicily and the second front in France.

"Of course, irony and the army's logic prevailed, and my orders came through for the Pacific theater."

Gertrude boarded ship in California and landed, after four weeks, at Hollandia, New Guinea. After a short stay there, she took an army transport plane to Leyte, an island in the Philippines. En route, she spent the night on the small island of Peleliu, part of the Palau group in the western Caroline Islands. Peleliu had recently been captured from the Japanese, and Gertrude found the odor of decaying bodies that had not yet been buried "indescribable."

"Leyte is one of the more primitive islands of the Philippine chain. It was here that U.S. troops made their first landing when the Philippines were liberated from the Japanese in 1944–45. The only occasion in my whole army experience on which I said to myself, Gertrude, how did you ever get yourself into this? was when, upon arrival, we were divided into groups of four or five and assigned a muddy patch of earth along with a pyramidal tent. This was to be our home for the next three months.

"I remember, too, the hordes of mosquitoes, the teeming tropical rains, mud, heat, and humidity. We were cautioned to take Atabrine daily as a protection against malaria. A side effect of Atabrine was that one's skin slowly took on a sickening yellow hue; here again youthful blitheness prevailed, as most of us didn't take our daily dosage.

"One of the bonuses of being the first women stationed here were the invitations to parties given by male GI outfits, to which we were enticed by such gourmet offerings as fresh oranges. I was assigned to a message center where army communications were coded, decoded, and rerouted—a fairly interesting job.

"My last station was Fort McKinley, a permanent army base outside the ruined city of Manila. One had only to see the bombed ruins of what had once been known as the Pearl of the Orient to reflect on the cruel folly of war.

"Manila was recaptured (by U.S. troops) in February 1945, and it was soon after this that our contingent of WACs arrived. We were never too far behind the advancing troops but were not exposed to any real danger.

"By the summer of 1945 the war in Europe had ended, but I don't remember thinking that it would soon be over for us in the Pacific. In the cocoon of army life, one was far removed from the happenings in the war; if we heard of the dropping of the atomic bombs on Hiroshima and Nagasaki, I don't recall it. The news of V-J Day in August came as an unexpected serendipitous event. Of course, our joy was intense; I remember quite vividly the celebration, which lasted through the night and the next day. Cold champagne could not have tasted better than the warm beer we drank."

The war was over, but now Gertrude had the problem of getting home. Transport space was limited and troops were returned home on priority basis, according to points earned. Gertrude waited. Her husband had returned from the European theater in July and was so impatient for her return that he actually went to Washington and met with Oveta Culp Hobby, the WAC commandant, demanding that his wife be returned immediately to him, a combat veteran with a Silver Star. Colonel Hobby pacified him, but he still wanted his wife home—now.

It was late October before Gertrude had a "long voyage home in a small converted fishing vessel whose creaks and rumblings sounded ominous." The trip seemed interminable.

"Then we arrived at the California coast. Sailing under the Golden Gate at sunset was a fitting termination to my year's tour of duty in the Pacific theater."

World War II was over. For Gertrude Morris, her experience in the WAC had been "a time of adventure, opportunity for development, and above all of service."

Recalling that period Gertrude felt that "World War II was the last patriotic war in which one could believe as a struggle for principles. It now seems to me that it was another life in a different world. Indeed, it *was* a different world, and we had every reason to be proud to have served in what was universally considered to be a just war. I often ask myself if I would have made the same decision to enlist had it been the Korean, Vietnam, or Gulf war. The world in 1942 was a simpler one, and we were fortunate not to have faced the more complex, difficult world situations that ensued."

After the war, Gertrude Morris resumed her teaching career. She took time out to care for two daughters until they reached school age, then returned to teaching until she retired in 1982. She was able to satisfy her love of travel and adventure during her many trips with her husband to Europe, Russia, and the Far East. They still continue their travels, and she is now involved with volunteer activities, in addition to sharing childcare for their eight-year-old twin grandchildren.

12

Little Carrier Pigeon

Christine L. Shanklin Hunt grew up in West Virginia, the youngest of eleven children. She had graduated from high school and traveled extensively through the United States with her family, but she had not decided on her future.

On December 7, 1941, Christine left the Orpheum Theater in Huntington and got into a cab. She was ready to tell the driver her destination when he blurted out the news: the Japanese had bombed Pearl Harbor. She felt "a deep sense of shock," and she knew that some of her eight brothers would be called into the service.

Three of her brothers did enter the service, and Christine joined the civil defense. But then she learned that the army would send women recruits overseas. She made her decision: She was sworn into the WAAC on December 19, 1942, when she was twenty-three years old.

Christine had volunteered for overseas duty, and finally, in January 1944, after basic training and duty with the Anti-Aircraft Artillery Command, she received orders to report for advanced

WAC Christine Shanklin poses as if on guard duty in Jullouville, Normandy, on September 10, 1944. The gun belonged to the photographer.

overseas training at Fort Oglethorpe, Georgia. Christine realized she was starting out on "the biggest adventure" of her entire life.

Overseas training was the usual grueling training. It was, as Christine noted, "to test our individual endurance, measure our emotional stamina, and fathom how much our nerves could endure."

After another training stint at Camp Shanks, New York, it was "zero hour." The women received orders to get packed, ready to leave camp. They marched to the train and then boarded the *Queen Mary*, which left the port late the next day, March 20, 1944.

The *Queen Mary* was armed with 40mm antiaircraft machine guns and many other weapons, in case of air or sea attack. Its

Corporal Christine Shanklin, left, in the war room in Rheims, France, points to the chair where German general Alfred Jodl sat when he signed the terms of surrender, May 7, 1945.

route this trip was by way of the North Atlantic, which was infested with German submarines, but it was the shortest distance between the two countries.

The *Queen Mary* arrived safely in Scotland on March 28, and the WACs trooped off to Kingston-on-Thames, a suburb of London.

Christine was ordered to report to SHAEF headquarters—Supreme Headquarters, Allied Expeditionary Force—under the command of Gen. Dwight D. Eisenhower. She was assigned to SGS—Secretary General Staff—the immediate section of General Eisenhower's office.

"I was required to circulate through the entire headquarters to deliver and pick up classified material and documents—some of which were classified as secret, top secret, bigot, and top bigot, which was the most secret. I also ran special errands and served as a receptionist. Sometimes I served the top brass their coffee and tea when they came to see General Eisenhower. It was interesting and exciting."

The war room at Rheims, France, May 5, 1945, where WAC Christine
Shanklin served as messenger during the peace talks.

While the WACs worked, the German buzz bombs came—day
and night. They were so frequent that headquarters personnel
became quite used to them. Sometimes they just watched them;
other times, they sought shelter in the trenches. Christine was
fascinated by them.

"These bombs resembled an airplane, only the fuselage was
miniature. In the rear was a red light that could be seen only at
night. As long as that red light was visible, one was safe, because
the bomb remained in flight. When the light went out, the
buzzing stopped and the bomb crashed to the ground with a
thunderous explosion. At night when we watched them fly over,
we wondered in suspense if the red light would go out in our
immediate area."

The red lights began going out. Some bombs crashed near
the headquarters, and Christine had several close calls with
bombs that splintered doorways, scattered debris, and created
powerful gusts of wind. As the raids grew more frequent, General Eisenhower became concerned and issued an order of the
day that *everyone* had to take shelter during a raid. Christine

shared an air raid shelter with the general and his staff. After the Normandy invasion on D-Day, June 6, 1944, a segment of SHAEF was selected to become SHAEF FORWARD to follow the invasion forces. Christine was among this forward group. On September 7, 1944, they left by air convoy and crossed the English Channel. They landed in Normandy.

"We were all crowded into trucks and rode for at least an hour and a half over rough, bombed-out roads, dirt and mud, and through bombed-out villages. Our headquarters was Jullouville, in a wooded area where German snipers were still lurking. The WACs were billeted in a large building that had formerly been used as a Nazi rest home. I slept on an old dirty canvas cot that was directly below a window that was impossible to close. I had no mattress, sheets, or pillow, and I had only one army blanket. It was hard to sleep because of the cold and the cot was so uncomfortable that my body actually ached from lying on those boards covered by a canvas.

"General Eisenhower's office was in a trailer in a secluded area. The other offices were sturdy wooden structures that were scattered over a wide area. Messages were delivered and picked up daily, rain or shine. So on some occasions, I trudged through the wet and sometimes quite muddy terrain. Even though the nights were very cold, the days were surprisingly warm in contrast."

SHAEF FORWARD's next move was to Versailles, outside Paris. They traveled in a truck convoy, which at times became rather disorganized. Christine rode on the truck floor, wearing her field uniform, which included leggings, helmet, field pack, pistol belt, first aid kit, canteen, gas mask, utility bag, and pup tent. She became filthy, her face, neck, and hair streaked with dust.

"The convoy passed burned out and wrecked tanks, trucks, cars, planes, and guns, German as well as Allied. There were graves with only crosses, with helmets hanging over them as markers.

"The majority of the towns we went through were practically level with the ground—all in complete ruins. Civilians were walking all along the way carrying huge bundles; some were pushing carts. We certainly received a tremendous reception as we entered their towns. The people joyfully greeted us, threw fruit and flowers, and yelled, '*Vive Américains!*' There were signs nearly everywhere reading Welcome to our Liberators. American, French, and British flags, and those of the Free French, were waving everywhere."

The forward group was slated to stay, temporarily, Christine thought, in the palace, but her new home turned out to be a horse's stall. Luckily it was only for a short time; she was moved to an old French garrison, where the WACs shared their living quarters, mess hall, and PX with the British ATS (Army Territorial Service).

"The French Morocco and Senegalese troops were also stationed in this garrison, but they lived across the courtyard on the opposite side. They were striking in appearance with their bright and colorful uniforms. They wore vests, colorful shirts, full, billowing pants, and sashes of various colors, and had long knives hanging from their sides. Bright red hats were perched atop their heads.

"We had trouble with them only once, when they had a fight with the French police. Shots were exchanged from both sides, and we were all restricted. Jeeps or staff cars had to bring us home from work if we missed the bus or worked late. Military police patrolled the streets to pick up any WACs or ATS to bring them to the billets. Tanks with guns were stationed in the palace area."

Christine found the old French garrison dismal, dirty, and cold, but she could walk to headquarters and visit the local shops and mix with the civilians on the way. She often used her chocolate bars and cigarettes instead of cash.

Then it was time to move forward again. The group's truck convoy continued to follow General George S. Patton's Third Army. SHAEF FORWARD moved to Rheims, France, to a former French vocational school constructed of red bricks. This was the first time headquarters and the WACs' living quarters were in the same building.

Christine was busy and obviously doing a good job. She was soon dubbed "Ike's little carrier pigeon." One day she heard that General Eisenhower had said that she was the "ideal and typical WAC." Needless to say, she was pleased.

The end of the European war was near. Christine wrote, "By the daily reports of our Allied victories, it was evident that Hitler would be forced to seek formal terms of surrender. He finally, of course, admitted defeat and agreed to peace negotiations. Hitler never appeared at SHAEF headquarters, but he sent two of his representatives of the German high command—Gen. Alfred Jodl, his supreme commander and advisor and the former chief of staff of the Wehrmacht, and Adm. Hans von Friedeburg. The peace talks were to take place in the war room.

"I felt honored to be chosen to serve the Germans, the Russians who represented Gen. Josef Stalin, headed by Maj. Gen. Ivan Susloparov, and Lt. Gen. Walter Bedell Smith, chief of staff for General Eisenhower. I felt so sorry for General Smith as he was so tired and he wasn't feeling well. One day he said to me, 'Virginia, would you get me a glass of water?' (The brass called me Virginia because I was from West Virginia.) I'll never forget the tired sound of his voice. When I served Russian General Susloparov his tea one day, he called me back and pointed to his cup: 'Too hard.' I thought he meant it was too hot and I started to pour a little water in it to cool it a bit. He repeated again, 'Too hard,' and made facial gestures so I knew it was too bitter and he wanted more sugar. He smiled and thanked me.

"I was serving the Germans on one occasion and attempting to straighten up the table with all the papers and other items. I picked up the bottle of alcoholic beverage that had been provided for them. Thinking I was going to remove the bottle from the room, General Jodl suddenly rose from his chair, leaned forward, and grasped it from my hand.

"There was a large assembly of the top brass present, waiting for the peace talks to begin. Only a few persons were allowed admittance, and the press outside would ask me if the surrender had taken place or if there were any new developments in the negotiations. I only could say I did not have the authority to give out that kind of information.

"I certainly did work hard during those days and I told one of the officers that as long as we served the Germans such good food, they never would surrender. I suggested serving them some of our C rations to make them sign the terms of peace.

"After many discussions of the terms of surrender the Germans agreed to sign the peace treaty on May 7, 1945, at 2:41 A.M. in the former red-brick school—later referred to as the Little Red Schoolhouse. Victory had been achieved and the mission accomplished, leaving us in a state of joy and relief."

After the peace negotiations, SHAEF was renamed the United States Forces, European Theater (USFET) and sent to Germany. The staff flew from Rheims to Frankfort on the Main, where they were taken by truck to the WAC area.

It was a warm day when they traveled, and there was a clinging, sickening odor as they passed through the heavily bombed out areas. It was, Christine learned, the smell of decaying bodies that had not yet been removed.

Here the WACs lived in relative luxury, in apartments with bathrooms and pink satin curtains at the windows. But freedom was limited. Their quarters were surrounded by barbed wire, and if they left the area they had to be accompanied by an armed escort.

USFET headquarters was in the I. G. Farben Building, one of the largest of the industrial buildings. It was here, on her duty rounds, that Christine had encounters with what she considered the very top brass. One day General Smith called her over to introduce her to Marshal Georgi K. Zhukov, chief of staff to Gen. Josef Stalin. Zhukov complimented her on her spiffy appearance. She had on her dress uniform and was wearing yellow gloves and a scarf. Pinned to her uniform was a yellow corsage.

Another day she had a brief meeting with General George S. Patton, who was later killed in an accident in Mannheim, an event that saddened everyone at headquarters, where he was liked and respected. Christine went to Luxembourg for his burial on December 24, 1945, in the U.S. military cemetery in Hamm.

One day Christine received a surprise. She was called into General Eisenhower's office, and instead of picking up a message to be delivered, was given a gift.

"The general had been promoted and had received another star, and was now referred to as General of the Army. This meant he was commander of the entire Allied force in the ETO. His new license plate had five stars. The staff handling the transfer of the plates decided to give the four-star plate to someone who worked in the office area—and they gave it to me! I was presented the general's four-star license plate as a 'signature souvenir!' I was touched and delighted. It was a wonderful gift.

"There were other moments of my service that I remember vividly. I had worked to help defeat the enemy, but now when I saw the defeated, I felt compassion. One day as I was riding through Düsseldorf, Germany, we passed an area that had been demolished, flattened no doubt by air raids and the big guns of Allied armor. I noticed a couple with their heads lowered, amidst the rubble that surrounded them. They stood in the ruins of what was once, I suppose, their home. Even though this was in enemy territory, I could not help but feel a sense of compassion for them.

"In Frankfort there were many German POWs who were marched to areas about the headquarters as part of their daily exercise routine. Often when I went out to make a delivery it was necessary for me to walk through their ranks. They appeared sullen, oblivious to their surroundings. Here in Germany we were regarded as conquerors and not as liberators.

"After a long absence from home, I was now making preparations to return to the United States. I flew to France to the port city of Le Havre, where I set sail on a small hospital ship, the *Blanche F. Sigman*. We had sailed only a short distance when we encountered heavy winds—so powerful that the crew lost control of the ship and it was turned around by the gusting gales and blown back toward Le Havre. After righting the ship, we finally started out again, headed for the United States. The trip was rough. The voyage back took two weeks and our insides rolled the entire way.

"What a wonderful feeling it was when we saw the Statue of Liberty as we approached New York Harbor. I thought back to the devastation I had seen, to the American graves with helmets as markers. I was glad the war was over and I was home again and I hoped all those who sacrificed their lives had not died in vain."

After the war Christine Shanklin (Hunt) found a job at the Owens-Illinois Glass Company, where she worked for over two years. Later, in 1959, she went to nursing school and became a licensed practical nurse and worked as such in hospitals until she retired in 1985. During those years she was married and divorced, and had two sons. She has traveled around the world, and most recently, in 1987, became self-employed as a sitter, a position she still occupies.

13

The WAC Code

Gertrude Pearson Cassetta was raised in an area of the Bronx that was still country, with cows, horses, sheep, and chickens living on farms nearby. Her mother died when she was five, and Gertrude assumed the responsibilities of an older child. After high school, she went on to business school and then secured a job in a bank. Reports of Germany's military aggression were prominent in newspapers and on the radio. Gertrude was well aware of the war clouds that were forming.

On December 7, 1941, Gertrude was riding with friends on a train in New York, on her way to a movie. When the train stopped at their station a man burst through the open doors, shouting, "Pearl Harbor has been bombed by the Japanese!" Gertrude knew that the news meant war for America.

After the WAAC was formed and announced that it would accept women for overseas service, Gertrude enlisted. She was sworn in at New York City's Grand Central Palace on January 23, 1943, when she was twenty-one years old.

Gertrude had two miserable months of basic training in Daytona Beach, Florida, which was experiencing an unusual freeze.

WAC Gertrude Pearson ready for coffee at a Red Cross Station in the field, Laval, France, August 30, 1944.

She was then assigned to administrative school right on the beach, which was pleasurable, since the weather had warmed up considerably.

From there Gertrude was sent to Maxwell Field Air Base in Montgomery, Alabama, where she was assigned to the signal office code room and learned to be a cryptographic technician. Finally she received much-desired orders for overseas duty.

On May 3, 1944, Gertrude was one of five hundred WACs aboard the troopship *Argentina*, the flagship of a very large convoy. As the convoy neared the northern tip of Ireland, it encountered a pack of U-boats; alerts were called frequently, and depth charges exploded constantly as the escort vessels searched for the subs. The women were told to stack their duffel bags against the heavy metal doors to keep them propped open, so they would not jam closed if they were torpedoed.

The ship landed safely in Scotland on May 14. The WACs were separated into detachments; Gertrude's was assigned to the Allied Expeditionary Air Force and would become the 385th Signal Service Company (AVN), stationed in Stanmore, England, a village northwest of London.

As D-Day neared the WACs' coding workload increased, and the women were instructed to try to jam the airwaves with increased volume to confuse German intelligence.

Then D-Day came.

"On June 6, we awakened at daybreak to the heavy drone of aircraft. We went outside and saw hundreds of bombers literally darken the sky as they flew on their missions to France. Seeing the planes come back later on D-Day was traumatic. Tears rolled down our faces at the sight of returning groups of planes that

tried to stay together in formation. There were gaps
where planes should have
been. Some had small holes
in their tail assemblies, others
had a propeller not operating. They were flying slowly,
ponderously, as they straggled
back to their bases."

Shortly after D-Day the
Germans retaliated, launching the buzz bombs. Sirens
wailed in London and in the
villages to the north. The
bombs came over Stanmore
in greater numbers. Gertrude
and the other WACs in the
coding area were not allowed
to leave their vans and seek
cover when a bomb came

WACs washing mess kits, Versailles, France,
October 1944. Gertrude Pearson is on the
left.

over—their machines and codes were much too precious.
They were lucky. The closest a bomb came was one that landed
some distance away and only blew out the windows of their
quarters.

Gertrude was one of twenty-one enlisted WACs to be ordered
to France. They landed on Omaha Beach at 5:30 P.M. on August
28, 1944, and the officer in charge of the beach area told them
to find a foxhole in the field above the beach and bivouac there
for the night.

They now were a mobile communications unit on their own,
made up of a small number of men and the assigned WACs. The
group was unusual because for the first time in World War II,
men and women formed a single company. As Gertrude said, it
was unique also "because it was the only instance in the war that
a cryptographic section of the Signal Corps was entirely staffed
and run by WAC personnel. Additionally, we were the first air
force WACs to arrive in France."

After the night above Omaha Beach, they left for Laval,

Lunch break on WAC and First Tactical Air Force (Prov.) convoy from Versailles to Vittel, France, October 29, 1944.

France, where they stayed a few days before moving on to Versailles. They set up their operations under some trees in the palace gardens and began to work around the clock.

They were a forward echelon, and when the rest of their company from England joined them toward the end of September, they were all quartered in the École de Combat, a large barracks establishment that housed women of the AEAF and SHAEF—WACs, WAAFs, WRENs, and ATS.

Organizational changes were then made. The Allied Expeditionary Air Force was dissolved, and the 385th with its WAC personnel was assigned to the First Tactical Air Force (Provisional), a newly activated command. There was much discussion about taking the WACs forward, until it was finally remembered that they had already been in service in combat zones—and that they were a necessary part of the signal unit.

Late in October their detachment moved to Vittel, France, a village that had been used by the Germans as an international internment camp for women.

"When we arrived we could clearly hear the artillery guns ahead of us—the front was about twenty-five to thirty miles away,

WAC convoy travels by truck to Vittel, France. Gertrude Pearson is at the far right.

and judging from the noise of weaponry, the fighting was still going on in the mountains and hills around us. Shortly after our arrival, we had a security lecture by an intelligence officer— there were spies in Vittel. We were forbidden to discuss the content of our work, or what we did (which we never did anyway). Later, we were to find that strangers often sat or stood close to us in the shops. We never did find out whether they were Allied intelligence personnel or spies."

Life in Vittel was difficult. Bunks were confiscated German military beds with wooden slats, no mattresses. The stove in each room in the small house where the women were quartered was also German—and inefficient. Wood was scarce and had to be dug out from under deep snow. Kerosene for their lamps was stored outside in large drums, and the women had to pump it into five-gallon jerry cans. Helmets were bathtubs. And, because the front was so close, regulations were strict—blackouts, challenges from the guards, curfews, and red alerts became routine. It snowed constantly and was bitterly cold.

"When von Rundstedt broke through our lines, signaling the Battle of the Bulge [in December], the WACs were told by our CO that we had become a target of enemy agents because of our work. She told us spies had and were parachuting into the forests and had infiltrated Vittel.

"One night we heard gunshots outside our house—the guards had apprehended and shot an enemy agent. Another time, a female agent arrived, saying that she had had plane trouble and was looking for a place to stay. She said she was a member of a British organization. She was clothed in British clothes, but I noticed her shoes were not or did not look British. I mentioned this to my first sergeant. The woman's room was searched and she was subsequently taken away by the military police.

"One of the larger hotels became the Twenty-third General Hospital. Soldiers were brought here from the field hospitals. Our room faced the railroad station, and for days on end during the Battle of the Bulge train after train pulled into the station filled with wounded. Medics on the train unloaded the soldiers on their litters to the platform, where they waited in long lines to be placed in one of the never-ending fleet of ambulances. It was bitterly cold and some had no blankets. When they arrived at the hospital—because they were arriving in such large numbers—they were again placed in long lines on their litters on the sidewalk leading to the entrance of the hospital. I saw this when I went to the hospital to donate blood. It upset me to see them lying wounded, waiting patiently in the cold for medical attention.

"At this time the overworked nurses asked for WAC volunteers to help the soldiers. Many volunteered. We wrote letters for them, read to them, wrapped and mailed packages, and if they were too weak to talk, we just sat by their beds for a short time, in the hope that our presence would give them comfort. Both men and women of our First TACAF gave blood whenever it was needed, on a regular basis.

"Here in Vittel we had seen the ravages of war—destroyed buildings, discarded German equipment, smashed and bloody German helmets, pierced by bullets, left along the roads as the enemy raced in retreat. But seeing our wounded men and the extent of some of their injuries was the worst. The fact that I could walk into a wardroom filled with soldiers and barely hear a murmur left a lasting impression. Sometimes we were requested to leave because a soldier required surgery in the ward because there wasn't room in the ORs! I shall never forget the white bed linens and their pale faces, almost as white, and the silence in those rooms."

Christmas in Vittel was bleak as the Battle of the Bulge still raged. It was very cold, and it continued to snow; the WACs worked harder than ever to keep warm. Large numbers of wounded kept arriving from the front.

"One day we woke up to find three army trucks parked in the backyard of our house. Our CO explained that the trucks were there to evacuate us to Mirecourt Airport, where a plane was stationed to take us to safety, if the enemy came too close. It was sobering. We continued our work as usual around the clock, coping with the snow and a diet of C and K rations and Spam and powdered eggs for breakfast. When we were off-duty we volunteered at the hospital; other times we walked to the village.

"The winter of 1944 and 1945 in Vittel was an important time in our military careers. We had been accepted into the First TACAF against the wishes of some who felt women belonged in the rear areas and were unsuitable for the type of work assigned to us. They felt that women were incapable of enduring the hardships and rough conditions of a combat area. However, our success and outstanding work changed many attitudes. We had remained reliable and stable while on duty under stressful conditions. It was the roughest winter any of us had experienced, and we were eager to go on."

When the Allied troops moved into Germany, a signal unit was needed. In April 1945 Gertrude was one of eight WACs assigned to Heidelberg to set up a signal unit with the air force. The trip from Vittel was far from pleasant. As they rode through the countryside, Gertrude could smell the odor of decay. She saw dead cattle lying on their backs, legs in the air. The lane on which they traveled had yellow markers at the sides to delineate the safe route.

Gertrude "prayed that those who had swept the lane for mines had not missed any. Perhaps because by now I was weary of the war, for the first time I was frightened by the thought of a mine exploding under our jeep."

She was just as apprehensive when they arrived at Ludwigshafen, a fairly large city on the Rhine River. The city had been mostly destroyed, and the bridge to Mannheim was gone, a string of inflated pontoons in its place. The current was swift, and as Gertrude looked at the two narrow planks that the jeep would drive on, she hurriedly undid her leggings and boots and unsnapped the strap of her helmet.

"If we went into the river I wanted a fair chance to swim and stay afloat." They made it safely across.

They arrived in Heidelberg, and "were promptly spat upon by three or four young teenagers standing at a corner." It was a dismal welcome, happily unlike later encounters with the Germans, who seemed genuinely glad that the Americans had arrived.

Gertrude and the WACs in her unit knew from their coding that peace was imminent, but when V-E Day came in May, there was no wild celebration. They had been warned that with the

Army personnel attend a church service May 9, 1945, in celebration of the end of the war in Europe at the cathedral in Heidelberg, Germany.

war still going on in the Pacific, they would probably be sent there. It was a sobering prospect.

Early in June the WAC cryptographic technicians were no longer needed, and they were transferred first to another base in Germany and then to Luxembourg as their signal officer tried to find a place for them to continue their coding. Finally, they were sent to Ansbach, Germany, a small town about 150 miles from the western border of Czechoslovakia.

Then the atomic bombs were dropped; the war was soon over.

"Life was now monotonous. It had been exciting while we were coding; now our days were idle. We tried to keep busy, reading, playing cards, and going for long walks."

In late summer they began the long journey home, via France and England, where they boarded the *Aquitania*. Gertrude arrived in New York Harbor on September 14, 1945.

When they docked there was a large crowd of people to greet them and a band was playing.

"It certainly was a happy homecoming. At the same time, I felt an emptiness knowing that I was leaving my friends and the service."

Gertrude was discharged at Fort Dix on September 19. The next day she was home.

After the war Gertrude Pearson (Cassetta) worked as a secretary for various concerns until after her marriage and the birth of her children, when she became a full-time mother. Later she returned to the workplace, employed as a secretary to a school principal, until she retired in 1984. She is currently a volunteer for community organizations. Her biggest regret is that she did not continue in cryptographic work after her discharge from the U.S. Army.

PART FOUR

WAVES (U.S. Navy)

In 1916 Congress passed an act creating the Naval Reserve Force. By 1917 Secretary of the Navy Josephus Daniels recognized that the United States would shortly become involved in World War I and would need the men of the navy for sea duty. He noted that the bill authorizing the Naval Reserve Force did not specifically use the word "male," but rather "personnel," and he proposed the recruitment of women for the naval reserve. On March 17, 1917, the Navy Department authorized the enrollment of women in the Naval Coast Defense Reserve.

The navy's first call to colors was immediately answered by one hundred women. Although the number of women actually serving with the navy during World War I was relatively small, the women assumed a number of vital jobs. Classified as yeomen (F), the women worked as translators, draftsmen, recruiters, and in various bureaus and offices. A few were actually sent overseas—to France, Guam, Puerto Rico, Hawaii, and the Panama Canal Zone. At peak enlistment, there were over ten thousand yeomen (F) serving the U.S. Navy during World War I.

After the war the Naval Reserve Act was revised. Despite their important service during the war years, women were to be denied admission to the navy; the 1925 act specified that only "male citizens of the United States" were qualified to serve.

By the end of 1941, the navy again became interested in the recruitment of women, and Admiral Chester Nimitz recommended that Congress pass a bill creating a women's naval reserve, which it did in July 1942. Thus the WAVES (Women Accepted for Volunteer Emergency Service) was born.

Officers' training was held in Massachusetts at Smith College and Mount Holyoke, while enlisted women trained at Oklahoma A & M in Stillwater; Indiana University in Bloomington; and the University of Wisconsin at Madison. Hunter College leased its campus in the Bronx, New York, for boot camp.

By the time the WAVES received their training, the war in the Pacific had accelerated sharply. The Bataan Death March had taken place in the Philippines early in 1942. The opening battles in the Pacific theater had been costly for the Allies, but a resounding defeat of the Japanese at the Battle of Midway had marked the beginning of the Allied retaliation. The WAVES, who were barred from overseas duty, eagerly followed the navy's victories from their posts in the United States.

Some WAVES became corpsmen, working in the naval hospitals, where they saw the physical and mental injuries caused by battle; others held secretarial jobs, working on future military plans. In Washington some of the WAVES secretaries were involved with top secret material such as the year-long planning for Operation Overlord, the invasion of Normandy that would take place on June 6, 1944.

WAVE radio operators in San Francisco kept in touch with the military ships at sea, were aware of the progress of battles, and formed part of an antisubmarine radio network. Some of the WAVES worked with secret reports from a special laboratory at Los Alamos, New Mexico, which was proceeding with the development of the atomic bomb.

The women with husbands on duty in the Pacific theater especially followed accounts of the leapfrogging tactics the Allies used against the Japanese. Combined assaults with sea and air power and amphibious landings enabled them to bypass islands with large concentrations of Japanese, letting the enemy become the victim of attrition while the Allies attacked the islands that were vital to the eventual defeat of Japan.

Marriage might be a reason for a navy woman to apply for service in Hawaii. If she had a husband who was stationed there, she was eager to join him, though officially her motivation was more patriotic. It was hard for the WAVES to continue working as storekeepers or typists when their loved ones were serving in the line of fire—and devastating when they received news of capture, injury, or death.

By 1944 the tide of the war had turned and the Japanese were running out of men, equipment, and supplies. By the end of that year U.S. submarines had sunk over 4 million tons of Japanese shipping. The Battle of Leyte Gulf, which took place on October 23–25, 1944, was the largest naval battle of all time and was the final decisive sea battle between the United States and Japan.

The navy women who served in World War II fulfilled their avowed purpose by freeing men for overseas duty. They greatly expanded their own horizons as well as they learned the skills they needed to work as control tower operators, aviation machinist mates, aerial gunnery instructors, photographers— even pigeon trainers. According to the navy, these women released 50,500 men to sea duty and filled 27,000 other jobs. At the end of the war there were about 8,000 officers and 76,000 enlisted personnel in the WAVES, with 8,000 more in training. These women had all served their country well and had helped in the effort for final victory.

The women's reserve was detached from active duty in September 1946. On June 12, 1948, the WAVES became an integral part of the Regular Navy as well as the Naval Reserve, providing a nucleus of officers and enlisted women to fuel any future expansion needed in time of war.

14

Operation Overlord

Betty Doolittle was twenty-two years old. She lived with her parents in Indianapolis, had a good job, and was taking a business course at night. One day in the fall of 1942 she decided to join the WAVES. It was October 2 when she was sworn in to become a member of the first class of enlisted women taught by the first officer graduates from Smith College.

When she told her parents what she had done, her mother was shocked, and her father was "so proud he almost burst his buttons." He had been in the army during World War I, and had lost the use of his right arm. His only question was why the navy? Betty answered that with a name like Doolittle, the army would expect too much. (Her father and Jimmy Doolittle were distant cousins. In April Colonel Doolittle had led a spectacular B-25 bombing raid over Tokyo.)

Betty Doolittle headed for Stillwater, Oklahoma, on October 9 and began her basic training, which was "college minus all the frills." There were classes all day, lots of homework, and very little social life. The women marched everywhere, and soon became a "crack marching group," mainly because they were so

frightened by their marine drill
sergeant, who was so tough they
thought "he could bite nails in
half."

After passing training, Betty
was assigned to naval operations
in Washington, D.C. She reported to the chief of the Naval
Operations Office on January
24, 1943.

"I learned that I was to be yeoman to Admiral Oscar Badger.
He accepted me kindly, but with
reservation, as I was replacing
his male first-class yeoman, who
was insulted that he could be
replaced by a yeoman third
class, and a woman at that."

Betty Doolittle salutes during WAVES
basic training at Stillwater, Oklahoma.

The yeoman, however shocked by the status of his replacement, decided to be nice and invited Betty to dinner on his last
night before leaving for sea duty. Betty remembered that he
said, "If I've taught you nothing else, I am going to teach you to
drink martinis." Betty didn't even know what a martini was, but
she learned quickly.

Admiral Badger was upset that he had a yeoman third class
working for him, so he told her to go out to the naval station
and take a test for second class—and to do it the next day. "If
you don't pass," he told her, "don't come back."

Betty passed, so she stayed with Admiral Badger. But then
came another test. Five other admirals had a meeting with
Admiral Badger, and Betty was assigned to take notes of the proceedings. She did, but when she was asked to read back her
notes, she "opened her mouth and nothing came out—for the
first time in my life I was speechless."

Admiral Badger suggested she go out of the room and type
up a rough draft, and when she got to the typewriter, she found
she could not read a word of her notes. Captain H. L. Challenger, USN, came to her rescue: He told her to try to remem-

WAVES marching to classes during basic training at Stillwater, Oklahoma.

ber the gist of the meeting, and together they assembled the rough draft, and it was accepted. It had been an unnerving experience, but obviously Betty was considered adequate for the job.

On April 8, 1943, she was assigned to the Joint Logistics Plans Committee, Joint Chiefs of Staff, as yeoman to Captain Challenger. Now everything was top secret. Betty and the other women were moved into a secured office building, which had been the old Public Health Building. Marine guards patrolled outside twenty-four hours a day. Everyone working inside had top secret clearance. And Betty was sent off *again* to take the test for yeoman second class.

"My duties were to set up an office of yeomen (secretaries) and set up a file room. Various personnel were ordered in to fill the quota. We had WACs, WAVES, marines, SPARS, and I was told we would be working on code name Overlord, the planned invasion of Normandy."

Everything was classified and top secret. The WAVES spent hours at the typewriters and many more hours waiting during meetings. They had to shred all wastepaper and carbons. The baskets were checked every night by the marine guards after the women had left. If anything was found, Betty was held responsible, so she checked all the baskets herself. It was hard work and lasted for over a year. The plans for Operation Overlord proceeded, coordinated with the British, who worked on the second floor of the secured building.

Now living quarters were also "secured." All WAVES on the project were housed together in an old three-story house, which had been made into apartments. The FBI took the women to work and brought them home. They were constantly cautioned that they could not discuss their work with anyone outside the JCS. The theory of having them live together, Betty said, "was that if we needed to talk, we could talk to one another."

Of course, much of the brass came to the workplace. Betty was impressed with the people leading the Allied fight. One time, however, an admiral appeared whom she did not know. As they waited together for the elevator, they casually looked at each other. The elevator arrived, and Betty stood back because of rank, and the elevator left them standing there.

"This happened three times, and he finally said, 'Young lady, will you get on the elevator,' and I said, 'After you, sir,' and he said, 'Let me tell you something, I was a gentleman before I was an admiral, please get on the elevator.'" Betty did and they introduced themselves. The admiral was Richard E. Byrd, the famous polar explorer.

As the planning went on for Operation Overlord, there were various conferences. The first big one was held in Quebec,

Canada. Congress would not let the WAVE personnel go, in spite of the fact that the officials working on the program wanted them to come along. The WAVES were permitted to serve *only* in the continental United States. Thus the clerical help made copy after copy of documents, and couriers went back and forth. The next conference was at Yalta, then Teheran. Still the WAVES could not attend.

By May 7, 1943, Betty had become yeoman first class and was recommended for officers' training school, but she opted to stay with the Overlord group.

"We got through a whole year of working and working, and in May 1944 we began to realize that the time was near, but no one knew the exact date. In the meantime tanks, weapons, personnel carriers, and jeeps, along with P-38s and P-47s, were stockpiled. Troops composed of Australian, Canadian, British, and American personnel were readied."

D-Day, June 6, 1944, came. The Allied landings in Normandy were a success.

Betty wrote, "We little people who had typed, retyped, made copies galore were so happy to have been a small part in breaking the back of the war in Europe."

Betty had been doing more than working: In February 1944 she had married Vernon Belcher, an Army Air Force cadet and a childhood sweetheart from Indianapolis. In November 1945 she was discharged—for pregnancy.

Almost fifty years later she noted, "In writing about my World War II service, I have laughed, cried a little, and done my best to remember. I loved every minute of my time in the navy."

After the war Betty Doolittle Belcher (LaFontsee) had three children. Her marriage ended in divorce after twelve years, but "the fine education given me by the navy" enabled her to get good jobs and support the children. Her son spent six years in the navy during the Vietnam era and was injured in the line of duty. Betty has five grandchildren; her grandson served in Desert Storm and Somalia. She recently retired from real estate property management in Las Vegas, where she lived for seventeen years. She is now working part-time in the retirement community of Sun City, Arizona.

15

Love and Marriage

Dorothy Barnes fell in love with James R. Stephens when she was attending Santa Ana Junior College in California. J.R. was an art classmate and a reservist in a Signal Corps photographic unit. In December 1941, after war was declared, the couple's future looked bleak. It was certain that J.R. would be called to active duty, but when? They both graduated in June 1942, and they decided to elope. They were married in Arizona in September.

When J.R. received orders to report to Fort MacArthur in San Pedro in February 1943, Dorothy decided to enlist in the WAVES. She did so on February 9, shortly before she kissed J.R. goodbye at the fort's gate. She was not quite twenty-one years old.

Dorothy went east to Hunter College in New York City for boot camp.

"Boot camp at Hunter is not a place I remember fondly. We hit the deck before dawn and fell exhausted into bed at 2200 (10:00 P.M.). Spud locker detail (as the navy called it), working in ankle-deep water peeling beets and potatoes, guard duty where I actually was given a baton and told to guard a gate,

WAVES decorating their Christmas tree in 1943, at Treasure Island
Naval Station, San Francisco. Dorothy Stephens is standing at right
(Photo credit: U.S. Navy)

classes in military organization, and learning navy songs used up
the day. After lights out I'd cry into my pillow.

"Close order drill and the constant marching from place to
place raised blisters on my heels. I caught a cold and my nose
ran constantly. But blowing one's nose while in ranks was not
only unthinkable, but absolutely forbidden."

Discipline was strict. Dorothy learned to thoroughly dislike the navy, but she rationalized that her service was a way to help get the war over sooner.

After basic training Dorothy was assigned to radio school at Miami University in the small town of Oxford, Ohio. There she learned radio operations, including Morse code, but as she said, "it was still the navy, despite the ivy-covered buildings, a fact of which we were reminded each morning when the public address system in our quarters assaulted us at dawn with, 'Hit the deck, you bloody sea dogs.'

"It seemed that every waking moment was in class: radio theory, procedures, and code, code, code."

Finally graduation arrived, and Dorothy learned that she was an honor graduate and was to be posted to Treasure Island Naval Station in San Francisco.

Dorothy and J.R. had seen each other from time to time, never knowing when he would be shipped overseas. It was heart-wrenching for both of them every time they parted.

At Treasure Island the radio operators—still called radiomen, despite their sex—worked hard and became a close-knit group. "Down in the basement radio room, we girls were now occupying all the operating positions, for the men had all been sent to sea. We operated Morse code with the ships mostly, but there were teletype machines and voice transmissions."

Dorothy heard from J.R. that he was taking jungle warfare training, and his address kept changing. Then there was silence. Dorothy continued to perform her duties and tried not to think about what was happening in the Pacific. Dorothy knew about MacArthur's return to the Philippines and surmised that J.R. was there with the photographic unit. Each day she dreaded the arrival of a telegram. She did receive one, but it was from her mother-in-law, inquiring why Dorothy had not written! Then she learned two important things: Her husband was back in Hawaii and likely to be there for some time, and the WAVES were now sending women overseas. Dorothy was jubilant. She applied for transfer to Hawaii.

"The big hurdle to get over in my application for overseas duty in Hawaii was the interview with the captain, commanding

Dorothy Stephens walking through the gate of the WAVES barracks at Mouna Loa
Ridge, near Pearl Harbor, July 1945. (Photo credit: J.R. Stephens.)

officer at Treasure Island Naval Station. I'd heard he was very
strict about whom he'd approve, that one had to convince him
of selfless intentions to get an assignment there, so for my interview I had memorized a little patriotic speech."

But when asked by the captain why she wanted to serve overseas, the speech was forgotten. She blurted out the truth—she
wanted to go because her husband was there.

The captain fidgeted, but then said, "Well, I'll approve your
request, Stephens, but the reasons you want to go will remain
between the two of us. All right?"

Dorothy thanked the captain, saluted, and "about-faced and
tried to keep from running out of his office."

Dorothy boarded ship, finally landed in Hawaii, and was
reunited with her husband. The work there proved a disap-
pointment. She was assigned to filing, a job the radio operators
loathed and thought was beneath them. Seeing her husband was
also difficult, unless their days off coincided. When J.R. came to
visit they had to meet in the recreation hut; regulations forbid
them to touch when on base.

"Even though everyone soon learned we were husband and

WAVES parading in Honolulu during V-J Day celebrations, August 1945. (U.S. Army photo by J. R. Stephens.)

wife, we were not allowed to so much as hold hands. (I think an embrace would have been looked on as a felony.)"

A break came when one of J.R.'s buddies' parents opened their home to them in Honolulu. They could come and go as they pleased, and stay as long as they liked. As Dorothy pointed out, this arrangement inevitably led to the start of their family.

Dorothy and J.R. knew that pregnancy while in service was looked upon as a major infraction, but they decided to "leave it up to God."

It was summer when Dorothy became pregnant. Three weeks later, Japan surrendered. The night of V-J Day was full of singing, dancing, and drinking. The ships at Pearl sent tracer bullets arcing across the sky.

In September Dorothy was back at Treasure Island, and out of the navy with her discharge.

"Finally home in Santa Ana, California, in a world at peace, I visited my obstetrician. The waiting room was full of ladies in my condition, and a very talkative bunch they were. One of them asked, 'And where is your husband, dear?'

"'In Hawaii,' I replied.

"'Oh,' she said, 'and how long has it been since he's been home?'

"Absently, I said, 'About three years.'

"The chattering ceased; the room became very quiet.

"'Oh,' she said, coloring.

"And that was that. I didn't bother to explain."

After the war Dorothy Barnes Stephens became a "full-time army wife," her husband having reenlisted in 1948. She raised four children, lived in Greece, England, and France before her husband left active duty in 1965. After the children left home, her daughter to the air force as a nurse and two sons to the navy, Dorothy worked as a part-time high school teacher in Florida. She and her husband both retired in 1979 to Tacoma, Washington, where they now live on five acres of pines in the Cascade Mountain foothills. Dorothy still does a little amateur radio, keeping in touch with their children and five grandchildren.

16

The Hazards of Harassment

Mary Jane Stutsman was seventeen and a college freshman in Columbus, Ohio, when the war broke out. She was too young to join the service, but she dreamed of the day she could enlist in a hospital corps. Her mother had died five years earlier and her father was very protective: she had been a frail and only child.

When she turned twenty she knew the WAVES could accept her with her father's permission. She enlisted on January 4, 1944; her father had signed the necessary papers because, Mary Jane would discover years later, he had secretly thought she could not pass the physical. She did pass, and received orders to report for boot camp at Hunter College in New York City.

At Hunter she adjusted well to the strict routine and felt that she really belonged in the navy. Eventually, she got her wish: she was assigned to hospital corps training at Bethesda, Maryland.

Mary Jane did well in all her classes, although she still had trouble making a bed with mitered corners. After completion of her training, she was assigned to a nearby hospital, the Bainbridge Naval Hospital in Bainbridge, Maryland.

The Bainbridge complex was huge. In addition to the hospi-

Mary Jane Stutsman in the WAVES, 1944.

tal it housed a boot camp for southern inductees and many special service schools.

Mary Jane was delighted to be at work in a hospital, but some conditions there disturbed her.

"I was assigned duty on an entirely black ward. In those days there was discrimination, and black meant stay to yourself and don't mix with the whites. There was difficulty getting WAVES, especially from the South, to work on this ward; if they did, it was only for a short time.

"I never saw any black WAVES, but they could have been somewhere else.

"This ward also had only black corpsmen. Discrimination against anything always bothered me. Finding Maryland still fighting the Civil War was amazing to me. I had never seen the separation of facilities between blacks and whites. As usual I was annoyed, but thought I would get lynched when I brought it up."

Mary Jane's first weekend liberty also brought a surprise. For the first time she experienced sexual harassment. She and her roommate visited a small town and attended a local festivity in the park, which was filled with townspeople and men and women in uniform. Two sailors joined them. Suddenly the WAVES were grabbed, pushed against a tree trunk, and the sailors "attempted to push up our skirts and grab us all over." The women managed to shove them away and escape from the park, but it was an unexpected unpleasant experience.

Mary Jane worked briefly in the hospital's galley, serving food to the patients from a large cart, but she showed such interest in medical matters that she was transferred back to work with the patients.

"I saw insulin shocks, eye problems—caused by constantly getting reinfected with gonorrhea—pneumonia, heart attacks, all types of respiratory ailments. I learned very quickly how to change a bed with a patient in it and to miter those corners correctly."

Mary Jane swabbed throats, inserted gastric tubes, gave hypodermics, passed out medications, gave back rubs, and volunteered for any type of care needed. She remembers that she "happily awoke every morning wallowing in my life of work in a hospital."

It was on her off-duty hours that Mary Jane ran into more difficulties. She became friends with a navy cook, who asked her for a date; she accepted. They went to a local restaurant that was patronized by the navy personnel, had a "nice dinner and lots of good conversation." It became time to return to base, and they were running late. The navy cook suggested a shortcut so they could get back to base more quickly.

They took the shortcut. "Suddenly I found myself on the ground with him on top of me trying to remove my skirt and pants." Mary Jane fought him off and in the process tore off the bandage on his hand, which he had cut working in the galley. Blood spurted out, her date got up to go to sick bay, and Mary Jane returned to her barracks alone. The WAVE officer on duty questioned her, since she had blood on her clothes, but she was too shocked to answer. The matter was dropped.

The attempted rapist was angry and spread the rumor that Mary Jane was "an easy lay." Invitations to go out on a date came rapidly. Mary Jane refused them all.

Mary Jane also had an unpleasant encounter in the barracks. As she said, "Homosexuality in the armed forces is now in the news constantly. It was not tolerated in 1944." Mary Jane had thought nothing of going to the head next to her room to shower each day. She walked the short distance nude with a towel over her arm.

"Someone was apparently watching and thinking I was 'advertising.'" One night, Mary Jane was relaxing in her nightgown; after leaning over the railing of the second floor open porch to look at the stars, she sat down. Suddenly she felt a hand going

up and down her thigh. A WAVE was the guilty party. Mary Jane
quickly got up, without saying a word, and returned to her
room.

The offending WAVE continued her unwelcome sexual over-
tures. She was finally reported and discharged from the navy.

Some of the ambulatory patients, on spotting the WAVES on
their way to the mess hall, would call out in unison, "We joined
the navy to ride the WAVES," amidst catcalls and whistles. The
corpsmen never joined in this harassment, for they knew how
important the WAVES were to the hospital.

There were other irritations. Mary Jane was put on report and
not allowed to leave the barracks except for duty for a week
when she returned from the ship's store, with both arms filled
with goods, and failed to salute a male officer.

Bainbridge Hospital offered specialized training programs,
and Mary Jane was accepted for heart technician training. She
learned how to do EKGs and basal metabolism tests. However,
she and the WAVE instructor clashed, and when her training
was finished, instead of being sent to the heart station, she was
placed back on the wards. She took care of returning sailors and
fleet marines who were hospitalized for all types of war wounds,
battle fatigue, malaria, or pneumonia.

"It was a busy time in the hospital as more and more men
were leaving for overseas duty. It was cutting into the male hospital staff."

Mary Jane had been on thirty nights of night duty, and when
it was over she was planning "on sleeping for days," but she
never got the chance: a replacement could not be found. She
became exhausted. She developed a severe cold and finally
ended up in the WAVES ward as a patient. After only a short rest
she was out and working on the contagion wards with patients
with scarlet fever and mumps. Her cold reappeared. She was
fatigued, and the doctors took pity on her and placed her in the
heart station, where duty was lighter.

Mary Jane's free time had been spent with a very special
sailor, and when V-E Day came, the atmosphere in the unit
changed and personnel began thinking of being able to return
home. Mary Jane and her sailor decided to get married. They

Mary Jane Stutsman Schneider and her husband, Bill,
on their wedding day, May 15, 1945.

had their blood tests and found a state where there was no waiting period. After their leave, they returned to the base and
found an apartment nearby. Then the Japanese surrendered.
The war was over, and married women were eligible for discharge. Mary Jane quickly signed up and was sent to Washington, D.C., where she was discharged on October 3, 1945. In January 1946, her husband was discharged from the navy.

They packed their belongings and took the train to Rochester,
New York, her husband's hometown.

Mary Jane Stutsman Schneider was not idle after she settled in
Rochester with her husband following the war. She first stayed home and
took care of her four children. Then in 1969 she entered the workforce

as a pioneer enterostomal therapist (a nursing specialty); by then, her husband's long-standing multiple sclerosis had ended his working career. In 1980 she received her B.S. degree from the University of Rochester, thirty-nine years after she started college at Ohio State University.

She retired in 1985. She has four grandchildren, and now keeps busy with gourmet cooking, bird-watching, reading, and relaxing with her husband.

17

Service Among the Brass

Vi Myers joined the WAVES on her twentieth birthday, January 20, 1944. She had no idea of what military life would be like. She arrived at Hunter College for boot camp in high heels and silk stockings, in the midst of a snowstorm, to begin what the navy called "indoctrination."

"The first day included rushing from class to class; from mental exam to physical exam; from needles in my arm to turmoil in my brain. The strangest thing is, I began to like it!"

Vi successfully made the transition from civilian life to regimentation, and after six weeks she found herself more than ready to "do her share." She was assigned to yeoman school at Oklahoma A & M College in Stillwater.

"The days flew by once we commenced our scholarly grind. We were up at six to the tune of reveille and from then on it was rush, rush, rush until ten at night. I never studied so hard in my life, as every Saturday we had a tough exam in each subject."

When the three months of learning were nearly up, the women had their last medical exam.

Vi Myers in front of the WAVES barracks at West Potomac Park, Washington, D.C., in 1944.

"The doctor put us all in one big room and said, 'How are you feeling—anyone sick?'

"No one answered.

"'Dismissed,' smiled the commander, and that was that."

Vi was assigned to the Bureau of Ordnance in the Navy Department in Washington, D.C. She and the other WAVES at the bureau found themselves too busy to do much with their little leisure time. Washington was a bustling place, and Vi often saw prominent military leaders. She had a chance to salute Adm. Ernest King, then chief of naval operations, and even General de Gaulle when he was visiting from France. Vi was still in Washington when President Franklin Roosevelt died in April 1945, and she solemnly watched the funeral cortege from a hotel balcony.

Vi had always considered that her job was dull compared with the work other WAVES were doing. Her roommate was called out at all hours of the night to help her boss, a commander in the bureau, and Vi was envious of what seemed to be an exciting job. Little did she realize then how important her job was: she was dealing with all the reports on Los Alamos, the New Mexico complex where the atomic bombs were being designed and built.

Regimental review for the commandant of the Ninth Naval District at the U.S. Naval Training Station at Stillwater, Oklahoma, on April 27, 1944.

One day in May 1945 the newsboys in Washington were shouting, "Extra! Extra!" The Germans had surrendered. The WAVES were exhilarated. Then, "when Japan gave up it was almost unbelievable. That was when we first began to think that perhaps someday before we were old and gray we would get to go home and live a normal life.

"It was quite a ceremony that took place the day I was discharged. As I was called to receive my discharge certificate, I saluted and shook hands with the officer in charge. And as I stood there and sang *The Star Spangled Banner* and *Anchors Aweigh* with the rest of the WAVES and sailors, I couldn't help but think of the day two years before, when a little frightened boot in high-heeled shoes set off for camp, and wondered if she could ever go home again."

Vi Myers married and returned to Brooklyn. She worked for a major textbook publisher until she left the job to raise her three children. The family moved to upstate New York, and Vi went back to work as an office manager for a benefit fund in Albany, which she continued to do until 1987. She now has eight grandchildren and works part-time when she is not traveling.

PART FIVE

U.S. Marine Corps Women's Reserve

During World War I a group of 305 women served as administrative clerks in the U.S. Marine Corps. These women, called Marinettes, wore the forest green uniform of the corps and learned simple drill movements, which they practiced early in the mornings on the Ellipse in Potomac Park in Washington, D.C. This small group set the precedent for women to serve in the Marine Corps.

The U.S. Marine Corps was the last of the four major services to organize a women's reserve in World War II. On November 7, 1942, the commandant of corps, Lt. Gen. Thomas Holcomb, who originally had been against the formation of such a reserve for the marines, gave his approval, as did President Franklin D. Roosevelt. The establishment of the Marine Corps Women's Reserve was made possible by an amendment, dated July 30, 1942, to the U.S. Naval Reserve Act of 1938.

The women reservists were to be called marines. They were the only women's service that did not have an acronym designation or semiofficial nickname. Perhaps more significant, they were not an auxiliary group, but were accepted as a full-fledged part of the U.S. Marine Corps Reserve.

The officers trained at Smith College and Mount Holyoke, the enlisted personnel at Hunter College, following the same course of instruction given to the WAVES. However, by July 1943, training and specialists' schools were transferred to Camp Lejeune, North Carolina. The women were trained for and performed in over two hundred job categories.

By the beginning of 1943, when the women were responding to the snappy marine poster calling for enlistment to free a man to fight, the Allies had taken the initiative from the Japanese in the South and Southwest Pacific, with victories at Guadalcanal and Papua. The Germans were still battling in the USSR near Stalingrad, and fighting was fierce in North Africa, Italy, and western Europe.

After learning the basics in boot camp, most of the women marines went on to train in specialized fields. Some studied auto mechanics and became adept at servicing trucks and jeeps. They learned to drive military vehicles of all sizes and provided transport on and to and from bases and even drove jeeps during war games. Some worked in vital statistics, notifying parents and wives about casualties, a particularly difficult job during the spring of 1943, when the troops were on the attack in New Guinea, Russell Island, and the Solomon Islands chain.

Some women marines were typists; some served in public relations, writing publicity releases about the marines in action in the Pacific for hometown newspapers. Some of the women, whose jobs were not directly involved with the war, felt far removed from the military action abroad. Others would check the bases' bulletin boards for news or even put up world maps pinpointing war engagements, such as the brisk fighting in Italy and the Allied penetration of Naples in October.

Some women marines were trained in airplane maintenance, some were in charge of supplies and payrolls. Still others were keypunch operators. Together, they created a strong system at home to support the men fighting overseas.

Nineteen forty-four was a hard year for the Allies in both Europe and the Far East, but the tide was turning. In June the Allied troops landed in Normandy, and the U.S. Marines invaded Saipan. The Japanese suffered defeat after defeat as the Allies conquered or recaptured the many Pacific islands. By January 1945, it was apparent that the Japanese had lost the war.

An overseas bill for women in the naval services had been signed by President Franklin D. Roosevelt in September 1944, and by January of the next year the Marine Corps Women's Reserve began serving in Hawaii. Women marines serving on the islands saw many of the men who had fought in the Pacific as they came through Hawaii on their way home. Some of the women were aviation maintenance personnel; they not only checked out the planes for pilots and kept them in flying order, but also directed the parking of planes, much to the surprise of the incoming crews.

More than twenty thousand women were in the marine reserves by the time the war ended. The women of the marines had indeed taken over many of the jobs, freeing the men to fight. Many felt that they did not have a big job, or did not serve heroically, but they all knew they had met a need. And somehow, they left the corps with a feeling of "Once a marine, always a marine." *Semper fidelis.*

All units of the Marine Corps Women's Reserve were disbanded by September 1946. On June 12, 1948, Congress passed an act establishing the women marines as a permanent part of the Regular Marine Corps, as well as granting them permanent reserve status.

18

Fraternization

When the Japanese attacked Pearl Harbor in 1941, Dorothy Lloyd lay in a hospital bed in Pittsburgh, paralyzed from polio. The doctors said she would never walk again. But Dorothy was determined to prove them wrong. By October 1942, she was walking and back at work.

In December, while Christmas shopping with her landlady, Dorothy passed a recruiting poster. Laughingly she remarked, "I should join the marines." Idly she went into the headquarters to pick up some literature. Before she knew it, she was taking a physical. She flunked because she was underweight. Undaunted, Dorothy returned to her rooming house and spent a week stuffing herself with food and liquids. She went back to the marine recruiters and passed the physical. She was sworn into the United States Marine Corps on December 19, 1942, when she was twenty years old.

Her trip to boot camp at Camp Lejeune, North Carolina, took two days and nights. Everyone aboard was in the service. It was a no-frills train: no dining car, no food provided. By the time they arrived at Camp Lejeune at 6:00 A.M. on January 22, 1943, they were a very hungry crew. Luckily, their first stop was the mess hall.

Boot camp consisted of six weeks of marching, saluting, and learning, six weeks of training as hard as the men.

"There was an enormous amount of information about the marines and our country thrown at us, a strenuous physical exercise program, and the cruelty of the male drill instructors."

The women marched two and three hours without stopping to rest. "If some girl fainted you were to step over her and go on, for if you stopped to help you got a demerit." (Dorothy got many.) The drill instructors were tartars. After shining her shoes for an hour, she would be told they were dirty. If a recruit forgot to button a button, it was roughly pulled off and handed to her. Hair was measured with a ruler to be sure it was the proper length. To work off her demerits, Dorothy stabbed paper and other trash on the grounds with a pointed stick, rain and shine. The women hated the drill instructor but they did as he said. They learned that a marine always follows orders.

Dorothy fell into bed each night tired and homesick, but she finished boot camp successfully and received her first stripe on March 2, 1943.

She applied for motor transport school at the camp and was accepted for a six-week course. She learned about motors and how to change tires, grease, and oil, and she became adept at servicing trucks and jeeps. By the end of the sessions, Dorothy was an accomplished mechanic and military driver.

Her next assignment had nothing to do with either mechanics or driving. She was posted to a desk job at Henderson Hall in Arlington, Virginia, across the river from Washington, D.C. She sent telegrams to parents and wives of wounded, dead, and missing marines. The Vital Statistics Department received daily reports of marine casualties from the fighting on New Guinea, from the drive up the Solomons, from the Russell Islands, from the battles for the capture of many small islands. The Allies had encountered stiff fighting, and the marines lost many men.

Marine personnel were to work for only thirty days sending telegrams to next of kin, for it was a stressful job. Dorothy had known some of the men on the lists from the Camp Lejeune base

Photo of Dorothy Lloyd, Marine Corps,
used in the MPs' pin-up picture contest,
which she won.

clubs. She was shaken to see the name of a favorite motor transport instructor. She felt as if she had lost a relative.

Not only was she under great stress, but Dorothy was eager to use her driving training, and after ninety days on the job she applied for and received a transfer to Quantico, Virginia. She arrived on June 10, 1943, assigned to duty as a jeep messenger for the Marine Corps schools.

Dorothy discovered that the men on the base hated the women marines.

"Their motto was 'First the blacks, then the dogs, and now the broad-ass marines.' They yelled this at us everywhere we went—shopping, to the PX, bowling, at the movies, or just on the streets."

The MPs always accompanied the women at night and checked on their barracks area every hour. Finally, after a year, with more and more women marines arriving at the base, the men began to accept them. They unanimously voted Dorothy their "pin-up girl" in July 1943. Eventually, they even became possessive. They did not want any of the women marines to date swabs (navy) or dogfaces (army)—only other marines. Many fights broke out when a swab or dogface took a female marine to the NCO club to dance or drink a few beers.

Dorothy began driving a station wagon on trips to Washington, D.C., with marine officers—the brass—because she knew the streets well, having been stationed in Arlington for three months. She also drove jeeps and vans and small trucks on maneuvers and on training exercises. She often would be the "lead" on a convoy to other bases, traveling to Cherry Point, North Carolina; Baltimore, Maryland; and the Philadelphia Navy Yard.

Dorothy was on a field trip in December 1944 when she had a serious accident. She was driving a jeep for Fire Control—firing power—during a war game. She ran over a stick of dynamite and the jeep turned over. The commander, who was in the jeep, was not injured, but Dorothy suffered internal bleeding. She recovered, but the damage done would return to plague her later.

By January 1945 Dorothy had become a corporal. She was transferred to ordnance officers' training school on the base, and she became a messenger for the colonel, as well as his driver on trips and during field maneuvers. She also picked up student officers who had arrived to attend the school.

In one of these groups she met Bill Hughes, a handsome warrant officer with curly brown hair and blue eyes. He had been a basketball player and a boxer, and now as a marine had arrived to attend the ordnance school.

Dorothy was smitten instantly, but it was some weeks before Bill asked her out. Officers and enlisted personnel were not allowed to fraternize, let alone date. Enlisted marines dated enlisted marines, and officers dated officers. Bill and Dorothy dared to break the rules.

On their first date they went double, with a friend of Bill's and a friend of Dorothy's. They drove to a Hot Shoppe in Arlington, fifty miles from Quantico, for a steak dinner, not willing to risk the chance of being caught dating on base. The other couple traveled to Washington, D.C., by cab to a nightclub. Bill and Dorothy went to the Tidal Basin. It was late April, and the breath of spring was in the air. The cherry trees were covered with pink blossoms, and a full moon shone on the waters of the Potomac River. By the time they returned to Quantico, Bill and Dorothy knew they were in love.

Their courtship lasted seventeen days, then they decided to elope. With Dorothy's best friend, Kathy, and Bill's best friend, Eddie, they found a small white church in Bethesda, Maryland, and a minister to marry them.

The newlyweds were on top of the world. Dorothy had passed her tests for sergeant stripes, and her future looked bright. However, two days later, at eight o'clock in the morning, Dorothy

Marine Dorothy Lloyd Hughes and husband, Bill, on their
wedding day, May 19, 1945. Dorothy was subsequently arrested
for fraternization with an officer.

was arrested in her barracks and hustled to the guardhouse. The
charge: fraternization with an officer. None of the MPs had
wanted to arrest her. In the past they had all turned their backs
when they saw Bill and Dorothy together. They drew straws.
The unlucky MP had appeared at the barracks with the bad
news.

The guardhouse was a part of the women's barracks set aside
for a jail: one person to a room, one window, a bed, a chair, no
books, no radio, and no visitors. Meals were brought in. The

inmates were allowed one shower a day in the head down the hall. A guard stood on duty outside around the clock.

Fortunately for Dorothy, the general thought twenty-four hours in jail was enough time for her to fully contemplate her sin. The next day she was brought before him for a day court hearing. It was the same day that the list for sergeants came out, with Dorothy's name on it.

"The general was very angry and did most of the talking, informing me that the only reason he didn't throw me out of the marines was because I didn't date on base, but I would not keep my sergeant stripes. I would not return to ordnance school."

Since Dorothy was a corporal, the general could not put her on KP, but he did place her in charge of the women marine officers' mess hall, which entailed making the menus, keeping the hall clean, seeing that the food was served hot, keeping the records of the officers who ate there, and billing them once a month.

The difficult times and the punishment were not over. Bill and Dorothy got permission to live off base and found a room with the operator of the town's beauty shop, whose husband was overseas in the army. The house was right outside the base's front gate. It was convenient, but cramped—one room with washing and kitchen privileges—for ten dollars a week.

The general had, indeed, been angry. He felt that out-of-rank marriages not only went against marine rules, but were bad for enlisted morale. He wanted to make an example of Dorothy. She had to be in her barracks at 5:00 A.M. every morning for roll call and keep her bunk and area clean for inspection. And she had to eat three meals a day in the mess hall.

"The captain in charge of our company was very kind and understanding, and thought the general had gone too far, but even though she could give me liberty passes to go off base each night, I did not get back my sergeant stripes. For three months we lived like this, seeing each other only at night and on weekends."

Respite came when Bill and Dorothy had three weeks of leave. In August 1945 they took a delayed honeymoon to the Great

Smoky Mountains in Tennessee. They were there when the Japanese surrendered.

When Dorothy and Bill returned to Quantico, he received orders to report to Camp Pendleton, California. Dorothy was to stay in Virginia. It was to be just as the general had told Dorothy on the day of her hearing: She would be punished for breaking the rules. Bill had received no punishment at all, not even a reprimand.

Dorothy had enlisted for the duration, and with the war over she was due for discharge. She longed for those papers to arrive so that she could join Bill in California, but by this time she was suffering from side effects of the jeep accident. By September 1945, she became so ill that she could not continue to stand duty. She had lost weight and suffered from anemia. Surgery was scheduled. Dorothy underwent surgery the day Bill left for California. She was in the hospital for three weeks, during which time Bill received no mail from her—it had been misdirected to Hawaii.

Dorothy recovered from the surgery and went back to jeep driving. Now all she wanted was her discharge. Bill finally got an eighteen-day pass, and he came back for Dorothy on October 11. Her discharge finally came through on October 18, 1945.

Although "it was hard at times," Dorothy was always proud and pleased that she had been a marine.

Dorothy and Bill Hughes stayed in California. Bill was discharged from the marines in April 1946 and enrolled in UCLA at Santa Barbara and earned his teacher's degree. They moved to Kentucky, where he taught for twenty-five years. Dorothy took a business management course and worked in that field for twenty years, until she had open-heart surgery. They have two sons and four grandchildren. Today Dorothy handles the paperwork for the remodeling company Bill opened after retiring as a teacher.

In May 1995 they will celebrate their fiftieth wedding anniversary by returning to Bethesda, Maryland, to repeat their vows in the same small church in which they were married.

19

Not a Really Big Job

Ruth Walters was an impressionable young woman of twenty-two in July 1943. The war in Europe and the Pacific was at its peak, and Ruth was captivated by the marine recruiting poster. There was a *woman* marine, looking "self-assured, happy, and wearing a handsome green uniform with a scarlet cord on her cap." Ruth pictured herself in that good-looking outfit and knew, as the slogan said, she would be "freeing a man to fight."

The next day she went to marine headquarters in Manhattan, New York, held up her right hand, and took the oath that made her a marine.

"I am sure," she wrote later, "that my heart beat faster, and I know I was thrilled and not a little scared."

In September she "packed a small suitcase with very unmilitary stuff—curlers, sweaters, a dress, and the sewing kit pressed upon me by my mother" and set off for boot camp at Camp Lejeune, North Carolina.

Boot camp did not exude the friendly atmosphere Ruth had found at the recruiting office. Now it was "overbearing sergeants who snapped orders faster than we could follow. Every move in boot camp was performed at top speed as if the Japanese were already at the camp gates. Every boot learned to move as though life depended on it. Routines were done at breakneck speed." It seemed to Ruth that everyone shouted, from the drill sergeant to the mess hall servers.

Unlike many of the boots, Ruth was enthralled by the marching. The weekly battalion parade was "the stuff my dreams had been made of. I thrilled to the surge of patriotic emotion I felt as I proudly marched behind our country's flag and our marine flag. The stirring pomp of 'Semper Fidelis,' the bright blue of the sky, and a thousand of us marching in strict cadence was pure joy. My heart was full and all the swabbing, shoe shining, KP, inspections, and punishments were as nothing. This was what it meant to be a marine!"

Boot camp came to an end, and Ruth was given what she thought would be a plum assignment in Washington, D.C., "the exciting hub of the nation's heart." There she found she had no real purpose. She was put on guard duty, which she felt was quite unnecessary, since the women's barracks were surrounded by a fence, with a male guard at the gate. But she did as she was told.

Ruth walked official beats at night, two hours on and four hours off, then a day off. "From the frenzy of boot camp to the near leisure existence was a culture shock."

She was cold during the nights, and the days began to blend into one another. In 1944, when the winter was over, she received orders to serve as recreation leader at Camp Miramar in San Diego, California. Miramar was a new base for the women, and Ruth was one of those responsible for the creation of its recreation program. A recreation hut was built and stocked with everything from anagrams to volleyball. Outside, baseball and softball fields were built. Ruth helped arrange trips for the women marines to town for ice skating and dancing, or tours to Mexico.

Life in sunny San Diego represented a big change from Ruth's early marine days, and she changed, too. Her love of marching had vanished. The colonel's battalion drill was "an exercise in torture. Standing there with reflected heat from the pavement increasing our misery, we watched helplessly as even hardened marines succumbed, dropping one by one like dominoes."

Ruth found that the days at Camp Miramar were predictable and long. There wasn't much to do.

"The war seemed distant. Intent on our daily existence, we were aware of it, but even the men did not discuss it."

One day passed pretty much like the others. By now it was the summer of 1945.

"I remember well the strange, unconfirmed rumors of a terrible bomb. It sounded like a Buck Rogers episode, but, no, it was true. Days later, after a second bomb, the Japanese surrendered."

Ruth was discharged from the marines in December and given two hundred dollars and a ticket to San Francisco.

"I had proudly been a marine for two and a half years. It was thrilling to see war and killing at an end and the new stages of peace. Still, I missed the unity and comradeship. As boots we were bound together in struggles to adjust, often causing misery. Later the strong feeling of being together as part of the best—marines—unified us. Looking back, I felt that even though I had not had a really big job to do, I had fulfilled a need and so perhaps had helped after all."

Ruth Walters married in 1948 and bore two sons and a daughter. Raising a family was "a cinch after having been part of the U.S. Marine Corps." One day she heard her nine-year-old son trying one-upmanship with a friend.

"My dad was a sergeant," said her son.

"So was mine," was the reply.

"Well, my mother was a sergeant, too."

That was the end of the discussion.

Today Ruth Walters Ward keeps busy taking writing courses at New York University. She is active in church affairs and edits the congregation newsletter. She and her husband travel, taking car trips or cruises whenever they can.

PART SIX

SPARS
(U.S. Coast Guard)

On November 23, 1942, the U.S. Coast Guard Women's Reserve was established. Known as the SPARS—derived from the Coast Guard's motto, *Semper paratus,* "Always ready"—the women's reserve would grow from a few recruits to approximately ten thousand enlisted personnel and one thousand officers by the end of World War II.

In December 1942 twelve WAVES volunteered to be SPAR officers, and they trained at Smith College and at Mount Holyoke. They received further training at the Coast Guard Academy in New London, Connecticut, where they were commissioned. Enlisted SPARS started boot camp at stations at Oklahoma A & M at Stillwater; Iowa State Teachers College in Cedar Falls; and at Hunter College in the Bronx, New York. On June 14, 1943, the first class of SPARS began training at the newly opened Coast Guard training station at Florida's Palm Beach Biltmore

Hotel. Starting in early 1945 the SPARS were also trained along-side their fellow Coast Guardsmen at the Coast Guard training station in Manhattan Beach, Brooklyn.

The SPARS' slogan was Release a Man to Fight at Sea, and the women who joined did just that. They became yeomen, store-keepers, clerks, parachute riggers, chaplain's assistants, air traf-fic controllers, boatswain's mates, coxswains, radio operators, ship's cooks, vehicle drivers, pharmacist's mates, and even manned the new loran long-range navigation station.

Many of the Coast Guard women were trained in communi-cations, especially coding and decoding, which was important to the Coast Guard's mission. Messages were constantly being sent out to ships, and recognition signals—the passwords allowing a ship into port—had to be established and checked. Some of the SPARS served in New York, which early in the war was bustling with naval activity as convoys set out for Europe. The port also maintained beach patrols to guard against possible attack from enemy ships prowling the Atlantic. The threat was real; in a six-month period in 1942, when shipping war matériel to Britain was a priority, almost five hundred Allied ships were sunk by German U-boats off the eastern coast of the United States.

Some SPARS served in Florida, assisting the U.S. submarines from the Groton, Connecticut base as they passed offshore on their way to the Pacific via the Panama Canal. The Coast Guard women maintained radio contact with these subs, and with the minesweepers and patrol planes on sea-rescue duty.

Within months the SPARS had taken over the majority of shore jobs at many Coast Guard stations. They performed a vari-ety of duties, from cooking to serving as personnel officers. As the war finally wound down, the SPARS were kept busy rerout-ing overseas mail to the guardsmen coming home from Alaska and the Pacific.

The women who had served as SPARS were aptly named, for they were indeed always ready to do the job at hand. They were a small service, but a necessary one.

After the war, the SPARS were separated from the service, although a few years later a reserve training program was established that allowed women to participate in the Coast Guard.

On December 3, 1973, legislation was passed allowing women to serve in the Regular U.S. Coast Guard; three years later, the Coast Guard Academy in New London became the first branch of the service to admit women into its ranks.

20

They Were Always Ready

Jan Thorpe was twenty-nine when she was accepted as an officer candidate in the U.S. Coast Guard on January 4, 1943. She left her California home on January 17 as a SPAR recruit, headed for the naval training station at Smith College in Northampton, Massachusetts. At that time Smith was the site of boot camp for the WAVES, and the SPARS joined them, since their facilities at Palm Beach, Florida, were not yet ready.

After four weeks of boot camp, Jan was assigned to communications, to study coding and decoding. The work was concentrated and demanding, but she mastered it.

Jan "could not have wished for a better assignment." She was ordered to duty at district headquarters at 42 Broadway, New York City. New York was a shipping hub. Convoys left for the battle areas, beach patrols and small boats offshore guarded the port. The dock areas were teeming with activity.

When Jan arrived in May 1943 there were only three SPAR officers in the whole district, and the "Code Board" office was completely staffed by men. This situation would change as more and more SPARS came. By mid-November, all the male officers

SPAR Jan Thorpe, left, worked in coding communications for the U.S. Coast Guard. In uniform, May 1943.

were gone. Jan was made officer in charge of the Code Board, now completely staffed by SPARS.

It was exciting and busy work, coding and decoding the confidential messages flooding into the board—messages to the harbor pilots who guided the ships in and out of the port, messages to the small boats offshore. All kinds of shipping messages needed to be decoded.

Jan was baffled one day in decoding. "I came up with the same word regardless of how many times it was checked. It did not make any sense and was a word I had never seen before, nor could I find it in the dictionary." Jan asked other departments for help, without success, and then checked with a captain in charge of ordnance. He knew. The word was *snorkle,* the name of a new device that allowed enemy subs to stay submerged for long periods of time.

It was while working at headquarters that Jan met Lt. Alan Macauley, who had come there on business; they began a romance that culminated in their marriage. They wed just before his ship, an attack cargo vessel, left port for overseas.

After V-E Day, Jan applied for and received transfer to Long

Beach, California, rejecting the option of going for duty to Hawaii or Alaska on the theory that she had best stay in the United States, since her husband was now in the Pacific theater.

After V-J Day, Alan's ship was sent to Japan, but by December 1945 he was home. They were both discharged from service on the day before Christmas.

After the war Jan Macauley and her husband set up a business that developed and supplied machines for professional motion picture and television use, which were sold throughout the world. Jan was executive vice president and treasurer of the firm until they both retired. They celebrated their fiftieth wedding anniversary in 1993, "which proves wartime marriages do last. "

Martha Lucinda Vaughn also enlisted in the SPARS in January 1943, when she was thirty, and was sent to Northampton for boot camp. As Martha put it, after four weeks, the SPARS "emerged from this punishment disciplined in mind and body and feeling great, ready for anything."

The "anything" turned out to be coding and decoding secret and important material. Martha was assigned to headquarters in Washington, D.C., in June 1943. After a short stay there, she received a transfer to Miami. There, Martha first corrected classified publications; she was then given the job of traveling to other bases to teach a new procedure for handling messages. She worked in Palm Beach, Fort Meyers, St. Petersburg, and Cedar Key and was finally assigned to full duty at Key West.

At Key West, Martha and the other SPARS got to know the servicemen who worked in the next office, the radio/teletype room. These men were busy conducting radio traffic with the fifty small navy minesweepers attached to the base. Martha recalls that "most of the men were very young and lonesome, and all were frightened."

The slogans on the recruitment posters had said Release a Man for Sea Duty, and Martha was probably one of the few who actually knew the man she released. The base's communications officer received his orders, and she stepped into his place. Her responsibilities enlarged. She now had custody of a large safe where classified documents were kept, and her SPARS were responsible for the recognition signals. Every ship that approached the port had to give the proper signal or be treated as an enemy. And when signals were changed, all units, and the navy, had to be notified.

As more and more enlisted SPARS arrived at the base, Martha's responsibilities increased. She had to help assign them to duty, and she found that while some of them could type or do other jobs, most had no skills. Some wanted to drive the jeeps. This offer was initially refused by the base commander, who did not want the women at the

SPAR ensign Martha Vaughn in 1944.

motor pool without supervision. Later, the women won out and were allowed to drive. Of course, no one wanted to work in the mess hall. Martha solved that problem by assigning rotating duty.

One problem followed another. One evening, the male officers were teasing her about not being able to handle her SPARS. She broke into tears and was consoled by them only when they said that they had much, much more trouble with their men.

In February 1945 Martha was transferred again, this time to the Coast Guard air station at Dinner Key, Miami. There she was assigned not only coding and decoding but also to other duties involving air/sea rescue.

Martha and the other SPARS also helped the patrol planes learn the locations of U.S. submarines. "We received long coded messages about where a certain sub would be and the time.

Those new submarines were en route to the Pacific. These messages, usually in strip, consisted of long strings of numbers and were tedious to decode. We then located the spot on a map, marked it with a pin and stretched a string to show the route. This was in a locked wall closet that the pilots consulted when they were preparing to go out. The crews also consulted the weatherman, and also filed a flight plan. Accuracy was important, for lives depended on it."

Martha also made arrangements for trips to Caribbean islands, usually by amphibious PBMs. Among her duties was to be at the base when the planes were readied; to personally see who boarded the plane; and to be a witness that those people were on the plane should it be lost. In the afternoon the crew would radio their estimated time of arrival and give a rundown of whom they had on board. Martha was to be ready to call an ambulance if needed, security if there were any prisoners, or immigration if there was an alien.

One day there was an alien. He "was a dapper English official with a rose in his buttonhole. A man stepped forward and took the rose. He had been there every time, but I did not know him." He was the plant inspector.

There were enough varied events during the day that Martha enjoyed her job, but in Key West she had heard so many people sing the praises of Seattle that she decided to apply for a transfer. Through a bit of maneuvering, Seattle requested Martha, and she moved on.

V-E Day was past and the war was winding down. Martha replaced the SPAR postal officer, who had enough points to be separated from the service. It was a busy time.

Soon the war in the Pacific was over, and the postal office was busier than ever, forwarding mail and taking care of paperwork for the returning men. Martha was so happy in her work that she stayed in the service until the SPAR program was terminated in June 1946.

After she left the Coast Guard, Martha Vaughn (Butler) worked in an insurance office in Seattle. She married in 1951, but in 1957 her

husband died of a heart attack. Martha went back to work, first for the
YMCA, then for an insurance office, and then at Santa Barbara City
College during registration. In 1957 she married David Butler, and
they traveled to Florida, Alaska, Idaho, and New Zealand. He died in
1983 of cancer, and in 1985 Martha moved to a retirement community.
She is active in volunteer work, adult education classes, in church, and
has been to most of the United States and thirty-one foreign countries.
She still meets with SPAR groups.

Doris McMillan was twenty years old and working in Houston when she decided to enlist in the SPARS in January 1943. She had been persuaded to enlist by an emotional surge of patriotism brought on by the Sousa march playing loudly at the nearby recruiting office. She convinced her parents to sign a waiver because of her age, and by the spring of 1943 she was at boot camp at Hunter College, training with the WAVES. She was sent on for further training at Oklahoma A & M to become a yeoman in business administration.

The Eighth Naval District in New Orleans needed many SPARS so that male personnel could be released for ship duty. Doris was assigned to New Orleans; she was first used as a recruiter, but she found that job so unrewarding that she requested a transfer to the personnel office, which she received. At that time, about 20 percent of the office staff were SPARS; within two months, 80 percent were Coast Guard women. Some of their male comrades were not happy to be released for ship duty.

Doris had an upsetting experience at that time. As she was riding on a streetcar in the city, a woman suddenly took her umbrella and began hitting Doris and screaming, "It's your fault that my son is now at sea. If he's killed, it's your fault!"

"Tears were streaming down her face and mine. I did not know how to handle the situation. I finally took her umbrella and left the bus at the next stop."

By December 1943 she received her yeoman second class rating. By early the next year the Coast Guard headquarters had expanded so greatly that all the SPARS were busy.

"The first eighteen months, we worked five and a half days a week. I was responsible for about sixteen file clerks. I learned to handle the problems, whether they were the filing or the personalities."

By spring 1945 some of the men were returning, ready to go back to their stateside duty stations. After V-J Day, the SPARS were told that they would soon be discharged. Doris was separated from the service on October 9, 1945.

Doris McMillan (Breed) married in September 1945, and she and her husband will soon celebrate their forty-ninth anniversary. They have one son and four grandchildren. As she wrote, she was "more housewife/ mother than career girl," though for the first few years of marriage she worked as a secretary and bookkeeper. Currently she has been diagnosed with pancreatic cancer, but she can still write of her "fond memories" for her stint in the SPARS during World War II.

PART SEVEN

Women's Airforce Service Pilots

At the beginning of the war, it was obvious that air power and superiority would be major factors in an Allied victory over Germany and Japan. Scores of male pilots would be needed to serve overseas; the country would need women pilots to step in to take over the jobs of the men being sent abroad.

To meet this need, the Women's Airforce Service Pilots (WASP) was formed, the direct result of the dedicated efforts of two women, Nancy Harkness Love and Jacqueline Cochran.

As the war clouds intensified, Nancy Harkness Love, an accomplished pilot, had decided to form a group of experienced women pilots to transport military planes throughout the United States. The U.S. Air Transport Command, realizing that male pilots were in short supply, supported Nancy Love's plan. Finally, on September 10, 1942, the Women's Auxiliary Ferrying Squadron (WAFS) was created, with Love as director. The program's twenty-five highly qualified pilots were assigned to the Air Transport Command (ATC) for ferrying duty.

WAFS headquarters was initially based at New Castle Army Air Base in Delaware; later, ferrying squadrons were established at Romulus, Michigan; Dallas, Texas; and Long Beach and Palm Springs, California.

At about the same time, Jacqueline Cochran, a prominent aviator, was promoting the creation of a separate corps of women pilots who would be trained to fly military aircraft within the United States, and hoped to establish a training school for that purpose. In the meantime she recruited a number of women pilots to serve with Great Britain's Air Transport Auxiliary (ATA). These pilots were the first American women to fly military aircraft for the Allies in England during World War II.

When Jacqueline Cochran returned from England in September 1942, the Women's Flying Training Detachment (WFTD) was established, with Cochran as head of the training program at Municipal Airport, Houston, Texas.

By the time the women had begun ferrying planes in 1942, the Americans were seeking to wear down German resistance by heavy air bombardment. Hundreds of air force members, freed for overseas duty by the women pilots, had been sent to England to train and organize for the bombardment of German-occupied Europe. Later that year, U.S. Army Air Force pilots would bomb Europe for the first time, while U.S. pilots would help provide an Allied umbrella for the invasion of North Africa.

Not only were pilots and aircraft needed for land-based bombing attacks, but they were also called to man the aircraft carrier planes in the Pacific. In July 1942 there was heavy air and naval bombardment before the Allied landings on Guadalcanal. Patrol planes searched the Midway area, and carrier planes attacked the Japanese fleet.

On August 5, 1943, the WAFS and the WFTD merged into one organization, the Women's Airforce Service Pilots (WASP). Cochran was named director of women pilots, and Nancy Love was named WASP executive of the Ferrying Division of the ATC.

Over 25,000 women applied to join the WASP. Of these, 1,879 were accepted, but only 1,074 successfully completed the training program at Avenger Field, Sweetwater, Texas. WASP training was rigorous; the women had to qualify to fly one plane after another, for they had to be able to perform any flying job the Air Corps asked of them.

The WASP flew almost every type of military airplane built for World War II, including fighters, bombers, trainers, and cargo carriers. They flew over 60 million miles in seventy-eight different types of military aircraft.

They ferried new aircraft from factories to overseas shipment points; they flew planes to repair depots; they tested the repaired planes; they towed target sleeves so the ground troops could practice their antiaircraft skills with live ammunition. They served as test pilots and instructors for male pilots; they flew searchlight and tracking missions, towed large gliders, and carried out simulated strafing, bombing, and smoke-laying raids.

In 1943, the WASP continued to train class after class to fly all types of military aircraft. The women made solo flights all over the country—sometimes routine, sometimes under frightening circumstances. As they continued to transport and test planes within the United States, American pilots were bombing submarine construction yards, airplane factories, oil plants, transportation systems, and other war industries in Germany.

By the end of 1943 there had been tremendous gains in aircraft production in the United States—more planes for the WASP to test, deliver, and ferry. More and more women entered the WASP program as the demand for pilots increased.

The next year was difficult for the WASP, which had been pushed hard to transport planes to reinforce the European invasion. In his semiannual report, Gen. William H. Tunner, commanding officer of the Ferrying Division of the domestic wing of the Air Transport Command, noted that 60 percent of all fighter aircraft had been ferried by 117 WASP. They had made hundreds and hundreds of domestic flights. He wanted more WASP as capable as those who had been flying.

The women pilots kept transporting and testing planes. Although the women of the WASP were under military orders and discipline, lived in military barracks, and flew military aircraft, they were governed and paid by the Civil Service Commission. Jacqueline Cochran, head of the WASP, began to press for their full militarization. As early as September 1943 a bill had been prepared for Congress that would give military status to the WASP, but the amended bill did not come up for a vote until June 21, 1944. Known as the Costello Bill, HR 4219 proposed that the WASP become part of the U.S. Army Air Force. The legislation was defeated in the House of Representatives by nineteen votes.

The defeat probably was the result of many factors. Director Cochran had not wanted the WASP to become part of the WAC, and she supported the Costello Bill. Male pilots were beginning to return from overseas, and many protested that women had taken over their jobs. There had been heavy lobbying in Washington, which had contributed to the bill's defeat.

The women were notified in October that the WASP would be disbanded, but they continued to fly until the organization was officially deactivated on December 20, 1944. The women were dismayed and disheartened. Their official service was over.

The war continued, and most of the WASP managed to keep flying. They had, as one WASP said, "made an important contribution to the war effort and had had an incredible experience in so doing."

In November 1977, following much testimony and persuasion by WASP leaders and with the backing of Gen. Hap Arnold's son, Bruce Arnold, and Senator Barry Goldwater, Congress finally passed legislation that granted the Women's Airforce Service Pilots military recognition and veteran status.

21

From Barnstormer to Fighter

In 1928 when Florene Miller was eight years old, she took her first airplane ride. She best tells her own story:

In those early years of flying, barnstormers would fly their open-cockpit planes over a town, pump the throttle, make a lot of noise to attract the public to the place out of town where they intended to land—on the prairie somewhere—to entice the public to come and buy a ride in their planes. When a plane would come over, my father would find me, we would dash out to the location, and we would take a ride. I found it exhilarating, an open cockpit with the wind in my face and my hair blowing and my feeling like a bird.

I took a number of rides in these barnstormers, and one day, on our way back to town, Daddy said, "When I get on my second million, I'm going to buy us an airplane!" We both laughed. Such pie-in-the-sky talk! But during my spring semester at Baylor University, he called me to say that he had bought us a beautiful silver Luscomb two-seater airplane. I could hardly wait for the semester to end.

Florene Miller, as one of the WAFs, before the ferrying squadron became a part of the WASP. Wilmington, Delaware, October 1942.

During my first year in college, my family moved to Odessa, Texas, and my father, T. L. Miller, opened five jewelry stores in the area. I took flying lessons at the Odessa airport and soloed after the prescribed minimum of eight hours of instruction. For many months it seemed that our Luscomb was in the air most of the time. One of us— my father, my older brother, LaMonte, younger brother, Dolph, or I—would lay claim to it. My father, Dolph, and I quickly got our private licenses. I was ahead of the others in acquiring my commercial and flight instructor's license. This was in 1940. At this time it was unusual for people to own airplanes and certainly unusual for four family members to be flying one. My father, a very perceptive person, told a reporter who was doing a piece on the "Flying Millers" that, although he could justify purchasing his plane for business purposes, what he actually had in mind was to prepare his children to be able to contribute to the war effort when and if America was to get into a war. We kids were quite embarrassed, but Daddy was way ahead of us and could see what Hitler was doing and where it would lead.

I began to teach flying in Odessa and went on to acquire my instructor ratings in all of the ground school subjects. The U.S. military realized that if America did indeed get into war in Europe, we did not have enough pilots, so they established the War Training Program to give free ground school instruction to military-age men who passed their physicals. Classes were com-

WAFS, photo taken on a delivery trip of P-17 Stearman planes from Great Falls, Montana, in December 1942. Florene Miller is second from right.

posed of fifty men each, and the men who got the top ten highest grades on their written work were given free private pilot's licenses with no strings attached. Although the United States had just started drafting men, they couldn't draft pilots. The program was designed to motivate the men who took the classes to volunteer for the Air Corps. I taught several hundred men in these classes—on the ground as well as in the air. My future husband, Chris Watson, was one of my students.

Chris and I had a date for July 4, 1941, and we drove to Ruidoso, New Mexico, to meet my father and LaMonte, who were to fly there. Since there was no airport, they would land on the golf course, or if they rejected the course, they would fly to Roswell, New Mexico, and come in by car. This is a mountainous area at an elevation of ten thousand feet. As Chris and I drove down the canyon highway to await their arrival, we turned the corner around a cliff, and there on the side of the road was the wreck of our plane, tail high, nose into the ground. There was no mistaking whose plane it was. We were told by bystanders

WASP Florene Miller flies a P-51 fighter out of Long Beach, California, in the summer of 1944.

and policemen at the scene that the plane had not been able to get enough altitude to get out of the canyon before it closed up. The plane had circled the small area three times, attempting to land on the highway, but the traffic was too dense. The plane hit the top of a tree, then tumbled down the mountain, landing by the side of the road. Both men had been taken to a nearby hospital. My brother was already dead, but we were able to be with my father when he died less than an hour later.

Since flying in those days was much more risky than it is now, our family had discussed the issue of a likely death of one of us. We agreed that we thought that we knew enough about scripture to know that God deals with us individually and not corporately, and if one of us were to get killed, it would not necessarily mean that any of the rest of us would go that way. So, when this happened, my brother and I decided to continue flying. We both volunteered to fly for the Army Air Corps.

I began to teach flying in Lubbock, Texas. I was in Florida on vacation the first week of October 1942 when I heard about the Women's Auxiliary Ferrying Squadron and the need for experienced women pilots who had at least five hundred hours of flying time, a commercial license, and a 250-horsepower rating and were between the ages of twenty-one and thirty-five. I was twenty-one. I did not go back home, but talked it over with my mother, Dolph, and my sister, Garnette, and caught the next train out

WASP Florene Miller with Bob Hope and Jerry Colona, Love Field, Dallas, Texas, March 1943.

for Wilmington, Delaware, to the Second Ferrying Group, Ferrying Division, Air Transport Command.

Those of us who qualified to ferry military planes from the factories to the airfields and overseas shipping points in the United States had been flying in a man's world for several years. Many of us had not known another woman pilot, so we established an immediate rapport. We found that there were many men on the base and only a few of us, but we were used to being in the minority. We adjusted to our new environment very rapidly. We were given an officers' barracks in which to live and army cots on which to sleep. The walls had no sheetrock, just outside materials and inside two by fours to look at and use as whatnot shelves. To get to our bathroom we had to pass a lineup of equipment designed for men. We always said that we were going to make curtains to cover this sight, but we never did. We were either too busy or out of town.

The auxiliary practice field we were assigned to fly out of unnerved us slightly. We were first checked out in an open cockpit low-winged training plane, a PT-19, and were asked to do our practice takeoffs and landings on a field that appeared to have

Florene Miller Watson chats with Bob Hope, almost fifty
years after their first meeting, at an Air Force convention
in Washington, D.C., September 1992.

been hewn out of a deep forest. It was, we thought, just about
the size of a postage stamp and covered with grass and surrounded by thick, tall trees. For some of us who had been used
to flying over relatively flat terrain with few or no trees, this field
appeared to be too small to land our planes safely. How were we
going to get over the trees and still land on the first part of the
runway so that we could stop at the other end?

We all had been flying for a few years and had learned the
slipping maneuver—raising the nose and severely lowering one
wing—that would cause the plane to lose altitude fast. Not too
safe a maneuver but one that many of us used more than once
to get down where we should. Some had to ground loop their

WASP marching in a graduation ceremony at Ellington Field, Houston, Texas, in 1943.

planes in order not to hit the trees on the other end. One girl had to stop so quickly that her plane went up on its nose. The field was *all* grass—no hard-surface runway—and the only other clearing in the trees was a cemetery nearby. We joked that we would get to the cemetery one way or the other if we had to make a forced landing there. The twenty-five girls who finally made up the group averaged eleven hundred hours each and had more flying hours than some of our military instructors.

Don Teel, one of my instructors in Odessa, ultimately flew bombers all over the world; for twenty-five years he was the chief aviation director for United States Steel. He and two other instructors had demanded precision in everything I did. I was never allowed to land a plane just anywhere on the runway but on a certain designated spot on the runway each time. I had practiced that discipline almost every time I came in for a landing, which gave me a degree of confidence that I could set the plane down where I should. This skill served me well twice in civilian planes when my engine went out and I had to make an emergency landing. It helped me again when I had an emergency landing in a military fighter on a very short runway.

Most of us encountered another new experience when, without radios in our planes, we had to find our way through heavy traffic of larger and faster military planes—B-17s, B-25s, P-38s, and P-47s—that were flying in and out of New Castle Air Base in Wilmington, Delaware, where we were stationed.

In addition to our flight training, we were given a rigorous physical exam and a month's ground school. The ground school consisted of navigation, meteorology, radio and Morse code, study of firearms, military courtesy and discipline, military law, and some instrument time.

All of our flying equipment was issued to us by the army. Every day in training we wore army green coveralls, of course styled for men but practical nevertheless. Other equipment issued to us was a light sweater, leather jacket, helmet, goggles, sunglasses, traveling bag, parachute, and a complete winter flying suit made out of lamb's wool with the wool worn on the inside. We WAFS bought our own dress uniforms, which were designed and made just for us—slacks, skirts, jackets, and a top coat with snap-out lining. They were gray-green in color and bore the Ferrying Command insignias on the shoulders. An overseas cap and a pair of silver wings completed the outfit.

We WAFS were still civilian pilots, as were some of the male pilot volunteers. We were on officer's status with all of the advantages and disadvantages. We were paid the same as a second lieutenant pilot, $250 a month. The enlisted personnel treated us the same as any other officers. The pilots and the officers in command of the base treated us with respect and for the most part acted as though they accepted us. The fact that we had already been flying planes for several years and had more time in the air than most of the men made a difference. We were not female activists, but we thought we could fly anything that the men could fly.

After the few girls in the WAFS had flown out of Wilmington, Delaware, for approximately three months, the twenty-five were broken up in groups to start bases at Love Field, Dallas; Long Beach, California; and Romulus, Michigan. In early January 1943 I was sent to Love Field with four girls, to be the commanding officer there.

Nancy Love was in charge of the WAFS. A few months after we began, Jacqueline Cochran enlisted girl volunteers to enroll in an Army Air Corps sponsored pilot training course offering the same training given the men pilots. These girls (after the first class that required two hundred flying hours) could enroll with thirty-five hours' previous flying experience. The first few graduates were sent to us in the Ferrying Command, but the majority of them were assigned to the Training Command to tow targets, test-fly planes after maintenance, and to do other needed flying jobs. The duties of the girls in the Ferrying Command were to take all kinds of planes from the factories to the airfields and overseas shipping points. About a year after the WAFS began, the two groups joined and became the WASP, the Women's Airforce Service Pilots. We changed uniforms from gray to blue.

The five of us WAFS at Love Field were the only women pilots there and the first women pilots the men had seen. The commanding officer and I had many discussions on how a women pilots' squadron should be organized and what rules we should follow. Men were concerned that we, at our regular period during the month, might somehow be weaker, sicker, or somehow more unstable—particularly the latter—and they wanted to restrict us from flying on those days. That experiment soon fell apart, since no once could prove who was lying.

Love Field soon became the base of first choice, with Long Beach a close second. There were plane factories near both of these bases and there were always plenty of planes to fly.

At Love Field I soon checked out in the BT-13 and the AT-6 and made deliveries. Later came the advanced trainers, the AT-17, AT-11, AT-9; the B-25, B-26 bombers; the C-47 cargo transport; the SB2C navy dive bomber; and an instrument rating. Instrument time was given in the air and on the ground in a mock-up cockpit trainer called a Link trainer. To my delight my instructor for part of my ground instrument training was my mother, Flora Miller, who had learned the skill and was teaching there. I stayed at Love Field for about a year.

One Sunday afternoon in December 1943, a few days before I was scheduled to go to Palm Springs, California, to attend pursuit school, I was given the chance by the operations office to fly a P-47, the most famous American fighter plane of the war. That morning I was given the technical manual to study, and then I spent a long time in the cockpit to familiarize myself with the plane, with my instructor giving me the characteristics of flying a P-47. The plane has only one seat, and there was no way for me to ride in it with an instructor before flying it alone for the first time.

The P-47 was the largest and heaviest fighter used during World War II. It has a huge radial engine up front, so large that, with its tail wheel, rather than a nose wheel, it is impossible for the pilot to see straight in front. In addition to the large engine, its enormous four-bladed propeller made an arc much larger than the engine. When taxiing the plane, the pilot had to turn the plane to the side so he could see straight down the runway, then straighten the plane's path and roll blind for a short distance, then turn sideways again in order to see ahead. To a lesser extent, the same procedure was repeated in order to see when coming in for a landing on the final approach. Forward vision was not good.

There were two main runways at Love Field. The long one, which was roughly north and south, was used probably 90 percent of the time. On this day, however, there were many, many new planes parked on each side of the narrow runway. Because of this danger to landing planes, the much shorter east-west runway was used, causing landings to be made into the setting sun.

In 1943 Love Field had not yet buried the high-power lines around the runway approaches, nor had they moved buildings and traffic lanes that were situated in the runway approaches. One had to fly over houses, businesses, a heavily used Dallas street, and a power line supported by large, sturdy poles, with six crossbars on each, all of which were at the immediate end of the runway. Fast planes were new to prewar aviation, and this runway was short enough that a P-47 had to be landed at the very beginning of the runway in order to comfortably stop before running out of runway.

The haze was very bad this sunny afternoon when I began flying the P-47. The haze continued to worsen as I made numerous practice takeoffs and landings; as the sun went down, flying into the sun and haze became more and more blinding. The tower told all of us in the area to get on the ground as the airport was being closed because of the danger of the sun and haze.

I had become very aware of all of the hazards over which I had to fly by looking straight down and counting them off, because I could never see straight forward. I knew them all by heart and intended to clear the telephone poles and high-power lines by about ten to twelve feet. I was anticipating a telephone pole to come into sight as I came in for this landing when— *crunch*—I was too low and flew straight into the pole itself. The nose of the plane shot up and the plane started to roll on its back. I jerked on the controls quickly and hard. I tried to give the plane full power, lift up the gear, pull up the flaps, and straighten out the plane all at once. Immediately upon hitting the pole, there had been a very loud, high-pitched sound as well as a violent vibration of the plane and instrument panel. When I finally looked at the instrument panel, I couldn't read a thing, it was all so blurred. The screeching sound finally stopped.

By the time I rolled the plane back, I, of course, was off the runway into the grassy area and three-fourths of the way down the length of the field heading straight into a hangar. I can see that hangar yet. There was a big open door as I approached. I just prayed, "Oh, Lord, let me get over the top of this hangar!" The plane on full power was going about half the speed it should have been going, and I barely made it over the top. My immediate thought, as I was holding left rudder and right stick to make it fly straight, was, "If I can get enough altitude, I'll get the heck out of here!" I turned toward the north because that was the shortest direction out of the populated area, out toward Lake Dallas. As I was flying, I was searching the terrain ahead to find a logical place to land.

The plane, at full throttle, gradually gained altitude. Other than the instrument panel vibrating badly, my having to cross controls to make the plane fly straight, and the slow rate of climb, there was a rhythmic clang, clang, clang going on at the side of the plane. I looked. It was a slender piece of metal still attached to the plane that must have torn off from part of the wing or flap that was giving such a musical beat. Then I noticed that the wing was damaged and a part near the flaps was missing. I somehow summoned up enough courage to look back at the tail and saw that part of the elevator was also missing.

With such a sick airplane, it was time for me to get out, and I had enough altitude. It was almost dark by this time. I unbuckled my safety belt and harness, opened the canopy, and started to stand up in the seat to bail out when the thought crossed my mind that the plane was under control, and although I was having to cross controls to keep it straight and I still couldn't make much out of the instrument reading, I was handling it.

Two other reasons for bailing out, though, had my real concern. Ever since I left the airport, I had tried desperately on every radio channel I had to get someone to answer me and I had not been successful; also, my instruments told me that my gear was not either up or down but was in an unsafe position. But since I was flying it straight and level, I hesitated to destroy the plane by bailing out before I tried working with it a little more.

Before a landing would even be a possibility, with or without a landing gear, I had to see if I could handle the plane in a stall. I didn't dare completely stall the plane as I throttled back to slow the plane down and raise its nose as I would do in a landing, but after several tries, I determined just how far I could throttle back before the plane wanted to quit flying. At its best, with the throttle wide open, it was flying at about half power. The plane wanted to quit me when I pulled the throttle back about a third.

By this time, it was pitch dark. Should I bail out or try to land when I did not know if my gear was up or down, or, if it was actually down, if it was in the locked position? Would it collapse upon landing? I could tell I had very little gas left. I was flying around at night with a sick airplane, low on gas, not knowing the status of my gear, no radio, the first day I had flown the plane and never having made a night landing before. I knew I had at least a little bit of gas left, so I decided to go back in the direction of Love Field while I kept trying to get someone on the radio.

I flew toward Love Field but it wasn't there! I looked in all directions, but I couldn't see it. I thought I must be lost. I had a sick, desperate feeling. I decided I must not panic. There were lights on some buildings to my left. If those lights were Dallas lights, then the Magnolia Building with the red horse rotating on the top would be there. I flew closer, and sure enough, I saw the red horse. That meant Love Field was to the west. I turned to what I thought was west, but still no Love Field. Finally, it came through to me that there were just no lights showing, that Love Field had to be in that black hole somewhere. It was a frightening feeling to be so mixed up when my life was at stake.

About this time, a radio repairman in the Lockheed Aviation hangar at Love Field heard me on a radio he was repairing and answered me. What sweet music to my ears! He told me that there were no lights on Love Field and that I must have knocked them out when I hit the big pole. I asked him to telephone the tower, tell them my plight, and ask them to shine their traffic gun on me as I flew over (provided I could find the tower with no lights) to see if my gear—both wheels—were down. We would not know until a landing if they were in the locked position. This was the way I communicated with the tower—through the radio repairman and by his telephoning the tower and getting back to me.

I found the tower, flew over it low, and was told that it appeared that I might have two wheels. I told them that I would like to land and to please hurry to get the emergency smudge pots out along the runway. No smudge pots. The sergeant in charge of them was away for the weekend and had the key to the storage in his pocket. I thought that maybe I should go to Ft. Worth, thirty miles away, and land, but what about my low gas? I decided I had better try to land right here by jeep lights.

By this time, the operations officer had come to the tower. Although I remembered from my study of the cockpit where the landing and cockpit lights were supposed to be, I was hesitant to be flipping toggle switches in the dark, in the event I touched the wrong one. I asked the officer to tell me specifically just which switches to turn on.

I asked if they could get some jeep light to mark the runway for me. I wanted no part of the short runway with the telephone pole I hit that took out the lights, so I requested to use the longer one with all of the airplanes parked on either side of it. I preferred to take my chances on not hitting the planes. Jeep lights were put at the beginning of the runway, but I could barely see them or distinguish them from the many lights from the traffic that was traveling on the road that crossed at the back of the runway. I told the tower that I also needed jeep lights at the other end of the runway so that I could know [in which] direction the runway was running. The police stopped the traffic at the back of the runway and had the cars turn off their lights. Then I spotted the weak jeep lights. Jeeps were then put at the end of the runway, too.

I told the tower that I wanted to make a pass over the field without intending to land, to be sure that I had spotted the right things. I made the pass, lined up properly, then pulled up. As I did so, a terrifying feeling swept over me. I had to make the decision if I was actually going to try to land or use the precious gas I had left to get around the field one more time or get altitude with it and bail out. It turned out to be a real life or death decision, because, as I was told later, I had nothing but vapor left in the tanks. I had long before switched to the high octane gas when I knew the other tank was empty.

I chose to try to land. On my final approach to the field as I got near to the end of the runway, my landing lights shone on one of the high oil-derrick-like transmission towers that supported many lines. Just like the telephone pole—I knew it was there, but I intended to clear it by a few feet. My heart jumped into my throat. I was too low and flying already at full throttle. I pulled back on the stick, hoping I would not stall as I tried to clear it. I made it. Once over it, I pushed the nose down quickly to get back my speed. I already, literally, had my hands full. Since I did not know if my landing gear would fold upon landing, I was pumping the emergency hydraulic lever to hold the pressure up.

The end of the runway was in front of me. I knew that I had to keep the plane straight upon landing so I would not plow into all of the new planes parked wingtip to wingtip on both sides of the runway. I pulled the throttle back about a third and the plane landed like a big rock—not a bounce. It had no flying speed left with which to bounce. I went straight down the runway and came to the first taxi strip leading to the hangar. A tremendous sense of relief swept over me. I knew then that the Lord was not through with me yet. I paused and started giving myself a lecture. "Now, stupid, you got down safely, just don't break your leg by falling off the wing when you get out!"

After taxiing a bit farther, I could see all the hangar lights were on and dozens upon dozens—it looked like hundreds—of people were standing there waiting for me to taxi up. How embarrassing! I wanted to crawl into a hole. I had already been afraid that my commanding officer was going to kill me. I had thought about that a number of times while I was flying. The war attitude we had already gotten from our superiors was "Kill yourself, but don't you dare scratch an airplane!" He would surely wipe me out. After I had taxied up to the hangar and turned off the engine, who was the first person to jump up onto the wing and stick his head into the cockpit but the commanding officer himself. He was talking a mile a minute telling me how glad he was that I got down safely and what a good job I had done flying. I suppose he was really glad. He didn't want anyone getting killed on his watch!

Just about then I began to hear loud comments from those around the plane. "Part of the tail is gone." "Part of the wing is gone." "Look at the belly of the plane. It's torn open like a can opener did it from the engine to the tail wheel." Then a loud expletive and "Part of this propeller is gone!" It was true. About a foot of one of the four blades of the propeller had been melted off when it hit the power line. The little melted drops of metal could be seen. After I got out of the plane that night, a maintenance man jumped into the cockpit and one of his feet went right through the floor. But I was safe now. I was on the ground, but it was a flying experience that I would never forget!

When I went to pursuit school that December to learn to fly

the fighters, there were about fifty men and four girls in our class. We always knew that we had to do a better job of flying with a minimum of mistakes or we would come under scorn from the men. One time I was standing in a group of men students and instructors at the school when a girl bounced her plane—a little, not badly—when she landed. The men, not remembering I was there, ridiculed the landing and said that girls should not be flying. Right behind her a male student landed his fighter and bounced so badly several times that it appeared that he might really crash. The same men said, "Well, it looks as if old Joe is having a bad morning!" Nothing was said about his not being fit to fly.

Later on at the same airport, I was standing on the end of the runway when my friend, Dorothy Scott, and her instructor were coming in to land. I could see a fast-moving P-39 attempting to land but making a different approach. The planes collided almost at the end of the runway where I was standing, waiting to take my ride with her instructor. I had to notify her family and accompany her body parts in the hearse to Burbank, California, which was near Palm Springs.

We received certificates at the pursuit school indicating that we flew the P-39, P-40, P-47, and the P-51. In February 1944 I was transferred to Long Beach and there was able to fly the A-20 attack bomber, the four-engine B-17 and the B-24, and the twin-engine P-38 fighter.

In April 1944 I left the Long Beach base and went to WASP Officers' Training School in Orlando, Florida. Later I was commended by the commanding general of the Ferrying Division for logging an unusually large number of hours on P-51 deliveries in June 1944.

I was fortunate to have spent time on all four bases in the Ferrying Division on which WASP were stationed. But sadly, in December 1944, the WASP were deactivated, and did not get their honorable discharge from the Air Force for their war service until 1977.

Florene Miller married her former flight student, Chris Watson, after the WASP were disbanded. They had two daughters. When the girls started school, Florene went back to college to finish her degree and to earn a master's in business. She then taught at the University of Houston for thirty years. She is still active in civic, volunteer, aviation, and women's club work. She has served as national chaplain of the Women's Airforce Service Pilots for many years and continues to give many talks to various groups about the role of women pilots in World War II.

22

A Few Problems

Frances Roulstone was raised in New York City, went off to Virginia for college, then returned home to become a shop manager at Best & Co. After war was declared Frances went out to Utah to work as the first woman engine test operator, at the Hillfield Air Depot.

Frances had heard of the formation of the WASP, and she was determined to get into what she considered an "elite" group of flyers. How she was going to do it, she did not know. She went to Springfield, Missouri, where her brother-in-law was stationed and began taking flying lessons.

Finally, in November 1943, she had her private license and the thirty-five hours of flying time that enabled her to apply to the WASP. Applicants no longer needed a commercial license and flying hours had been reduced from the original required two hundred.

Over twenty-five thousand young women applied and less than two thousand were accepted. Of those, roughly half made it through training. Frances applied; she was called to Sweetwater, Texas, for an interview and was accepted. She was twenty-four years old, ready to learn to fly every type of plane the Army Air Force had.

Training was demanding, and the flying could be harrowing. Frances can still remember her first long solo cross-country flight from Abilene to Brownsville, Texas, roughly three hundred miles over the uninhabited, rugged Uvalde Mountains.

"It was a bleak, drizzly morning. The ready room clock was ticking noisily overhead. It was 7:00 A.M. and a group of young female trainee pilots nervously awaited takeoff instructions. Suddenly it was time. The girls picked up their gear, weather reports, and plane assignments and headed for the flight line. With my parachute seat pack buckled on, I briskly inspected my PT-19 Fairchild trainer, then hopped up on the wing and climbed into the cockpit. It was a nasty morning. The sky was an ominous gray and a light rain was falling. The Fairchild was an open-cockpit, low-wing, single-engine plane with 175 horsepower and did not offer the luxury of a radio. The flight was to be made by dead reckoning, using only compass and map for navigation.

"As I yelled 'clear' and the engine kicked over, I thought about the conversation I had overheard a few minutes earlier between my flight leader and the tower operator who questioned sending a bunch of rookie students out into what appeared to be a front moving in. Our leader had laughed, said he had a hot date back at the base in Sweetwater and he planned to be there for it, front or no front. What no one knew was that there also had been a wind shift since we were given our report, so every one in the group would be flying off course.

"Little shivers of anticipation were soon dissipated by the job at hand. The Fairchild roared down the runway and into the air. Each girl took off ten minutes apart so as to be on her own. As I throttled back to cruising speed, adjusting my heading, I ran another quick visual check of the instruments. All was well. A rush of exhilaration swept over me. I didn't even mind the light rain, which meant I'd be soaked before the flight was over. Looking down at the rugged peaks below, there appeared to be no sign of habitation anywhere. It was time for that crucial first checkpoint. Where was it? Anxiously peering through the drizzle, I saw nothing but rugged peak after peak, rocks, towering pines, and rain. Thanks to the wrong wind report, all of us would fly just enough off course that those precious checkpoints never appeared.

"I wiped the drops of rain off my goggles and checked the instruments again. Then I did a double take. The oil pressure gauge was on zero. That can't be, I thought frantically. It must be a faulty gauge. The engine was still running. I had worked on aircraft engines for a year prior to joining the WASP in anticipation of doing just that. I had attained a ground instructor's aircraft engine rating and knew the limits of the engine. Aircraft engines do not run without oil pressure. It was as simple as that.

"Fighting back the impulse to panic, I reached down within myself to my early upbringing. If God was everywhere, omnipresent, then He was all around that plane. I kept repeating, 'Underneath are the everlasting arms.' I repeated it over and over, never allowing any other thought to enter my consciousness. And I flew, flew hour after hour, constantly proclaiming the protection and presence of God.

"Suddenly the Brownsville airport appeared below. Having no radio to signal trouble, I rocked the wings as I lined up for the final approach to the runway. The tower had seen me and the fire truck and 'meat wagon,' as we called the ambulance, came speeding across the tarmac. No sooner had the wheels touched down than the engine quit dead and the plane rolled to a stop. It was like a giant hand had reached out and caught the propeller in an iron grip, freezing it motionless. Shaking, I climbed out of the cockpit, jumped down, and watched a jeep tow the plane off the runway.

"The nightmare was not over. The flight leader accused me of burning up the engine by flying with a wide-open throttle for two and a half hours and promised a court martial on our return to the base. But God never takes us only halfway. They pulled the engine log for that plane and discovered that it had been taken off the flight line because of serious oil leaks but had somehow been assigned for this cross-country trip by mistake. The engine was indeed frozen solid, but I was exonerated and commended for bringing it in at all. The flight leader was reprimanded for sending the girls out in unfit weather and not rechecking the wind report. It was considered nothing short of a miracle that the girls had somehow found the airport and that no one was hurt or lost by being off course. So ended that memorable first solo cross-country."

Frances was in the WASP class of 44-W-4, and Jacqueline Cochran, the head of the program, flew from Washington, D.C., to attend the graduation ceremony. After the women had had the silver wings pinned onto their Santiago blue uniforms, Cochran announced that the names of all the graduates from the East Coast would be put into a hat, and one name drawn out. That person would be the winner who would fly back to Washington with her as copilot. Frances's name was pulled from the hat.

She well remembers the trip. Frances and Jackie Cochran climbed into the cockpit of the twin-engine Cessna. Mrs. Patterson, the wife of the secretary of war, and an Army Air Force captain also boarded the plane. Frances plotted the trip, and they took off for Washington.

"All went well until we ran into a severe electrical storm just outside Roanoke, Virginia, and all the flight instruments went crazy. Jackie kept trying to find a hole in the storm and changed from heading to heading so rapidly that it was impossible for me to keep track of our position, although she kept asking me what it was every few minutes. The captain, to make matters worse, informed her, after some time, that it appeared that we were over Versailles, Kentucky. Miss Cochran told him we were nothing of the sort; we were just outside Roanoke, but I noticed she was putting her rosary to good use. My state of mind was not improved when she muttered she wouldn't have had this happen for the world with Mrs. Patterson on board. (Never mind the rest of us, I thought.)

"Mrs. Patterson meanwhile was peering out the cabin window at the scenery, which was now only about five hundred feet below us, exclaiming how exciting this all was and she wouldn't have missed it for the world! The captain, still being helpful, said he recognized the buildings below and we were definitely over Versailles. Well, a look at our empty gas gauges meant a landing was called for, no matter where we were. Jackie found a large empty pasture and down we went. We rolled to a stop just feet from a ditch and barbed wire fence. We were so close, in fact, that we had to get out of the plane and pick up the tail to turn it around.

"We were down and it was Versailles, Kentucky. Miss Cochran knew people everywhere and it wasn't long before we saw a limo bouncing across the field to pick us up and we were the house-guests of a colonel she knew for several days until the weather cleared and the plane was checked over."

Frances's first assignment after graduation was to Williams Army Air Field in Chandler, Arizona, just outside Phoenix, where she was to be a test pilot of the AT-6 advanced trainers. Williams ran schools for training in the AT-6s, and also in air-craft mechanics.

Frances was to discover that not all the mechanics had mas-tered their subject.

One sunny morning she visually checked her first test plane of the day, climbed in, tried the controls, the ailerons, and rud-der. All seemed to be in working order. She took off and flew to eleven thousand feet and popped the plane into a spin. When she attempted to pull out of the spin, her problems began.

"The AT-6 kept winding up tighter, picking up speed well past the red line. The ground was getting uncomfortably close. I tried everything I could think of to break that spin; finally, when I reversed the normal procedure, it miraculously pulled out at a mere five hundred feet above the desert floor. When I returned to the flight line, we discovered that the controls were working all right. They had just been hooked up backward."

Frances felt that her guardian angel had been riding with her, and she vowed to be a more careful and humble flier thereafter.

Frances served for several months as a test pilot at Williams, and was then sent to Yuma, Arizona, along with a number of other WASP from various fields, to see if they could handle and be checked out in the B-26 twin-engine bomber. This "infamous Martin Marauder" was "affectionately known as the 'flying coffin' due to its accident record." Yuma was using them to tow targets for the trainee gunners in B-17 bombers.

The WASP had two days to memorize the cockpit instrumentation of the B-26. Frances recalled that there must have been over one hundred instruments. In addition, they had to pass a blindfold cockpit check. Then they were ready to be tow target pilots.

One day Frances went out on what was to be a double high-altitude mission. The first B-17 was already up, and the B-26 waited at thirty thousand feet for the second to join them, but it seemed to have some difficulty on the ground. The four crew members—pilot, copilot, engineer, and radioman, all on oxygen—had been up for several hours, and the wait for the second B-17 seemed long.

Frances ran into a problem. As she well knew, military aircraft were built on the assumption that they would be flown by a male crew, and the facilities were designed for men. Frances recalled what happened.

"There was a relief tube, which was little more than a small funnel attached to a hose. That little funnel was no help to me. We were trussed up in heavy fleece-lined flight gear and bulky seat pack parachutes. I examined my options. There was the gaping, open tow target hatch, or I could have an accident where I sat. The former appeared the better choice.

"I asked the engineer to bring me a portable oxygen supply so I could check on the tow target banner. He assured me there was no need, everything was fine. I finally got across my problem, so he came forward, unhooked my oxygen, and hooked up the portable oxygen, with its limited two-minute air supply.

"I gingerly picked my way down the catwalk in the belly of the plane, noticing that they had hung a pair of flying pants in the bulkhead opening to give me some privacy.

"By this time everyone had figured out why I was struggling to the back of the plane, parachute banging against my legs and with a very brief supply of oxygen. The tow target hatch yawned beneath me, the earth thirty thousand feet below, and the temperature in the minus thirties. After I finished, I made it back to the cockpit, gasping for breath. The B-17 finally joined us."

Frances later heard the story of the escapade when she returned to the East Coast. She was eternally grateful that no name had accompanied the tale of the WASP in the tail of the B-26.

In 1944, when Frances heard that the WASP would be deactivated, she felt it was a blow to all of them, but, as she said, they "were the leading edge of equal rights for women, dispelling forever the traditional role of women as housewives, teachers, or secretaries. And we opened the door for women fliers in the Air Force. We had made an important contribution to the war effort and had had an incredible experience in doing so."

After the war, Frances Roulstone married Ray Reeves, a former army flight instructor, and together they opened a private flying school. A year later, when it had closed, Ray was killed while crop dusting. Frances went back to retailing until she remarried six years later. She had three children, but returned to buying for thirteen years when her youngest was only two years old. She then left to form her own manufacturing company, Frances Reeves Originals, and designed and manufactured the first preteen dresses. After ten years her business partnership was dissolved, and she went into insurance and financial planning, which she still does today "on a rather laid-back basis." Her second marriage ended in divorce after thirteen years. Frances has two grandsons and one great-grandson.

23

Once a Pilot . . .

Bee Falk Haydu grew up in Montclair, New Jersey. The Depression was in full swing, and the family felt it could not send both of their children to college. Bee's older brother was given the opportunity, and she went out into the working world.

"I always felt badly that I had not gone to college. One day I said to myself, Stop complaining and do something about it. I felt aviation was here to stay, so I decided to take aviation courses at night school. This was 1942–1943."

Bee was fascinated by the ground school classes, and she decided to learn to fly. Since parts of New Jersey were classified as a defense zone, Bee's instructor, Charles Grieder, had to move his flight school from Teterboro to Martins Creek, Pennsylvania.

Bee went to Grieder's school on weekends, spending most of her salary on lessons. It was at the school that Bee met six other young women who were determined to apply to the WASP. They were accepted and took the train to Sweetwater.

At this time Bee Falk was twenty-two and had "more time behind the 'wheel' of an airplane than a car."

Bee Falk, wearing her "zoot suit" and forty-pound parachute, on the
wing of a primary trainer (PT-17 Stearman) at Avenger Field,
Sweetwater, Texas, 1944.

Bee tells the rest of the story:

Avenger Field, Sweetwater, where we were trained, was similar
to "camping out" except that there were many restrictions. We
were assigned barracks, which we called "bays," given men's coveralls, which we called "zoot suits," slept on cots (six to a bay),
ate at mess halls, marched to ground school and flight lines.
Since the class prior to ours had been held up in getting their
flight time because of bad weather, we only had a half-day of
ground school, and the other half free time.

Senator Barry Goldwater, seated, at a meeting with the WASP before a Senate hearing on granting military status to the WASP, March 17, 1977. WASP president Bee Falk Haydu is third from left. At far right is supporter Bruce Arnold, son of Gen. Hap Arnold, chief of the Army Air Forces in World War II, who testified in favor of the legislation at the hearings.

Finally, after two weeks we were able to start flying lessons. Half of our day was spent on the flight line. We were assigned to a civilian flight instructor, usually four to an instructor. The airplane in use at that time for primary was the PT-17 Stearman open-cockpit biplane, with a 220 horsepower radial engine. This aircraft had a narrow landing gear, making it susceptible to ground looping on landing. You have to be very alert and ready to use the rudders quickly when landing because of this characteristic. We had seventy hours of training, both dual and solo, in the PT-17. The reason this type of aircraft was chosen was because we were being "experimented" with. The usual training given to male cadets were PTs (primary trainers), BTs (basic trainers), and then ATs (advanced trainers). They wanted to see if they could skip BTs and go directly from PTs to ATs, which they did in our case. I suppose the theory was that if the women could do it, then anyone could.

And so after our PT-17 seventy hours, we were placed in AT-

6s. This aircraft had many features that weren't found in PTs. We had retractable landing gears, flaps (to slow you down on landing or assist you on takeoffs), a 650 horsepower engine, much faster flight (about 160 mph as compared to 90 or 100 in a Stearman), a radio to contact the ground, etc. I would sit by the hour in the cockpit blindfolded (on the ground, of course) touching various things in the "busy" cockpit as one of my class-mates tested me. We would do these things in our free time so we were proficient in locating any item in the cockpit without having to look down.

There was a lot of air traffic at this one field. The Stearmans would fly to auxiliary fields to do their practicing, leaving in the morning, returning at noon, leaving again in the afternoon, and returning in the late afternoon. They had no radios and would be "told" they could land by a green light pointed at them. The AT-6s used the same main field and were directed by radio, as were the BT-13s, which were basic trainers used for instrument practice flying. We had to have our heads on a swivel. I know of one accident where two planes did collide in the traffic pattern, killing both people. (Each aircraft had a certain pattern to fly when taking off and landing, so it was not chaotic.)

Of course soloing any one of these airplanes was a big thing. We had a wishing well on the field and were unceremoniously dunked after anything special, such as soloing or completing ground school. The wishing well was where we would toss coins for good luck prior to a check ride, a test of our flying abilities by civilian and military pilots.

After about thirty hours in the AT-6, both dual and solo, we were provided with another instructor for instrument training. We were given approximately forty-five hours in a BT-13 for this training. We had to practice under the hood (there was a cur-tain-type arrangement in the back cockpit of this low-wing air-craft that closed you in so you had to fly by the instruments and radio only). If we were not flying with the instructor, we would fly with another student who sat in the front seat, took off, land-ed, and looked out for other aircraft. These were called buddy rides. We would practice at the radio range in Abilene and would land there. I recall that my buddy found a puppy there, which she snuck into the aircraft and took back to Avenger Field. He became our pet, was well fed and cared for.

In each phase of flying we were tested by a civilian check pilot and an army check pilot. If you did not come up to the standards demanded, you were asked to leave the program—you were "washed out." If an instructor felt you could not meet the standards, he would request a check ride, and if you failed, you were finished. This threat constantly hung over our heads. It was not a matter of being able to learn to fly, it was a matter of learning to fly in the time allowed by the program. The washout rate with male cadets was about 50 percent. Our rate was a bit lower. It was always sad and emotionally heartbreaking when someone had to leave. Some never got over the feeling of failure. We had been told from the beginning that if we felt there was a personality clash with the instructor we should request a change. Some of the women thought this would be held against them and so did not make such a request.

After the instrument phase in the BT-13, we went on to the final phase, which was cross-country. This was done in the Stearman and the AT-6. The Stearman had no radios, and so navigation had to be accomplished by determining course headings, the effect the winds aloft would have on the headings, and various other factors. Of course, we had charts that showed in great detail what was on the ground so that we could compare what was there with where we were. The AT-6 cross-country was a bit easier, since we had the assist of radio. However, one still had to plot the course, taking wind and other factors into consideration. We had about fifty-five hours of cross-country, both dual and solo. In addition to that, we had to fly night cross-country and practice takeoffs and landings at night.

The half-days we spent in ground school consisted of courses in navigation, aircraft and engines, mathematics, theory of flight, link trainer (a make-believe airplane in which we sat and practiced instrument flying; today they are called simulators), and meteorology.

I liked cross-country flying the best. My solo cross-country in July 1944 in an AT-6 started at Sweetwater and took me back to Sweetwater via San Angelo and Brownwood. While approaching

Brownwood, where I was scheduled to land, I noticed fire coming from the exhaust stack of the aircraft, just outside the cockpit. I debated with myself whether to jump, using my parachute. I knew this would entail an investigation, check ride, and possible dismissal from the program.

Since the fire did not seem to be spreading, I decided to contact the tower at Brownwood, since I was so close to it, and ask for an emergency landing, which meant that they would clear traffic and allow me to come right in. After landing, the maintenance crew located the trouble, and within a couple of hours I was on my way back to Sweetwater. I do not recall what was wrong with the plane, but it must be remembered that we were not flying the best of equipment during training. Sweetwater was notified about my predicament, and so there were no repercussions when I returned.

In addition to ground school and flying, we had gymnasium, calisthenics, and marching. Each month a class graduated and we would do marching as part of the graduation ceremonies. We looked pretty sharp, if I do say so myself.

When we first arrived at Sweetwater we were issued army coveralls with pockets everywhere. I used to put fruit and other goodies in the pockets to be later shared on the flight lines and at the auxiliary fields. We were not issued any dress uniform until graduation. Since they wanted us to look the same when marching and attending graduation ceremonies, we purchased army-issue pants (called "pinks") and white shirts and wore overseas caps. The pants became known as generals pants because there was one occasion at the field when six generals attended the graduation.

Since the powers that be were not certain whether women could fly as well as men or could fly military aircraft, we were paid by civil service. During training it was $150 per month from which they took our room and board. We had to pay our own expenses to Sweetwater, and if we washed out, had to pay our own way home. When we were issued uniforms, we were given one dress uniform, one overcoat, one work uniform, which consisted of slacks and an Eisenhower jacket, and cap. (My original uniform is in the Smithsonian.) After graduation, we received $250 per month and from this had to pay room, board, and personal expenses. This was not quite equivalent to second lieutenant pay.

After graduation you were either assigned to the Ferrying Command or the Training Command. I was assigned to Pecos (Texas) Air Force Base, Training Command. This was a twin-engine flight school. Initially I had to be given instruction as to how to fly a twin-engine aircraft, having only flown single engines in training. My job was engineering testing and utility pilot. If, for instance, something had been written up on a plane by a student that might indicate something wrong with an instrument or something minor about the engine (nothing dangerous, of course) we would fly the airplane and check out the complaint. Also, when an airplane had had an engine overhaul, it had to be flown in a certain manner for some hours. We would do that. There were times when ground personnel had to be flown around the country. That would be an assignment. In other words, we flew where and when we were needed. We lived on the base, ate in officers' quarters, and were on call.

The type of aircraft being flown when I arrived at Pecos was the UC-78 (utility cargo), which had many nicknames—Double Breasted Cub, Useless 78, Bamboo Bomber. It had two engines, each with a 225 Jacobs engine.

We were disbanded on December 20, 1944, due in large part to opposition by male cadets and civilian flight instructors who, because the need for pilots was decreasing, were facing the walking army. They lobbied in Washington, D.C., against us and succeeded. General Hap Arnold, Jacqueline Cochran, and many others wanted us to remain, but we were defeated by a small margin of votes in the House of Representatives against a bill to put us under the Army Air Force.

Bee Falk's need to fly was still there. She wrote to every airline and aircraft manufacturer she could think of, trying for a piloting job. "I never heard 'no' said in so many different ways. I realized I had to make my own way if I wanted to stay in flying." Bee obtained her instructor's rating and started a business under the name Garden State Airways, ferrying aircraft from manufacturer to distributor. She then secured a Cessna Aircraft dealership and subsequently joined a group of ex–military pilots in the ownership of a flight school in New Jersey, where she first taught flying and then ultimately ran the operation. The company was put out of business by the construction of the Garden State Parkway. Bee, ever resourceful, then got a job as a buyer for an aircraft company in India.

Bee Falk married Joseph Haydu in 1951 and had three children. Her husband had been a primary flight instructor during the war, and they bought and flew many aircraft for their own pleasure. Bee considers her greatest contribution to the WASP was being instrumental, along with many others, in seeking military recognition for the women who had been denied it in the war. As Bee said, "Happily, in November 1977 President James Carter signed into law the bill that recognized the Women's Airforce Service Pilots as veterans of World War II." Bee and her husband are still flying. Their latest airplane is a Russian Yak-52 aerobatic trainer.

24

On a Wing and a Prayer

"I've been waiting for you to wake up," said the general in a very disapproving tone. "What the hell are you anyway?" WASP Geri Lamphere roused herself and sat up in the plane seat next to him and began to explain.

Geri Lamphere Nyman recalled the incident clearly almost fifty years later:

"Flying to the East Coast, I got a little north of Atlanta when I hit a tornado. I saw a small field, and four of us went down as quickly as possible. We had people running out to tie us down and we grabbed our briefcases and left the B-4 bag and parachute in the plane. The tornado struck, and not a plane on the flight line was spared. We were in the one hangar, and suddenly the roof flew off and we were a mess of rain and mud. The tornado had not hit the other side of town, and late that evening I was able to get a commercial flight out. I left my parachute there to be repacked and with a soaking B-4 bag in hand I got a seat on a flight back to Long Beach, California.

"I had no change of clothes and was a total mess. Too tired to care how I looked, I immediately went to sleep on the airliner.

WASP Geri Nyman in C-47 cargo transport.

When I woke up I was being stared at by a very spit and polish general in the seat next to me. He had just returned from Africa and didn't know women were flying army planes. He listened to my tale of woe and then smilingly admitted he had never seen anyone such a teetotally absolute mess, especially one wearing a uniform with pilot wings."

Geri had been flying for two years before the Japanese struck Pearl Harbor. She had graduated from college when she was nineteen and immediately sought a job in Oregon. She found one at a radio station, which paid twenty-five cents an hour. Because it was so boring and paid so little, Geri went out and took flying lessons and became "hooked" on flying. But even when she received a raise to fifty cents an hour, she could hardly afford the fifteen-dollar lessons, but the flying instructor was still interested in teaching her because he needed ground school personnel. He said that if she would get the ground ratings needed to be a ground instructor, he would give her free flying lessons.

And Geri did just that. Within a year she had all five of the necessary ratings, in addition to her commercial and instructor's rating. She had, of course, spent almost every waking hour at the airport. But her time there had paid off, and she became a full-time instructor.

Instructing could be hazardous. Geri had several forced landings during the time she was in the Northwest. These emergencies ensured that she drummed forced landing techniques into her students, such as performing a stall landing with wheels up if faced with landing on the top of trees.

When the Pearl Harbor attack came, all fields within two hundred miles of the Pacific coast were shut down. Geri went to New York. She instructed and she worked, but most important she contacted Jacqueline Cochran, the famous aviatrix, who had taken a small group of women to England to fly for the established British Air Transport Auxiliary. She had returned to the United States, planning to supply the ATA with a second group of flying women. Geri signed up. She was twenty-three.

Two weeks before she was to fly for the British, Geri was called by Jacqueline Cochran and asked to join the group of the first twenty-five women who would make up the newly authorized Women's Airforce Service Pilots that Cochran had persuaded Gen. H.H. "Hap" Arnold to establish. Geri, along with the other women, assembled at the Howard Hughes Municipal Airport in Houston, Texas, on November 16, 1942. All twenty-five received their cadet training at Howard Hughes. (Later, when the classes grew larger, the school was moved to Avenger Field in Sweetwater, Texas.)

In January 1943, Geri was on a cross-country flight when the engine suddenly quit. She was over an area of farmland ridged with high furrows.

"I applied my teaching and landed in two-foot-high furrows with wheels up and as easy a stall as possible. It turned out okay as all I had was a little bend to the prop and a bump on my head. The airplane was later able to fly out after repairs. It turned out the trouble had been vapor lock."

The women who ferried planes from factories or airports or acted as test pilots often ran into trouble. Geri had her share.

"Flying again to the East Coast I took off from El Paso. About one hundred miles from Abilene the engine began to miss and stutter. I coaxed it along and as soon as possible radioed Abilene for a straight-in approach. I came in high and side-slipped to the field. I knew it would be a dead-stick landing but managed to hold it and get it down. I was towed to the repair shop and the mechanic was waiting. He took one look at the engine, then shook his head in wonderment. 'Lady,' he said, 'that there cylinder and valve looks just like a cauliflower. I jest don't see how y'all made it.'

"An investigation turned up a nasty fact: Not only was the plane not pretested at the factory, but worse yet, the steel used in the valves was the wrong kind. I guess that was one time that you could say I came in on a wing and a prayer.

"Another evening, I had a late start out of Long Beach but felt I could make it to Phoenix. Everything would have been fine except that I hit one of those dust storms just before Phoenix. I landed in a field at Tonopah and then the radio said I couldn't get into Phoenix but could land at Luke. Up I went and immediately was surrounded by dust—no visibility.

"I looked for another place to land, and right below me was a vague runway at Goodyear. It called for a close-in and low approach so I wouldn't lose sight of the tiny runway. Suddenly I felt something I couldn't explain, but I was aware of a power taking over the controls, shoving the control forward against every instinct. It looked like a perfect landing, but whatever it was that took over made me land with the nose in the soft sand and the prop right up against the fence at the end of the runway. Just bent prop tips, but I was horrified to think that I hadn't landed on the runway.

"Out of the dust came people from all angles, thinking there had been a miracle. I was overcome by what they said.

"'Thank God you're okay! You would have flipped on that runway—it's just been coated with heavy asphalt! Lady, you've got some kind of angel riding on your shoulder.'

"I knew it was true, and deep down I knew I would never be the same.'"

Incidents, accidents, and near-accidents kept plaguing the WASP. In mid-1944 Geri had an accident that would have kept her from flying for several months. Since she was "anxious to go back to private flying," she took a medical discharge from the WASP.

Geri Nyman did go back to her flying school, and she continued to fly. She specialized in charter flights but also taught navy pilots. When her husband returned from overseas, they went to Alaska, where they owned and operated a bush pilot service. They had three sons and now have eight grandchildren. They recently celebrated their fiftieth wedding anniversary. Geri, now seventy-four, is windsurfing.

PART EIGHT

Office of War Information and Office of Strategic Services

During World War II a need was recognized for the dissemination of war news and information at home and abroad, and for the collection of intelligence that would be essential for the successful prosecution of the war.

To meet the country's information and intelligence needs, the Office of War Information (OWI) and Office of Strategic Services (OSS) were formed from the old Department of the Coordinator of Information in June 1942.

The OWI had two branches: the Domestic Operations Branch and the Overseas Operations Branch. Within the United States, the OWI, under the direction of Elmer Davis, was responsible for the dissemination of all official news relating to the war, and, through educational programs, for the support and building of American morale.

The overseas branch provided foreign countries with information about America and its contribution to the war effort. Its more dramatic role was to conduct psychological warfare in enemy territory by disseminating news and propaganda through radio broadcasts, leaflets, newspapers, and any other available outlets.

Perhaps the OWI's most significant psychological warfare was conducted against the Japanese, carried out from the territory of Hawaii and in the forward area on Saipan.

From both places the OWI sent out radio broadcasts and leaflets to the Japanese civilian and military population designed to influence them to surrender and inform them about the Western way of life. The OWI spread word to the Japanese about Allied victories, information that their government obviously would not give to them.

The leaflets urging the Japanese to surrender were translated into Japanese in the Honolulu office and transmitted by radio photo to the Saipan office and printed there. They were then picked up by B-29s of the Twenty-first Bomber Command and dropped onto Japanese cities.

One of the last leaflets the Honolulu office produced was made shortly before the atomic bombs were dropped on Hiroshima and Nagasaki. The leaflet listed ten of the largest Japanese cities as possible bombing sites and urged the civilian population to evacuate. The leaflet was dropped by the B-29s over the ten cities named, which included Hiroshima and Nagasaki. Unfortunately, the message was ignored.

The Office of Strategic Services, under the leadership of Maj. Gen. William Joseph Donovan, was charged with obtaining information abroad that would be significant to the Americans in the prosecution of the war. Its members sought to ferret out intelligence about the conditions behind enemy lines, and to act as liaisons with anti-Axis resistance groups in occupied countries.

OSS operators were stationed in London, where they worked in cooperation with the British Foreign Office. The women lived through the anxious times during the Normandy landings, constantly busy with the stream of messages from France. They experienced the buzz bombs and lived on the meager British rations. They were in constant contact with the Free French and with the members of the Resistance, who provided the Allies with valuable information. Many of the OSS women were still in London in 1944 when the Germans launched the V-2s.

As the troops fought toward Berlin, many OSS members moved to Paris. The women worked hard to secure political and economic information that would help the Allies. They deciphered radio traffic and debriefed agents who had been dropped behind enemy lines. Some were still in Paris when it was bombed in December 1944 during the Battle of the Bulge.

When V-E Day came, the women of the OSS knew that they had helped to bring the European war to an end; and when the Japanese surrendered the OWI women felt that they, too, had played a role in the Allied victory.

The Office of War Information was terminated on August 31, 1945. Eventually the State Department took over the foreign program with the establishment of the International Information Administration in 1952. The next year, the functions were transferred to the U.S. Information Agency, whose major project is the Voice of America, a world-wide radio network.

On October 1, 1945, a few months after V-J Day, the Office of Strategic Services was disbanded. In 1947, the Central Intelligence Agency was created to take its place.

25

First Names Only

Grace Dolowitz (Levitt) went to work for the OSS because her father, Alexander Dolowitz, was friends with one of the founders. She later discovered that he also worked occasionally for the organization. The OSS advised her to take translators' exams offered by the civil service, which she did—in French, German, and Italian. She was appointed to the OSS soon after. She traveled to Washington, D.C., from her home in Brooklyn in October 1942. At that time, OSS was located in a group of Quonset huts. Grace was assigned to counterintelligence.

Grace recalled her OSS service:

They were waiting for me, it seemed, because they had recruited a cleaning lady at the Vichy embassy who smuggled out the contents of the wastebaskets, and for a week or two I ploughed through those papers, vainly searching for something of interest. Then the United States broke relations with Vichy and interned their ambassador, and the embassy, of course, closed down.

Part of the time I worked in Washington a member of our unit had contacts with the French Resistance. I remember translating pages and pages of plans for a better French government after the war. Other documents given me were rather haphazard and seemed of little practical use.

I do remember talking with some American boys who were to be dropped in Spain. Later we learned that they had been captured, and that our then ambassador to Spain, Nicholas Murray Butler, would do nothing to help them, as he feared jeopardizing our relations with Franco.

Around March 1943 I was asked to transfer to London, and after a sharp tussle with my mother, who accepted my brother's service overseas but didn't see why I should go, I arranged to do so.

It was June 1 when three of us left by neutral Pan Am seaplane from La Guardia (the fourth girl in our group was delayed by her father's illness). It was my first flight; I remember my excitement as we rowed out to the plane. We stopped in Newfoundland overnight, at Botwood, where there was only a newly erected barracks in the wilderness, manned by some lonely naval personnel. The next two days we started out but met with adverse winds and were forced to return to our base. On the third day it was decided to try with a lighter load, so we three girls were left behind for a week to wait for the next plane.

Later I learned that the plane before ours was shot down. It was the only Pan Am plane fired on by the Germans, supposedly—and this was all hearsay—because of a rumor that Churchill would be on board.

Our fourth OSS companion was on the next plane and we four arrived in neutral Ireland together. From Adair we were taken by BOAC plane to London.

We were greeted by Norman Holmes Pearson, a Yale professor who was head of the Spanish Desk and important in the organization. He told us that we were to eat everything possible. If we took coffee we were always to add milk and sugar. Actually, we had no food problems at all, since the British did not collect coupons in restaurants, as was done in France. We used to eat out six days a week, and on our day off pool our coupons and invite some of the men to dinner. I had a friend in Luton and used to trade my lard ration in return for some onions that she raised in her backyard. (She even kept chickens. Her children had never seen a banana.)

There was an air raid during our first night in London at an OSS flat in Grosvenor Mews. I was sleeping on a sofa and didn't wake up, and was quite chagrined to hear about it in the morning. The others had watched the spectacle from the windows.

My first year in London I served as secretary to the French Desk, which was headed by Robert Blum, a talented, hardworking, good man. In London the OSS contingent occupied a number of rooms in the British counterintelligence building. In the beginning our work consisted of preparation. We read source material and tried to relate it to what we already knew, made précis of it—and typed a lot. (This of course was before the time of copying machines or computers for office use.)

At one time we had several army personnel assigned to us, both male and female. The office was heated by coal fires, and the male army personnel were asked to light the fires in the mornings. For some reason, they felt this to be an insult to their sex and fought the order. Finally, to keep the peace, the girls took over the job.

On the British side, almost all the girls were secretaries, and of quite aristocratic backgrounds. Women were drafted in England, and apparently work in our outfit was considered desirable. It was apparent from their accent that nearly all were "top drawer." They were friendly and rather delightful, though it took me time to learn to understand them. In the first days some of them invited me to lunch. In the restaurant I could not understand what they were saying; I thought that if I were in France listening to French I would comprehend better!

The only British women who worked above the secretary level were those maintaining the "Library." It is no longer a secret that our work was largely based on deciphered German radio traffic. After deciphering, anything radioed by German secret intelligence was sent to our office. The women in the Library typed each message as many times as it mentioned a name or an obvious code word or other important word, and built files where one could look up every mention of that name or word. For a long time—years, even—they seemed also to hold it all in their heads and were able to help out the Desks in many ways. Everyone in the Library was female.

At the beginning of my second year—June 1944, when the invasion of France began—we reorganized. A war room was set up, in which I served as an American representative. We responded to questions from our people in the field, where they followed in the wake of the armies (and in at least one case strayed behind enemy lines and were captured). We continued to read incoming intercepted material, and were now able to exploit it.

When I first started in the war room I had a little trouble gaining acceptance. One British officer explained that whenever he delegated work he came to regret it. After much argument, protest, and persuasion I got him to let me take over one minor task. But soon a very fine Britisher, a former Oxford don, Colin Roberts, took over our section, and I soon became, if not an equal, at least the chief assistant to Colin.

Social relations in our British-American outfit were extremely agreeable. For security reasons, only first names were used, and this introduced a pleasant informality. Also for security reasons, and because we worked long hours, we tended to mix with one another rather than with outsiders, although I did have a few outside contacts. I was young, I enjoyed the work, and at times I was mildly in love. I remember it for the most part as a happy time.

We almost never went to shelters during air raids. The only time I can remember doing so was when I got caught in the street. The tube stations that were used as shelters could not be kept clean in wartime for lack of manpower, and the walls were moldy and covered with fungus over large areas. People who had been bombed out slept on cots, and I'm sure if you were scared enough, you would certainly do so. We were lucky; sometimes our windows were broken, and once a partition between rooms just crumbled away from the vibration, but we had no serious trouble. One British officer in our building was killed at home in a raid. Once the windows blew out in our war room office. Colin and I hid under a table, and we worried that our top secret papers would fly out into the street. After a raid, people would calmly go into the streets, and one could hear them busily sweeping up the broken glass.

In December 1944, at the time of the Battle of the Bulge, the Germans as a general precaution changed all their ciphers. For about two weeks, while the new ones were being broken, no material came into our London office. I was offered a trip to our Paris office during this time.

Paris was cold. The buildings, unheated during the occupation, remained bitterly cold. The boys at the office drove around in a jeep, which was no protection against the weather. I was grateful to be wearing a lovely warm WAC uniform (without insignia); at the time, General Eisenhower didn't want Americans in civilian clothes wandering around Paris. The French were very apprehensive that the Germans might reoccupy the city. In the hotel room there were still signs in German advising the (German) occupants never to go out singly. People were still madly grateful to Americans—they would stop us in the street, and in one case we were taken home to dinner. Food was scarce—mostly lettuce and cabbage. Our hostess rubbed each leaf with lard to make it more palatable. We were forbidden to go to French restaurants in order not to use up their food; we ate at an army mess.

My most interesting adventure in Paris was a visit to a German defector. He had been studying hotel administration in France when the war broke out. He did not obey orders to return to Germany, but when the Germans invaded, they picked him up and assigned him to a sabotage unit that drove around southern France leaving delayed-action bombs in churches and other public places. His name and unit had appeared in our messages. When the German Army withdrew, he deserted and came to Paris. He offered his information to the Free French, but at the time they would not trust any German, so he came along to the OSS. OSS set him up in a house and began exploiting his information. He had been threatened over the German radio; they would get him when they came back.

I interviewed him (just for the experience) at the Paris office; he spoke perfect French, but heavily accented English. At the conclusion, he invited me to dinner at his house. He picked me up at the OSS office, wearing a Humphrey Bogart-style overcoat with a gun in each pocket. At his house a bridge table covered with machine guns stood in the vestibule. He was living with a French girl, and there was an elderly housekeeper and a young sister of his mistress. I sat and chatted with these two for some time. Finally we went in to dinner, and after we were seated the mistress appeared. She was blond and pretty, dressed in a slinky black gown with a large, squarish white collar covered with sequins. She was in a very bad mood. I thought perhaps she was embarrassed to be the mistress of a German while I was wearing American army uniform. The German did most of the talking, and about two-thirds of the way through the meal, she burst into tears and flounced out. I heard later that eventually he returned to Germany, where he had left a wife.

On one occasion I sat in on the interrogation of a French Resistance fighter who was the sole survivor of his network, and for that reason had fallen under suspicion of having betrayed his comrades. He seemed a strong, likable man, and the conclusion of the interrogation was that at worst he might have become punch-happy and relaxed his vigilance. I hoped he did not realize that the interrogation was not simply a debriefing. At one point he expressed the opinion that women Resistance fighters, if they were in love with another member of their group, when captured by the Germans stood up to Gestapo torture better than the men, in their resolve to protect their lover.

Returning from Paris, I met a British officer from our outfit at the airport who said he could offer me a ride back to London if I was not in a hurry. He was escorting a captured spy to the prison at Wormwood Scrubs in a Black Maria. I quite enjoyed the experience. The spy was a Belgian citizen born of German parents. I felt some hostility toward him, but my British friend was gentle and reassuring. When he was delivered to the prison the guard gave my friend a receipt reading "Received from Major T., one live body."

I returned home shortly after V-E Day, in June 1945.

Grace Dolowitz Levitt died in 1994.

26

The Lights Go on Again

Elizabeth Davey Velen wrote this account of the OSS days shortly before her death in 1993:

In the winter of 1943, as a recent graduate looking for work
in Washington, I stopped for lunch at a cafeteria in one of those
wartime makeshift buildings constructed in Foggy Bottom to
accommodate the overflow. Weaving my way toward a table, I
accidentally brushed the shoulder of Dr. William Langer, professor of central European history at Harvard.

"Professor Langer, what are you doing here?" I asked in surprise.

I could not picture him any other way than standing at a
lectern facing an awestruck group of Radcliffe undergraduates,
filling our minds with an uninterrupted flow of facts and anecdotes about the era of Bismarck without benefit of notes.

"I am heading a branch of a new intelligence agency, the
Office of Strategic Services," he answered in the rasping nasal
twang for which he was famous. "And you, Miss Davey, what are
you doing?"

"I'm looking for work," I answered.

"Then why don't you apply to us?" he suggested.

And so I did.

When my application was accepted I was sent to join the Western European Section of Dr. Langer's Research and Analysis Branch, which unlike the operational branches of OSS was engaged in producing background political and economic reports compiled from intelligence sources. The branch was housed in a red-brick building known as the Annex at the corner of Twenty-third and E streets, N.W. Once inside I was struck by the number of familiar faces I encountered in the corridors. Most of Cambridge, it seemed. In a week I had run into three of my former professors.

My main assignment with the OSS began in May 1944. It was a glorious spring day in Washington and the atmosphere on the Potomac was permeated with high-riding optimism over the turning tide of the war. In the Research and Analysis Branch, an administrator was making his rounds. His job entailed distributing mimeographed instructions to the professional staff, a potpourri of university professors, their former assistants and students, journalists, linguists, refugees from Nazi Germany and German-occupied countries, and army enlisted men whose special nonmilitary, intellectual, or linguistic talents had earmarked them for assignment to R and A, as the branch was commonly known.

On this morning the administrator approached each one of us to ask if we would like to serve overseas. The immediate destination was London.

For me, the opportunity was compelling.

Our orders, delivered by special hand, instructed us to appear one evening at an address on New York Avenue. When I arrived at the appointed time and place I was puzzled. The only thing visible from the street was a barbershop, obviously closed for business. I entered and stood hesitantly, expecting a trap door to open or a voice to speak from the walls. No one was there to direct me, no sign, nothing. Then I noticed an inconspicuous door at the back. I opened it and walked through into a small windowless room dominated by a large oval table. Seated on one side were four or five OSS colleagues, some looking apprehensive, some dubious. Facing them on the opposite side were two men and a woman who, I soon learned, were psychiatrists attached to the Washington School of Psychiatry.

The secrecy of the location and exercise under way were by today's measure quaint. We were first given association and mechanical aptitude tests, then asked to write our life histories. This material was collected by the psychiatrists, who studied it before making appointments to talk with us individually.

The object of the interviews—of the entire proceedings in fact—was to probe for some discordant note, some frail aspect of character that, if uncovered in time, might save the organization later embarrassment. My own appointment was with the woman psychiatrist. In her cross-examination she pursued the assumption that my desire to serve overseas was sparked by the opportunity it would afford to sleep with a wide selection of servicemen. And my prior sex life—such as it had been at twenty-three—was trundled forth under rigorous cross-examination.

At the end of May, bolstered by shots against tetanus, typhus, and typhoid, our group, which now numbered about twenty, boarded a troop train for New York.

We proceeded to the Brooklyn Port of Embarkation, a gray military wasteland surrounded by a high barbed wire fence not far from the notorious Red Hook section. There we were issued gas masks and helmets, and instructed how to use them. Finally, we were given top secret orders to go to Pier 90, North River, at midnight.

The ship we were boarding, it turned out, was the *New Amsterdam*, converted to wartime use and now under a joint British-Dutch command. It had been refitted to accommodate eleven thousand troops.

The eleven young women in our group were the only women aboard. We were quartered on the promenade deck surrounded by young B-52 bomber pilots, most of them still in or barely out of their teens.

We were somewhere in the middle of the North Atlantic on the fourth day out when we were awakened sharply at 5:00 A.M. by the ship's alarm, followed by the urgent announcement of the Dutch captain, delivered in a thickly accented bass over the public address system: "These ees enemy attack! Everybodee to ees emergency station! Prepare to deesembark!"

We scrambled into our clothes, then moved quietly in an orderly line as we had been trained along the corridors, up the stairs, assembling numbly at our appointed places on the open deck. Over our heads two five-inch cannons were firing salvos with a deafening roar skyward and out to sea. In the pale gray early light we strained our eyes for the site of enemy planes or subs. The mist was thick, and except for our own guns, the calm was complete. We waited for fifteen minutes or so in a state of disembodied half-wakefulness before the captain's harsh Dutch accent again rolled forth from the speakers commanding the deck.

"I have an announcement to make. At four-thirty thees morning the Allied Expeditionary Forces landed in France!"

As the full meaning of the exercise sank into our befogged minds, we clapped, but under the circumstances our exhilaration over D-Day was subdued.

A few days later we awoke to the sight of blue-green, rough, rolling pastureland on either side of the ship. We were cruising up the Firth of Clyde. All around were gray ships.

From the dock we boarded directly a troop train, which once under way backed and filled through Glasgow, then puffed on across the Scottish countryside, heading for Edinburgh and the east coast on the first leg of a twenty-four hour trip to London.

As night fell after a dinner of K rations—a can of cheddar cheese laced with small chunks of ham, and a chocolate bar— we arranged ourselves to attempt a night's rest, so far as possible on the wooden seats of our compartment. I ended up stretched out beside a navy warrant officer who happened to be in my compartment. The two of us not so comfortably took up the space normally reserved for three behinds.

At dawn the next morning we pulled into King's Cross Station, London. From there we went by cab to the Hotel Principia, where rooms had been reserved for us by the OSS London office. A block away from Oxford Street and a few blocks down from Marble Arch in London's Mayfair district, the Principia was a modest hotel that emanated a musty odor of boiled cabbages and potatoes. Still, it was reasonably comfortable and close to our office on Brook Street, just around the corner from the American embassy on Grosvenor Square, which had been unofficially renamed "Eisenhower Platz" by the British.

In the late afternoon that first day, which I slept away, the naval officer who had shared our wooden seat on the train came to my room and invited me to dinner. A few steps short of Marble Arch we found a restaurant one flight up on the mezzanine floor. The dining room was large and well appointed. A band was playing swing in one corner.

My new friend and I talked for what seemed like hours until we were abruptly interrupted by the manager, who approached our table in great excitement, waving his arms. "Get below!" he shouted at us. "Didn't you know there's an alert?"

"An alert, what's that?" We looked at each other and at the now empty dining room. We descended quickly to the foyer, where we joined a group of people sitting huddled together, talking quietly. On everyone's mind was the question, What was Jerry up to now? There had not been an alert for many months, not since the little blitz two years previously. The faces around us expressed forbearance rather than fear, weary expectation, and some anxiety that this time around, after what they had survived, they might not be so lucky.

"We must get back to the hotel, they'll be wondering about us," I said to my escort. A woman who overheard me turned to face us. "But you cannot go out without helmets!" In the end we decided to make a dash for it.

Out in the street the sky was ablaze with bursts of fire. Shrapnel rained down on us as we raced the few blocks back to the Principia.

We later learned that the noise and shrapnel came from anti-aircraft emplacements in Hyde Park just at our backs, and that Jerry was not dive-bombing that night but launching the first of the V-1 pilotless planes, most commonly known as "buzz bombs."

Early one morning a few days after my initial experience I was awakened by a series of explosions close at hand. Sleep being out of the question, I decided to dress and go down to the hotel lobby. The only person about was the night porter, a dour Scotsman who spoke with a thick burr. He asked if he could make me a cup of tea. I was grateful for the offer. We sipped our tea in silence as we listened to the rumble around us. Suddenly we heard the scream of a bomb descending. He stared somberly at me, his eyes reflecting the dark assurance of disaster. "Here it comes, mum," he said. The bomb landed near enough to crack but not shatter the window in the lobby.

During that summer in London the pervasive presence of the V-1s, or "doodlebugs," "buzz bombs," "robots," "the things," and "pilotless planes," as they were variously known, became normalized in our subconscious. While the press of our daily work banished them from our thoughts for hours, once the alert was sounded, a secret mechanism was released; our ears pricked to the air lanes overhead and, as keen as radar, we could spot the approach of danger. When the motor stopped, the plane, which bore a thousand-pound warhead, would drop.

I slept through alerts and blasts, but if a bomb was approaching in a direct lane over the hotel, I would wake up before I could hear a sound. Bombs fired from a launching pad, usually at the rate of five at a time, followed a set course. This fore-warning gave me time to throw on a bathrobe and descend to the cellar, where in my second week in London I had installed a three-quarter-length mattress, all you could buy then, on top of an abandoned bathtub that had been covered with wooden planks.

At the Hotel Principia as the summer progressed, a companionable nucleus of cellar mates was formed. We didn't feel safer there, but calmer.

Among those who opted for the cellar were a retired Australian admiral, his wife, and a robust Junoesque Irish cook who wore her hair in tight paper curlers and prayed after each blast, "Oh, Holy Mary, Mother of God, deliver us!" The other regular cellar mate was Phyllis Johnson, a quiet, reflective Bostonian from our OSS Brook Street office.

Despite the nightly lamentations of the cook, the cellar society was genial and generally in good spirits, ignited by thimblefuls of scotch supplied by the admiral, who was privy to some secret supply of this then rare and precious drink. Stray guests

at the hotel joined us from time to time. Talk of the war, the big
and little blitzes, swirled around us, spiked by rumors and sick
jokes. While I learned more than I wanted to know, I was mes-
merized by these sessions.

During the day at the Brook Street office we were too busy to
be more than intermittently aware of the war around us. Our
small R and A group, now limited to the French Section, worked
long hours in preparation for the time not far off when we
would move on to Paris.

My own work was to gather information on leading French
political personalities, officials of the Vichy regime as well as
prominent members of the Resistance. The main collabora-
tionists were known to us, but we knew little of the Resistance
leaders, quite naturally, since they operated under aliases.

Information came to us from various sources. We worked in
close cooperation with our British counterparts. We relied on
intelligence reports from OSS agents in the field. Most infor-
mative and useful was the Resistance press, which was smuggled
out of occupied France. About midsummer I was given access to
the files of an arm of British intelligence, the Political Warfare
Executive, or PWE.

Through some high-ranking German officers captured by the
British in the Allied drive across France we learned the identity
of some of the major players involved in the July 20, 1944, plot
to assassinate Hitler. The German officers were confined together in a military prison, where they were free to move about and
meet together, unaware that secret microphones were recording
their conversations. This was heady material to have in hand in
the weeks just following the ill-fated attempt on Hitler's life.

On nighttime excursions we met the average Londoners,
bone weary from four years of bombardment, blackouts, long
hours of work, and tragic casualties among their families and
friends. Their good cheer was unflagging, and their wit—the
wry, sardonic wit of the London people—was undulled.

After dinner, often at a favorite Greek restaurant in Soho, we
sometimes visited a pub near the concrete bunker-style building
that housed the BBC. Over the entrance was a sign warning
patrons: "In case of a direct hit this pub will close immediately."

Inside we collected in a booth in an oak-paneled room dimly lit by shaded lamps. The atmosphere was thick with cigarette smoke and the smell of beer. Behind us on a shelf running along the back wall sat a large goldfish bowl to which someone had attached a handwritten note cautioning the pair inside to "Mind the glass, dearies." Glass was the killer that summer. It was blown in and out of windows, shredded to fine shards and needles.

As we moved around the city we became increasingly sensitive to the toll of four years of war. The scars on the face of London from the big and little blitzes were largely hidden behind high wooden fences, but the faces of the homeless, especially poignant, who had been bombed out could not be concealed. Hundreds lived in a natural shelter deep in the London Underground. At each train stop the walls were lined with tiers of double- and triple-decker bunks, which by early evening were filled to capacity. Those who had no bunk lay rolled in blankets on the pavement. The light at that level was dim and the air suffocatingly close.

While the average American and British citizen may never have been as close as in that ambiance of direct communion and immediate danger, there was resentment of Americans, and it was felt in small ways. At the home of the father of an English friend I was berated for the way American servicemen were eating fresh oranges on the streets of London. And I was made embarrassingly conscious of the open display of fruit juice, cigarettes, and other scarce items that Americans were supplied by our post exchanges, in full view of people who had known only the strictest austerity for four years.

As the summer moved into August we followed the course of our armies in France with heightened expectancy. We were scheduled to move on to Paris when the time came. The buzz bomb activity had slackened, and we began to move around London more freely.

The liberation of Paris was one week away. The skies over London were clear, except for occasional squadrons of Flying Fortresses headed for the Channel and daylight raids deep into Germany. Although one or two V-2s, much more powerful and deadly missiles than the V-1, were dropped on London, we never did receive the command to march to Pett's Wood (the dispersal area in case of a need for evacuation), nor the maps giving the routes.

On August 24 I wrote home: "The biggest event of the week occurred today after the news of the liberation of Paris. This noon I joined the throngs on their way to St. Paul's, where the first salvo of bells was scheduled to ring out. The square around the cathedral was jammed with people as far as the eye could see, and the tricolor and the Union Jack were raised above the massive bulk of St. Paul's. Cameras flashed and a great cheer rose from the crowd—London's tribute to *le jour de gloire*. It was an historic occasion: the London of St. Paul's, battered and beaten, but unbowed, pealing its bells for Paris, which in the words of one spectator 'is with us again.'"

By the second week of September we were ready, as our colleagues who were to remain in London put it, "to escape to the Continent." Those of us who were civilians were ordered into uniform, WAC officers' greens, since we would be entering a theater of combat.

In another letter home I wrote: "It is an unusual feeling to go out into the streets and be recognized as an American. The military takes considerable more notice of you, I expect because they are not quite sure what you are. In the last two days I have managed with some embarrassment to return three salutes, two from naval officers, one from a GI. And along my way to our office I have been identified: 'Oyee, look at the wicky-wacky' or the 'wacky-wacky.'"

Early on a gray Sunday morning in mid-September fifteen OSS women in our new WAC greens were driven in a U.S. Army truck to a military airport somewhere outside London. The airport was wrapped in a heavy fog. Once strapped into our bucket seats in a C-47 transport plane and on our way to Paris we could make out through patches of mist a geometric pattern of green and brown fields interspersed with woods. The white cliffs of Dover—a chalkline—marked the English coast; then water and more fields, deeper green and marred by the ravages of war, and villages with church spires reaching up through billows of clouds over which we skimmed and through which we bumped. Finally, an airport, Le Bourget, and a hairy landing on a runway pockmarked with bomb craters.

At the airport we were picked up by a military bus manned by a contingent of the ATS, the British women's army auxiliary. It seemed odd, because up till then we had been under the jurisdiction of the U.S. Army. We were driven into Paris to the Place Vendôme, where we were greeted by an ATS sergeant, decanted, and herded into another bus that shuttled us to the Hotel Majestic, which had been commandeered by SHAEF (Supreme Headquarters, Allied Expeditionary Force).

At the Majestic we were ushered into the lobby and given lengthy questionnaires to fill out. Considering the fact that the OSS had complete and detailed information about us, to fill out more forms seemed superfluous. But we complied docilely.

We wrote down our names, ages, places of birth, years of education, work experience, typing speed (words per minute), and shorthand (words per minute)—if we had any shorthand.

When we had finished, another sprightly and efficient ATS sergeant gathered up our forms and asked us to wait for further orders. It was past noon and as we waited we began to wonder where our office and male colleagues were, and when and where we could set down our blankets and duffel bags.

It was a long wait. Two hours later a U.S. Army captain accompanied by the two ATS sergeants appeared at the entrance to the lobby. The captain looked perplexed. "Who the hell are you?" he asked peremptorily.

"We're with the OSS," we said.

"Oh, my God," he expostulated. "We were expecting fifteen telephone operators for SHAEF!" With that he turned on his heels and left. We looked at one another bleakly.

Now what? We had the address of the Elysée Park Hotel just off the Champs-Elysées at the Rond-Point, where we were to be billeted. We decided that the best thing would be to try to hitch a ride.

We picked up our duffel bags, threw our GI-issue blankets

over our shoulders, and emerged into the street. Finding a lift
was something else again. Except for bicycles with sidecars there
wasn't a vehicle on the streets of Paris.

So off we trudged in the direction of the Étoile. The wide
sidewalks of the Champs-Elysées barely yielded stepping room.
Families with children, old people, young people, all in their
Sunday best—the women wearing their hair piled in foot-high
coifs stuffed with papier-mâché, the fashion of the postliberation moment—were weaving their way up and down the wide
avenue.

It was very warm, and warmer still in the WAC winter greens.
We were fifteen hot, hungry young women dragging duffel bags,
altogether a somber olive drab contrast to the chic and colorful
Parisians. They stared at us in disbelief. Were we leftover Germans? They had never seen an American woman in uniform. We
were the first, it turned out, in Paris. Then we were recognized
by the U.S. on our lapels.

The maroon velvet and gilded lobby of the Elysée Park was
light years away from the spare mid-Victorian appointments of
the Hotel Principia and the austerity of wartime London. A bell-
boy—could there still be bellboys in this war? I wondered—conducted me to the lift, a glass cage enclosed in a wrought-iron
frame.

We rode smoothly to the top floor, where I was shown a room,
part of a suite that encompassed the entire top floor. The view
from the terrace spanned half of Paris, reaching from the white
dome of Sacré-Coeur on the left to the Eiffel Tower on the right.

The windows of the French doors leading onto the terrace
had been pierced and cracked in several places by bullets that
were still embedded in the walls opposite. The hotel, which had
been occupied until less than a month before by the Luftwaffe,
had come under fire by the Forces Françaises de l'Intérieur
(FFI), the military arm of the French Resistance, who had established a perch on the roof of the Petit Palais during the battle
for the liberation of Paris. There was no way now to replace the
panes because of the acute shortage of every sort of material in
Paris. Still, even later, when the fall temperatures anticipated the
coldest winter in Europe, the light, the view, the quiet elegance

of the room outbalanced the icy blasts that came through those shattered windows.

Our offices were a few blocks up on the Champs-Elysées, at number 79, one of those portly concrete Second Empire buildings that line the Champs-Elysées leading toward the Étoile. During the German occupation it had served as the headquarters of the Todt organization, which specialized in the "recruitment" of forced labor. In the spacious, cold, and drafty interior, a wide marble staircase and an elevator led to the upper floors. The offices of the French Section of R and A were on the fourth floor.

My own desk was in a large corner next to a window that looked out on the Champs. The room was used as the section library. It was pleasantly light and I never lacked for company, since it was used to seat transient staff coming in from London or back from the front.

Each of us covered a special aspect of the work, which by now with the liberation of France was less intelligence gathering than reporting in depth. My male colleagues followed the political changes in society, the reversion from Vichy France to a new democratic society grounded in the wartime French Resistance and the Free French movement led by de Gaulle.

Our best sources were no longer classified reports from the field, as they had been in London, but the daily press, interviews, political party meetings, and debates of the Consultative Assembly, which members of our section attended as observers. The information gathered and analyzed was passed along to OSS R and A Washington, and from there to the U.S. government agencies concerned, most notably the State Department, in the form of weekly reports.

My own work in the year in Paris, until December 1945, was to compile and edit a *Who's Who in French Politics*. The purpose of the work was to facilitate the contacts of American officials with their counterparts at various levels in the new French provisional government under de Gaulle.

My sources were the twenty-one postwar Paris dailies, representing every political stripe. I was also obliged to pore through the *Journal Officiel,* the official French record of laws and decrees and of election results down to the departmental prefects (all eighty-nine of them) and subprefects, a virtual Sears Roebuck catalog of French elected officials.

Another valuable source was information passed on to me— impressions and biographical footnotes—by my colleagues who from time to time interviewed party and Resistance leaders. The number of French actively involved in the Resistance has been estimated to be proportionately small. But those we knew of had shown extraordinary heroism and nerves of steel.

One of the assignments of the Research and Analysis Branch of OSS abroad was to collect and sift documentation abandoned by quisling regimes such as the Vichy government or by the retreating Germans. Other official agencies were also involved in this work, and efforts frequently overlapped. At times information was shared, at times not. Usually a cache of documents went to the first intelligence diggers at the site.

In the fall of 1944 we were given official permission by the then provisional French government to sift through the contents of the offices of a Vichy documentation agency known as Inter-France. Preliminary reports suggested that the offices contained extensive biographical files. As I was the section biographer, I was invited to go along in the two-and-a-half-ton truck we had at our disposal.

When we arrived at the scene we discovered rooms filled with a floor-to-ceiling library of sturdy blue and gray cardboard folders alphabetized by name. Excitement was high. At first blush it seemed an intelligence-gathering bonanza. But as we leafed through these files we quickly realized why the French had no use for them. They contained four years of newspaper clippings from the French collaborationist press. Material on leading Vichy and Nazi personalities was notably absent. What we had in hand were massive files on Roosevelt and Churchill, and less bulky ones on Wendell Willkie, Fiorello La Guardia, Frances Perkins, Thomas Dewey, and John Garner, to name a few.

Further ransacking of desks yielded nothing more notable than a 1936 Baedeker of Paris and the 1921 edition of the New York Social Register.

Unwilling merely to leave our prize, possibly because of the sheer bulk of it, we decided to store it in gunnysacks and transport it back to our office. There the sacks were stacked in the corner of an empty room and left to gather the dust of history. A year and a half later, the army gunnysacks turned up in Washington, D.C. A young Foreign Service officer found them in the mail room of the State Department.

From the time that the OSS civilian women were placed under U.S. Army command, our exact status was a puzzle and a problem that nagged the Regular Army officers in charge of our care and feeding. To be mistaken for telephone operators on the day of our arrival in Paris was just one case in point.

As the fall advanced the top floors of the Elysée Park Hotel began to fill with young women from the other branches of OSS: SI (Secret Intelligence) and X-2 (Counterintelligence). Later that winter, hot water appeared miraculously in the Elysée Park. And the OSS girls billeted there played hostess to our GI colleagues for warm baths.

We had our regular bath customers. Mine was a young Jewish refugee who had come to the U.S. from Austria and was inducted shortly after into the U.S. armed forces. He enjoyed lounging in the tub.

They were unusual GIs. Some had been assigned to the OSS directly from training at Camp Ritchie, a proving ground for talented linguists, writers, and artists, many of them refugees from Germany and German-occupied Europe.

In the early days of the fall of 1944, although we worked an eight-hour day, seven-day week, we were out every night on a continuous round of parties given by students of the graduate faculties of the Sorbonne and by us in reciprocation.

One night in late November we were awakened at the hotel by the unmistakable sound of exploding bombs. After about ten minutes of quiet the air raid alert sounded. On the top floor of the hotel one of the bellboys was running from room to room shouting, *"Il faut descendre immédiatement!"* In slippers and bathrobes we congregated in front of the elevator cage. The little red button of the elevator continuously registered *"occupé."* And as in normal circumstances the simple tactic of opening the iron gate just as the cage passed did not work.

So we took to the stairs. On the ground floor we were herded together by a member of the hotel staff at the elevator gate. We were then conducted in groups of four by the lift down into the bowels of the hotel. The elevator came to rest in a murky, dimly lit sub-basement. From there we were led forward by candlelight along a rough dirt path.

We were thunderstruck when we were ushered into a large, brightly lit bar furnished with chairs and booths lined with red leather cushions. Everything looked sparklingly new, from the chrome bar top to the burnished brass buttons of the tooled red leather cushions. The bar had been built by the Germans as an air raid shelter. The bar shelves had been empty since their withdrawal.

The bombing of Paris in December 1944 occurred at the height of the Battle of the Bulge. Two German planes flew over and dropped four bombs. One landed in the Tuileries garden; the others did little, if any, damage. The fact that the French authorities, the de Gaulle provisional government at the time, sounded the alert after the bombs had fallen indicated that Paris would have been ill prepared had the Germans ever reneged on their agreement that it be treated as an open city.

The weeks following were bitterly cold, reputedly the coldest winter in fifty years. News of the Allied losses from the German ambush at Bastogne were sobering. The war had entered a new and ugly phase. Rumors came back from the front that the German army, heartened by the near success of their surprise counteroffensive, would mount another, more massive attempt to recapture ground and block the Allied advance into Germany.

At OSS headquarters in Paris, sandbags were mounted at the entrance and stairway. GIs with machine guns stood guard. German parachutists were said to have been sighted. And there were rumors of spies everywhere.

After the German air raid Paris was put under a curfew. As a result of the curfew we saw our French friends less. Relations between the Americans and French had cooled since the fall honeymoon. The reasons were understandable. Foremost, perhaps, was the lingering sensitivity of the French over having lost the war. There were constant reminders of this in relations between the two, of our primary and their secondary roles. U.S. enlisted men at times openly demonstrated their lack of respect for the French, and this attitude became especially galling from the time Paris began to receive the first GIs on leave from the front. Among them were hardened combat troops who were getting their first taste of liberty since the Normandy landings. They were battle weary, thirsty, and hungry, and heartily adopted Paris as their playground. Reports of incidents were frequent, of clashes between American soldiers and French youths, of prostitutes being beaten up, of general rowdiness. That Paris should have become a leave center for U.S. troops was regrettable, but could not have been prevented.

Toward winter's end, as our armies moved across the Rhine and into Germany, the ugly character of the war was brought home to us. We had heard persistent rumors of extermination camps, but we were unprepared for the terrible reality. As the first camps were liberated and reports and photographs came through to us, we were stunned by the enormity of the crimes committed.

Early on the morning of April 10, crossing the Champs-Elysées on my way to breakfast at the Doucet, I was struck by the great number of people queuing up at the newspaper kiosks. They looked somber, stricken. I fell in with their mood when I read the large, black banner headlines: *"Roosevelt est mort."*

As the long, quiet day wore on, the clusters of Allied flags that had flown so gaily from every window at the time of the liberation began to reappear, this time tied back to their poles with a black ribbon in the French manner of mourning. Out on the streets some Parisians were wearing black sleeve bands; others were weeping openly.

On the afternoon of May 7, *Libération Soir,* one of the few afternoon dailies that had managed to stay afloat in competition with some twenty-one morning papers representing every party and political stripe of postliberation France, hit the stands with the banner headline *"La Guerre Est Finie."*

It's just like *Libe Soir,* we thought, trying to jump the gun, printing another of its false scoops.

But there was more than something in the air. After dinner I went with a friend to sit on the terrace of my top-floor room. It was a balmy, almost summer night, quiet, lit by a pale crescent moon. As we sat and talked, the world around us slowly came alive.

First a few planes flew low over the city, dropping flares. From the Ninth Air Force, we thought, stationed near Versailles. But why the flares? We stood and looked down into the street. People were emerging from homes and cafes, listening and lingering. The atmosphere was filled with wonder and portent. Suddenly, just below us a fountain that had been dormant since France fell in June 1940 burbled up into the air; seconds later it was illuminated and danced, disembodied, in the light. As we watched, spellbound, the Arc de Triomphe commanding the wide sweep of the Champs-Elysées to our right was flooded with light. Then to the left of us the white dome of Sacré-Coeur in Montmartre was lit up against the night sky. The war had turned off the city for five years, and its sudden illumination was like a touch of magic.

This must be it, we thought, and we started a night-long vigil to see Paris awake to V-E Day.

In the first pale light of dawn a hurdy-gurdy started to play on the Avenue Matignon just below. A group of people sang along with the organ-grinder; others began to dance. More and more people were filling the streets, holding hands, kissing, singing and dancing. Clusters of Allied flags, this time floating free, were unfurling from windows.

The wait, the long winter was over. And when it came Paris was way ahead of the official announcement. The celebration that had started with a muffled rumble had built into a great human roar.

When we descended to the street strangers took our hands and we "snaked" with them through the growing crowds to reach the nearest cafe for breakfast. All day long we wove hand in hand with friends and strangers—the only way you could move—up the Champs-Elysées and down, across the Place de la Concorde, along the Seine to the Ile de la Cité and Notre Dame. Exhausted, we sprawled on the grass before the cathedral with thousands of others and waited for de Gaulle to appear and put his official seal on the news.

Later, still exhilarated and swept along in the swirling human current, we made our way back to our office, where we perched on the wide cement windowsills overlooking the Champs, watching the singing, dancing, undulating multitude, the world of Paris unfold.

In the waning daylight U.S. combat planes on their way home flew single file at tree-top level down the Champs-Elysées, buzzing the flowering chestnuts. And as they rose up and over the Arc de Triomphe in a breathtaking show of bravado, they tilted their wings in salute to the unknown soldier buried there beneath the eternal flame, a spontaneous gesture of camaraderie with the French who had fallen in the war.

PART NINE

American Red Cross

The Red Cross had its roots in the Geneva Convention of 1864, when the delegates sought to establish national organizations to aid the sick and wounded of wars. The first large-scale Red Cross effort occurred in 1870 during the Franco-Prussian War, when Red Cross workers cared for 510,000 sick and wounded.

The immediate predecessor to the American Red Cross was the United States Sanitary Commission, formed during the 1860s to give relief to soldiers on the battlefields during the Civil War. However, it was Clara Barton who really sparked the formation of the American Red Cross.

Clara Barton, working independently, had volunteered among the Civil War wounded and was popularly called the "angel of mercy." After the war she went to Europe and served with the Red Cross in the Franco-Prussian War. She returned home and worked successfully to secure government adherence to the Geneva Convention (1882) and to found a Red Cross society in the United States.

The first major American Red Cross effort was a disaster relief operation for the victims of a forest fire in Michigan. The Red Cross served in the Spanish-American War in 1898 and in World War I. Its expanded service in social work, public health nursing, and disaster relief earned the Red Cross popular support and deserved recognition.

During World War II, the American Red Cross operated all over the world. The Red Cross established over eighteen hundred recreational facilities for the soldiers overseas, and staffed hundreds of clubmobiles, the mobile canteens that dispensed coffee, donuts, and cheer to soldiers in the field. Volunteers worked in hospitals, packed thousands of food and medical parcels for prisoners of war, and aided thousands of military men and women. Twenty-nine ARC women died in service, the first on the Anzio beachhead.

The American Red Cross women serving overseas were vital to the morale of the American troops. From the beginning of the massing of the servicemen in England preparatory to the assault on Fortress Europe, through the occupation of Germany and the demobilization of the troops in the Far East, the women worked to keep the spirits of the U.S. forces high.

They formed or served in Red Cross clubs in England and drove clubmobiles throughout the countryside. They were subjected to German bombing as they followed the army into Europe after the D-Day landings. Some were billeted in tent cities, in a monastery, in village hotels, even in a former German house of prostitution.

Some of the Red Cross women were sent to Iran, where they worked in station hospitals, exposed to sandstorms, heat, and disease. They served in hospitals in Cairo and in Dakar, cheering the patients from the CBI theater of war. Others were sent directly to the Pacific, to New Guinea, where they saw the heavy losses of battle. They saw the troops in full jungle warfare gear board ships on Christmas Eve 1944 for the further assault on the Pacific Islands. They went to Leyte and Cebu. They worked in field hospitals on the Hawaiian Islands.

The Red Cross women set up recreation centers wherever they could. Some Red Cross clubs in civilized areas were elaborate, providing food, drink, all kinds of games, music, and dancing, and even beds for overnight military guests. Other clubs had only Little Red Wagons offering cold drinks and snacks to the troops.

Red Cross women were sent to India, some continuing on to fly over the dangerous Himalayan Hump into China, where they set up clubs for the servicemen taking off for the Pacific battles. They experienced the *jingbao*, the Japanese bombing attacks. They traveled to outlying areas where they were joyously welcomed by troops that had not seen American women for months.

After the Japanese surrender, Red Cross women worked in China—in Tsingtao, serving the marines who had come from the Pacific Islands, and in Shanghai, helping to entertain the men who were waiting to be demobilized and sent back to the United States.

The war was very real to the women of the Red Cross. They all gave of themselves to make the life of the U.S. fighting troops a little bit easier. That they did so is of great credit to them. They too were women of courage.

The American Red Cross, with its 2 million volunteers, continues its peacetime service, but is ready to expand into wartime duty whenever and wherever needed.

27

Foreign Lands

One of the first areas overseas to call on the help of the American Red Cross women was the British Isles, for it was here that U.S. troops were massing for deployment to the European continent.

In the spring of 1942 Marion Hamilton was twenty-eight, working for an advertising concern in New York City, when she decided to join the Red Cross. After a long delay because of the North African invasion, which caused a shortage of transport ships, she sailed to England. She was sent to Kettering, seventy miles north of London, to help establish a club for American servicemen.

The club opened on New Year's Day 1943, and "the soldiers poured in, took instant possession of all that we offered, found the stack of records beside the Victrola, and within ten minutes Glenn Miller's 'Moonlight Cocktail' was loud and clear, a ping pong game was under way, along with a billiard game, and in the dining room an ever-hungry crowd of GIs had lined up. We were under way, and that was pretty much the way it was to be for the next three years."

Marion Hamilton in formal Red Cross photo.

Problems did, of course, occur. First came the need for more space. More disturbing was "a racial situation that had begun without warning."

A company of black soldiers from Louisiana with their white captain from Indiana had suddenly arrived in town, and one Sunday they strolled into the club through the back door. No sooner had they come in than all the white servicemen in the lounge and snack bar got to their feet without a word and walked out the front door. Marion and the staff managed to calm the situation, but they knew that the superficial mutual tolerance would not hold true at dances. They found an empty hall in the town, helped the army find a band, and arranged a dance for the black company for the same night the usual club dance was held. When the new Red Cross club with more space and facilities was opened, the old one became the club for black soldiers with a "Negro staff" in charge.

The clubs continued to provide recreation, food, and beds for countless servicemen long after the Normandy invasion, through the capitulation of Germany, and even past V-J Day, which found the staff dancing in the streets. Marion Hamilton did not return home to America until April 1946.

After the war, Marion Hamilton had a number of jobs in the education field. During 1946 she was registrar of summer school at the University of Virginia. She then served as dean of students and assistant professor of English at Westhampton College of the University of Richmond until 1950, when she received her Ph.D. in English literature. For the next

Red Cross worker Janet L. White on a trip to Giza with patients from the Thirty-eighth
General Hospital, Cairo, Egypt, 1944.

*three years she was assistant professor of English at Wellesley College in
Massachusetts. She then became a headmistress, first of the Ellis School
in Pittsburgh, then of the Williams School in New London, Connecticut, where she served until her retirement in 1978.*

Not all Red Cross women were concerned with the recreation
and feeding of American troops. Some, like Janet L. White,
worked in remote hospitals. Janet had been a medical secretary
at St. John's Hospital in Brooklyn, New York, for several years,
and was working as a volunteer staff assistant for the Red Cross
after business hours. By chance she learned that the Red Cross
needed hospital secretaries overseas.

In February 1943 she applied and was accepted. Within
months she was stationed in Khorramshahr, Iran, assigned to
the Twenty-first Station Hospital.

Khorramshahr was a miserable place, south of the junction of the Tigris and Euphrates rivers, reached by crossing the desert from Basra. The name meant City of Happiness, but, as Janet wrote, "why anyone should bestow such a name on that particular hellhole I never discovered. It was hot, dirty, and smelly, and the people, for the most part, were ragged, the children naked, with flies swarming over everything."

It was desert, heat, dust, bugs, monotony, and discomfort. At the hospital the doctors and nurses treated malaria, dysentery, broken bones, appendicitis, smallpox, VD, and mental illness. It was no wonder that when Janet received orders in April 1944 assigning her to the Thirty-eighth General Hospital, outside Cairo, she was more than glad to leave Iran.

At the Thirty-eighth Janet was promoted to staff aide. One of her pleasant new duties was to take transient ambulatory patients sightseeing. But this varied job did not last long. Dakar in French West Africa needed a Red Cross worker for the Ninety-third Hospital there, and in the summer of 1944 Janet decided to take a chance on service in Dakar, in spite of the plague prevalent there. She was the only Red Cross worker and was in charge of all American Red Cross activities at the hospital. Janet felt that her most worthwhile work was to attend to the patients flying in from the China-Burma-India theater, who were being returned to the States.

Late in April 1945 the Ninety-third Station Hospital received orders to move to Tripoli, Libya, and Janet moved with them, to stay until the middle of August, after the war was over.

After her stint with the Red Cross, Janet L. White went back to being a secretary at a stock brokerage firm. Then she joined the United Nations in New York, where she worked as an administrative assistant in the Dag Hammarskjöld Library for fifteen years. She then became the first executive secretary for a branch store manager of Bloomingdale's in Stamford, Connecticut. In 1969 she moved to Vernon, Vermont, where she worked in the record room at the Brattleboro Memorial Hospital until her retirement in 1977. She is currently part of a senior's program that works monthly at the Vermont National Bank.

Eunice Wardwell with the Red Cross in the jungles of Milne Bay, New
Guinea, a staging area for other Pacific islands.

Although the minimum age to apply to the American Red Cross
for overseas duty was twenty-five, Eunice Wardwell persuaded
the organization that she was qualified for service when she was
only twenty-three. She had been raised in upstate New York,
graduated from Mount Holyoke College in 1943, and had started a job as a lab technician in the biochemistry lab at Harvard
Medical School. After eight months of taking the rectal temperature of sick white rats, she was ready for a change.

Eunice wrote daily letters to the Red Cross until she was finally accepted. Instead of being assigned to Europe as requested,
she was ordered to Milne Bay, New Guinea, where she was to
spend a year living in a grass hut, surrounded by barbed wire.

Milne Bay was a staging area for other Pacific Islands and it
was crowded with servicemen. The Red Cross women were kept
busy providing food and recreation at the Base A Artillery Club.

"Off-duty GIs could relax, have a snack composed of warm
Aussie lemonade and bully beef sandwiches, play cribbage or
cards, or just spend time talking with the girls and one another." Sometimes the women took the Little Red Wagon, a jeep,
out to the work sites.

In New Guinea the Red Cross women provided all the recreational facilities and activities they could think of—dances, parties, swimming exhibitions—anything to pass the time for the men. Christmas 1944 was difficult with frenetic activity, but it gave Eunice a warm feeling knowing how much better it was to give than to receive.

Halfway into 1945, Eunice received orders to proceed to Leyte to help run a canteen at the airstrip. Then came another transfer to the island of Cebu, to work at a rather elegant Red Cross club—a far cry from the grass huts of New Guinea. It was on Cebu that Eunice met and married her husband. Japan had surrendered, and since husband and wife could not be stationed on the same base, she opted to be sent back to the States instead of forward to Tokyo.

After the war Eunice Wardwell Maupin and her husband raised five children in Hawaii and Westport, Connecticut. They then moved to the U.S. Virgin Islands. For eighteen years Eunice taught science in a large public high school in the Virgin Islands, and when she retired she settled in Seattle. Her marriage lasted thirty-five years. Now she continues to enjoy her extensive travels. When in Seattle she works part-time at the Pacific Science Center as an interpreter. Her volunteer work involves teaching sailing at Seattle's Center for Wooden Boats as well as facilitating a mothers' support group at the Seattle AIDS Support Group.

In spite of the chaotic war conditions in China, with the Kuomingtang and the Communists fighting each other, and the Japanese bombing both of them—and many civilian areas—and dogfighting Allied planes wherever they could find them, the Red Cross had no difficulty in securing volunteers willing to serve in the Far East. The women were braver than they realized.

The takeoff point was an airfield in Chabua, Assam, in northeast India, next to the Burmese border and not far from Tibet. The heavy monsoon rains proved hazardous, but the women discovered a more dangerous venture, the flight over the Himalayan Mountains, the Hump, familiarly known as the Aluminum Trail. As they flew over, the volunteers could see the reflections

New Red Cross dining room canteen opens in 1945, in China. Betty Heath is at right.
Two weeks later, a rainstorm washed the whole room away; it had been made of mud
bricks that were not quite dry.

from downed aircraft below, among the jagged mountain peaks.
The four-hour trip into China, flying at fourteen thousand feet
without additional oxygen, took courage.

Betty Heath was one of the Red Cross women who possessed
that courage. She flew over the Hump to her assignment at General Chennault's Fourteenth Air Force, headquarters of the Flying Tigers, near Kunming, "The Gateway to China."

For two years Betty served, fixing up three different Red Cross
clubs. She hid in trenches as Japanese Zeros and American P-40
fighters had dogfights overhead; she scrounged food from the
countryside to feed the men who filled the clubs. In March
1944, when the Air Transport Command was losing a plane a
day flying the Hump, Betty helped keep the airfield canteen
open twenty-four hours a day. One night when a group of ATC
crews showed up, all Betty had to feed them was a case of peas,
tea, and bread.

Betty became a club director, and her problems mounted. A
ping pong tournament at the bomb squadron recreation hall

had to be canceled: The prospective participants had gone off on a raid, and most of them had gone down in the China Seas.

One night during a dance, a *jingbao*, Japanese bombing, came. The crowd of men and Chinese university women serving as hostesses dashed into the slit trenches—slit trenches for two. Later the women were forbidden to attend the dances. Nine who had shared the trenches during the *jingbao* had become pregnant.

Nineteen hundred and forty-four had been a disastrous year for the Allies. There were rumors that the Japanese were targeting Kun-

Betty Heath stationed with the Red Cross at the Fourteenth Air Force base headquarters of the Flying Tigers.

ming. The colonel told the women that if the Japanese did come, they should take off to hide in the hills. And if anything went wrong, he added, knowing how the Japanese treated women, he had given orders to his officers that they should shoot the women.

It was a nerve-wracking time. Betty wrote: "As the days in China went by, I found that I was emotionally and physically burned out." She received a thirty-day pass and was soon on her way home.

There had been so little news available in the Far East that when Betty returned to America she felt she "had been gone from this planet a long while. I had somewhat of a time trying to readjust."

Betty found her mother ill; she asked for and received assignment to the Oakland Naval Hospital, where she worked with the injured, including many marines, for the next five years. She felt fortunate "to be back in one piece." She had lived at the end of the world for two years, where a plane came and went every three minutes. Now, when she hears the crop dusters in their propeller planes flying over her farm in Idaho, she often thinks back to the joys and sorrows of those days.

Betty Heath Oberst married after her service with the Red Cross in the Oakland Naval Hospital, and she and her husband had three daughters. Besides being a housewife and mother, Betty took in foster children and spent almost thirty years manning the telephones for the local chapter of the Red Cross for much of its Service to Military Families program. She has also done volunteer work on behalf of laws on child abuse and domestic violence. Today, after quadruple coronary bypass surgery, she leads a quiet life on the family farm, which includes some babysitting for her three grandchildren.

Phyllis Braidwood Dolloff performing with the Flying Tiger Band, Kunming, China, 1944.

Red Cross worker Phyllis Braidwood Dolloff at a small gate in a
village near Kunming, China.

Phyllis Braidwood Dolloff was thirty-two and married when late
in 1943 she also flew over the Hump to Kunming, the home
base from which the women were posted to outlying areas. Phyllis was assigned to work for the men of the Signal Corps, who
were dug deep into the low hills. After a short time there orga-
nizing special recreational events for the men, she was transferred to Yangkai, about two and a half hours by jeep from Kunming. Yangkai was a bomber base where the B-24 and B-25

squadrons were stationed, along with the ATC fliers. While she was there, so many planes and crews were lost that Betty wrote in her diary: "Damn war! Damn, why is it that young men will never live again! The emotional strain is hard to take."

One trip out in the field included a station where the ground troops were training Chinese army units and a Signal Corps unit near the Japanese-held border of Laos. Phyllis found that the ground troops were completely different from the men at the air bases. With the GIs, she wrote, "one could almost reach out and touch their loneliness."

The men everywhere in China were overjoyed to see the American Red Cross women, and though there was filth, disease, overcrowding, injustice, poverty, and constant fear of the Japanese bombers, many of the women, like Phyllis Braidwood Dolloff, hated to leave the Chinese people when the war was over.

After her service with the Red Cross, Phyllis Dolloff had been very active in both state and county health matters. She also found the time to co-author a sociology textbook and has traveled extensively, visiting sixty-three different countries.

In June 1945, when she was thirty-five, Gene Sawyer also became a Burma Rooster—one who had flown from India over the Himalayas into China. At Kunming, Gene was the only Red Cross woman in the group who would not remain there. She was assigned to Kweiyang, five hundred miles up the Burma Road, the supply lifeline to China. Kweiyang in Chinese meant "Expensive sunshine," and Gene noted, it rained most of the time. Since no flights were available, Gene made the trip to Kweiyang by army truck convoy. It was a rugged, tough, and dusty trip. When she reached Kweiyang, Gene found that it was so isolated that the only recreation for the servicemen was the Red Cross club with its snack bar, sports and game programs, popular music, and news from home.

One morning she woke up to the wail of an air raid siren, signaling the Japanese surrender and the end of the war. As the men slowly filtered home or on their way to reassignment, the club was closed. In October Gene was assigned to Tsingtao to open a Red Cross club for the Sixth Marine Division there. She arrived in Tsingtao two days after the Japanese surrender, and found the once-popular luxurious resort city on the Yellow Sea a ghost town. Only the poorest of the Chinese residents and the European refugees from the internment camp remained.

The Red Cross Club was organized, the first ever to serve the marines. "Four thousand marines came to our grand opening and from then on we were swamped. Most of them had come from Pacific Islands instead of going home after the war."

Official photo of Red Cross worker Gene Sawyer, who served in China until June 1946.

By New Year's 1946, men were converging on Shanghai from the surrounding war areas to be demobilized and sent back to the United States. A Red Cross club, with its recreational programs and companionship, was sorely needed. In March Gene was sent to Shanghai to help found it.

The club became "a service center for men and women in the military, navy, OWI, USIS, and United National rehabilitation agencies that were beginning to arrive." It was plush for China: offices, lounges, locker rooms, swimming pool, bowling alleys, ballroom, and canteen. Gene's job was publicity, which kept her busy preparing a club newspaper and articles for the Shanghai press and radio.

By Easter, the rest of the military personnel began to leave Shanghai. "The city seemed more and more Chinese. Army units moved up north to join the marines in their final mop-up operations. Navy men came on leave from Okinawa, Korea; others came from the occupation forces in Japan."

American forces thinned by the end of June. The China theater closed, along with the club. Gene returned to America. She looked out from her bucket seat in a tired military plane as it flew over San Francisco Bay and saw huge letters on a hillside spelling out a message for returning war-weary Americans:

WELCOME HOME, WELL DONE.

The American Red Cross had indeed done well in China.

Gene Sawyer worked in Hawaii as a radio announcer, producer, and writer after the war. In 1950 she became a Foreign Service officer and served for fifteen years in Burma, Indochina, Indonesia, and Washington, D.C., as a writer and producer for the Voice of America. She continued to work for the Voice of America in Honolulu from 1966 until 1970; from 1970 to 1980 she was a student and volunteer at the University of Hawaii.

From 1985 to 1992 Gene edited the United Nations Association newsletter, and was a tour guide for the Friends of the East West Center in Honolulu. In addition, she was a volunteer for a number of community organizations including the symphony society, where she is currently a volunteer, and the Mission Houses Museum.

28

With the Army
Through Europe

Alice Niestockel was twenty-three when she joined the American
Red Cross to serve overseas. After she arrived in England, her
first days were spent learning to make donuts and giant quanti-
ties of coffee and how to drive a huge truck. She and the other
Red Cross women mastered the techniques and took the clubmobile all over Britain, serving the American troops training for
the invasion of the European continent. Sometimes the GIs were
wounded or killed in the pre-invasion exercises. As Alice noted,
"The work was hard and tiring—working long hours and seeing
firsthand what a serious, deadly matter war was."

It was not until mid-July 1944, after the successful Allied land-
ings on Normandy on June 6, that Red Cross Clubmobile Group
B was told to report for shipment—it would be the first Red
Cross clubmobile unit to land in Normandy. The eight Red
Cross two-and-a-half-ton trucks were loaded onto an LST, and
the twenty-four girls assigned to the unit joined the throng of
GIs swarming about the landing craft.

Alice Niestockel, sporting GI shoes, in England with the Red Cross, June 15, 1943.

They crossed the Channel, and on July 16 the LST landed close to a pontoon bridge. The trucks were driven over the bridge, onto Utah Beach, which the Americans had captured at the end of June. By the time Alice arrived, the beach had been cleaned up somewhat, but it was still strewn with barbed wire and scattered wrecked vehicles. As the women landed they were greeted by a French farmer who offered them all a drink. Alice took a few swallows and hated it. It was Calvados. The farmer had obviously enjoyed it. He was "one happy fellow."

Later that day the women drove on to Cherbourg, where they stayed briefly, and then continued on to Trévières, where they were attached to the First Army, V Corps, on July 25. From that time on they would follow V Corps, always behind the front, from Normandy to Czechoslovakia. Wherever V Corps went, the Red Cross girls went. At this point their unit had eight Red Cross trucks, three supply trucks, and one cinemobile. Two enlisted men were assigned to their group, to serve as technicians. Officially the Red Cross women were attached to the Special Services group, and the girls went out into the field to serve the troops wherever Special Services sent them.

At Trévières the women lived in tents, as did the men of the First Army. They lived eight girls to a tent and slept on the cots and bedrolls they had brought with them. From headquarters at Trévières they were sent out to different units each day. Sometimes they parked in open fields, sometimes in the woods. They

Red Cross clubmobile at AAA Group in Normandy.

ate in the army camps, in open-air messes. In their tent city at Trévières they ate in the chow lines with the GIs.

The women had learned to put lipstick all around the edges of their flashlight lenses so that only pinpoints of light shone when they were turned on. It was strict blackout in tent camp. Security was also strict. Every tent was given the password for the day. Special Services informed the Red Cross girls before they set out for the field what the password was. It could be a word like "strawberry", or "orange", or the name of an American sports figure. It was needed to enter the tent city again.

Eventually, V Corps left Trévières, and the women followed the tanks and the trucks. The roads of Normandy were very dusty, and they passed pastures full of dead cows, lying on their backs, bloated.

Anytime Alice ate or drank something, she felt she was smelling the scent of death in the air.

One day when the military caravan had briefly stopped, one of the GIs came up to the Red Cross truck and asked Alice if she wanted to see a dead German.

"I was curious, so I went with him down the road a bit, and there I saw her." It was a dead German woman in a camouflage suit, in the fork of a tree alongside the road. She had obviously been a young sniper.

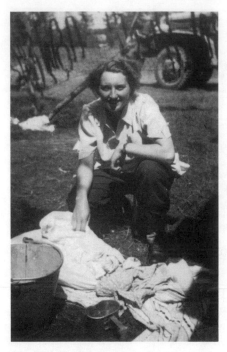

Alice Niestockel attending to business on laundry day in Normandy.

"I stood there and stared," Alice recalled, "and was relieved that she was no longer alive. One more sniper gone!"

V Corps was headed to Paris. The army passed through Ste. Mère-Eglise, where the Allies had beaten back the Germans, on to St. Lô, which the First Army had fought for and won on July 18. As they went along the narrow streets, the Red Cross women had to drive their wide trucks slowly, skirting the rubble of bricks and debris. Alice did not see a single civilian. Most villages were as quiet as tombs. The Red Cross clubmobile continued to follow the First Army, V Corps:

"We proceeded on, traveling as always in convoy.

"Whenever we stopped, if it was for any length of time, we were sent out from the encampment to serve wherever ordered. But we always had the army with us. An armed guard in his own jeep shepherded us.

"The next place we put into was Château Balleroi. It had been a German field hospital, but now it was only a shell of a building. There was no running water. The toilets did not work properly and overflowed. There were German pants and belt buckles scattered about in the yard. In the garden was a patch of freshly turned earth, and we decided to dig underneath it, thinking that wine was buried there. We dug, and did find a bottle—an empty one with the name of the German soldier who was buried there. We quickly placed the bottle back and covered it with dirt. We had learned that the French and Germans were extremely clever about hiding their wine supply, and it was a

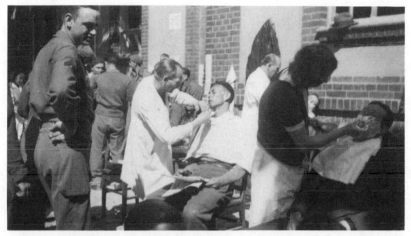

American POWs getting cleaned up by German civilians, Naumburg, Germany.

game with us to locate it. We had found wine under coal and wood piles and in one instance under a manure pile.

"The château had received no bomb damage, but the inside of the building was completely empty. The Germans had obviously left in a hurry, taking with them their wounded from the Normandy fighting.

"We brought out cots from the clubmobile, and our helmets. When we were traveling we had to use our helmets as latrines, for there was no toilet facility in the truck."

Still following the First Army, the women's next field assignment was in the Chambois pocket of France. The Chambois pocket had seen close, deadly fighting, a prelude to the forthcoming Battle of the Bulge. One of the GIs told Alice he was dismayed that the Red Cross women had been sent there. There were, unbeknownst to Alice, seventeen hundred German prisoners of war in a valley near the village.

Alice noted her impressions of the village on scraps of paper that she rediscovered in a suitcase side pocket almost fifty years later:

"We entered the town, and there were trucks, and tanks, and papers all over the street. Smoke was still coming from the houses. Outside in the fields were dead Germans stacked, awaiting burial. There were piles of guns, cameras, binoculars, and so on,

Red Cross clubmobile in Pilsen, Czechoslovakia. (Photo credit: Signal Corps, U.S. Army, 166th Signal Photo Co.)

which had been removed from the Germans, stacked on the street sides. Out in a field I saw a horse that had been hit. It stood looking like a statue."

Returning from the field assignment to the Chambois pocket, they returned to the command post, following a tank with two German prisoners riding on the fenders. Alice noted that the prisoners seemed very young and frightened.

There was one jarring incident on the way to Paris. As they were driving along a narrow street in a little village, someone threw tomatoes at the truck. It was not the splatter that bothered Alice, it was the thought that here were French people who were German sympathizers. A little farther along, the contents of a chamber pot were thrown at the clubmobile from the upper window of a house flanking the street. Alice shrugged off the incident, which was so unlike the warm welcome they had received on most of their trip.

Just on the outskirts of Paris, V Corps and the Red Cross truck stopped in Sceaux, where the girls were billeted in a private house that had been occupied by a German general before his troops had been forced to retreat. He had obviously left in a hurry, for the furniture, including the beds, was still there.

The next day, August 25, 1944, the whole convoy drove into Paris with the other Allied forces. It was liberation day.

"The crowds were crazy. They were happy, they were screaming, and they were kissing the GIs. The Parisians were in a riotous, joyful mood. They were liberated! They waved bottles of wine in the air, they drank wine, they hugged any soldier they could reach. One old Frenchman came up to me, commented on my uniform, and asked what I did. I said that I served

German POW doing KP with his pockets bulging with Red Cross clubmobile reject donuts. Pilsen, Czechoslovakia.

a thousand to two thousand men a week. '*Mon dieu, les Américains!*' he said, shocked. Because of the language difficulties he really believed I was a lady of the evening. I walked away and then looked back. The old man was still shaking his head.

"We were there only for that day. The French and the GIs marched in a parade. They looked tired, but sharp. I was proud of them. Then we moved out and traveled toward the front."

The convoy of the V Corps, followed by the clubmobile, now headed toward Belgium. Finally they stopped outside Liège.

The Red Cross girls were billeted in a monastery. They parked their truck in the huge open compound—the first women ever to be allowed inside. Using the monastery as a base, they traveled out into the field. It was cold. The women put their Red

When the Red Cross clubmobile women had to evacuate Eupen, Belgium, Kay Cullen was ill, and had to be left behind. She was taken to Verviers Hospital, where she was killed during the German bombing of the Battle of the Bulge. Alice Niestockel later visited Kay's grave in the Henri Chapelle Cemetery near Liège.

Cross raincoats on over their uniforms, and often wore their helmets. Alice had secured parachute boots, and wore them. She also wore long underwear, both top and bottom. "Anything to keep us warm, for often there was snow, mud, and ice."

In spite of the cold, the women cheerfully dispensed their donuts and coffee and put the favorites on the record player: "In the Mood," "Sentimental Journey," and "Paper Doll." "Paper Doll," a sad lament for a loved one who has chosen someone else, was often requested by an unhappy GI who had received a Dear John letter from back home. And there was dancing, even in the snow. The front, for a moment, seemed far away.

The women snatched whatever free time they could to wash their clothes. They washed their underwear with army soap and dipped their slacks and jackets in gasoline. Their blue battle dress began to assume a reddish haze from the gas. The pants and Eisenhower jacket would eventually drip dry, and then be aired out.

When they were at the monastery the monks would often come into the clubmobile to talk to the girls and watch them make the donuts. Many times they brought gifts of tomatoes and eggs.

From the monastery the V Corps, with the clubmobile trailing, stopped at a small village, where the girls were assigned quarters at a very prosperous-looking house. They went in to settle down before going out into the field and were quite surprised at the lushness of the furnishings. In the bedrooms were wide, low-slung beds, with red velour drapes at the windows. It was only when Alice went to bed that night that she realized where they were. Under one pillow were fifty new condoms. Exploring further, she found a whole gross under another pillow. It was, indeed, a former house of prostitution.

The convoy pushed on eastward and next set up camp in the Hürtgen Forest, where there had been heavy fighting in late November. It was cold and it was muddy; it rained and then snowed. It was a tent city again, and the girls were fortunate to have a potbellied stove in their tent; when in camp they kept it stoked with wood. Some of the GIs in the forest slept in pup tents, and as the snow came down it would pile up on their shoes, which were poking out. From the tent camp the girls were sent out to adjoining areas, one of which was a replacement depot, which housed newly arrived troops ready to replace the soldiers on the line who had been killed or injured.

On assignment the driver of the clubmobile had to pay close attention, for there had been mines all over the area. Now signs were posted, "Mines cleared to ———." The point could be a hedgerow, or a line of trees.

There were guards stationed around the perimeter of the tent camp. If anyone tried to enter the area, he was challenged and asked for the password. One day one of the GIs had a shock as he tried to return to camp. He was asked for a letter of the password of the day, "omelet," and since he did not know how to spell "omelet" he couldn't give the answer. It took a lot of talking for him to be passed by the guard. The GI swore that he was going to learn to spell before he got shot.

Christmas 1944 was spent in the forest. Cardinal Spellman had come to celebrate mass with the GIs. There was snow on the pine trees, and it looked as though they were in a fairyland, the war far away. The mass meant a great deal to the GIs.

The convoy continued eastward. The next stopping point was Eupen, in Belgium, not far from Malmédy, where the infamous massacre took place. The Red Cross women were billeted in the attic of a small hotel. Before they had time to be assigned to serve the troops out in the field, they were routed from the hotel in the middle of the night. The Germans were shelling the village. An officer came into their room to tell them they had to leave immediately. "And don't take anything with you," he ordered. They had been sleeping in their clothes; now they began tossing their trunks, duffel bags, and suitcases down the stairs, hoping to see them again—someplace. They had to leave the cots and the Christmas presents. Alice grabbed a radio and three light bulbs, and they all hastily got into their clubmobile and joined the convoy heading out of the village. One of the Red Cross women, Kay Ann Cullen, assigned to another club-mobile said she was sick, and so the officer decided that she could not leave. "He said he didn't know whether we would be captured or whether we could secure food or shelter." But she had to be left behind. (Alice heard later that Kay Ann Cullen had been evacuated to a hospital near Liège, which was hit by a bomb. Kay was killed.)

The convoy drove all night, with no lights. The moon was not bright, so the going was slow for the eight Red Cross trucks and the supply trucks. It was also cold. The truck wasn't heated, and since it had only canvas panels on the sides, the bitter wind came in. They finally arrived in Herve, a small town in Belgium.

Word came that the Germans were breaking through into the area from all directions. The women were told that they must try to find a place to stay, since the U.S. Army's First Division was billeted in the town. The women went to several houses before they found one where the attic could be made available to them.

There was no water in the attic and no toilet, so they had to go down to the living quarters to use the facilities there. Alice went down to ask for hot water so often that she was known as Mme. Hot Water. The family was obviously very poor. The girls gave them some PX supplies, but they could not give them any food. Alice was able to speak to them in her rudimentary French and understand their Belgian-French. While they were in Herve, the Germans kept sending over paratroopers, and GIs were posted in the center of the town, shooting at them with rifles. Alice never saw them hit one.

When the weather cleared, thousands of American planes

passed overhead on their way to bomb the German position in the Bulge area. Alice remembers that there were so many planes the women could hardly see the sky.

The convoy went through village after village, sometimes stopping to set up camp, followed always by the clubmobiles, which would be sent out into the field. The GIs the Red Cross now served were both the replacements and the combat weary. They treated the Red Cross women like queens.

When they hit Germany, there was a new feeling in the air. Fraternization with the enemy was not allowed, and the Germans had been evacuated from the villages where the troops were camped. The villages were closely guarded at a set perimeter. Now the Red Cross's records were not to be played over the loudspeaker. The atmosphere was definitely different, but the girls continued to go out to the troops, making donuts and coffee, and they were grateful when the luggage and Christmas presents they had to abandon in Herve suddenly appeared again.

Eventually they were stationed at Naumburg, Germany. The Red Cross trucks were asked to go out to the prisoner of war camp, which the Americans had captured. It had been used by the Germans to hold American prisoners, and it was now being used for German prisoners. Most of the American prisoners were still there, and Alice was dismayed when she saw them. They were dirty and ragged looking, and their khaki shirt collars were so filthy they looked as if they were made of leather. Before the men started to get cleaned up, they came to the Red Cross truck to drink coffee and eat the donuts. They then went off to have their hair cut and faces shaved by local German men and women barbers. When they came back to the clubmobile it was hard for Alice to recognize them, with their cut hair and clean faces and clothes.

By the time the convoy started off to cross the Rhine River, the bloody Battle of the Bulge was over and the First Army had seized the bridge at Remagen intact and Allied troops had poured across. V Corps had built the pontoon bridges for their crossing, and now Alice and the others were to go over into Grafenwöhr. The GIs guarding the bridges were somewhat apprehensive. Alice was sure that they were worried that the women would have trouble aligning the truck wheels with the tracks of the bridge; if they skewed to the side, the whole convoy would be delayed. But the women got the trucks over safely.

They were billeted in a huge military barracks that the Germans had used for their tank crews before abandoning it. The place was dirty and the walls were covered with all kinds of filthy graffiti.

The convoy went from town to town, and the routine was the same. As the military took over all the Germans were asked to come to the town square and drop their guns, their binoculars, and their cameras in a huge pile. The women were billeted in the houses in the towns but sent out into the field. In Elsenborn, where the convoy arrived in April 1945, the women were stationed in a house that had a huge shell hole in the roof that went through the second floor and down to the kitchen. Lying in bed, Alice could look up through the shell hole and see the stars. At night the air was filled with the sight and sound of the buzz bombs—the V-1s that the Germans sent streaking across the sky, aimed at London.

On the convoy's way to Czechoslovakia, the army wanted to show the Red Cross women Buchenwald. The army asked for volunteers to go there and see the results of the German atrocities.

Alice volunteered, and it was a sight that she will always remember. Dead bodies were stacked in trucks. Bodies were stacked like cordwood next to the incinerator; inside, Alice could see partially burned bodies. The only people alive were sick and emaciated. When Alice looked at the bodies lying on the floor, she couldn't tell which ones were alive and which were dead.

Down in the basement she saw the hooks where the Germans had hung the prisoners like slabs of meat as they tortured them. There were the firehoses that, they heard, the Germans had put in the rectum or mouth to torture the inmates. Everywhere were signs of ugliness. The ground was covered with bloody bandages, ashes, dirt, and old clothes. There were empty black boxes stamped with the swastika, awaiting the ashes of the cremated. A scoop lay nearby. Alice saw the lampshades made of human skin. She was shocked and angry. "Death is too good for the Germans responsible for these outrages."

The convoy headed out again, traveling fast since there was no German resistance in the area, though there were still snipers about. In one German village, the women were housed in a beer garden-cafe complex. As Alice was going in the door, she heard a shot. A piece of the concrete step struck her foot as a bullet ricocheted away.

In Pilsen, Czechoslovakia, the Red Cross group was billeted in an old German army barracks. The army used the German prisoners to help clean up the camp area. Alice noticed one prisoner in particular. As he was cleaning Alice could see his pockets bulging with donuts that had been in the garbage, the rejects from the first batch of the day. She also often saw him taking and then eating handfuls of fat, congealed in a tin, which had been discarded from the donut machine earlier in the day. Obviously he was starved for fat, since the German fat supplies had been commandeered for the war effort.

It was also in Pilsen that the Red Cross and the GIs had a gala celebration, a dinner dance held in the barracks hall. There were twenty-four Red Cross women and many, many GIs. Some of the women had carried their evening gowns with them from England, and this was the first chance they'd had to put them on.

Eventually, Alice became a section captain, and she now no longer made trips out into the field. She missed the GIs—in spite of the war, the GIs were a happy lot when they visited the clubmobile. They joked and they laughed, and they had a great sense of humor. Now that the war in Europe was over, many were eager to go off and "fight the Japs." Alice was promoted and put in charge of scheduling, and the time in Czechoslovakia passed quickly. V-J Day came and the Red Cross women were ordered to go home on leave. The end of the Pacific war was anticlimactic for Alice's Red Cross unit, whose world had been centered on the European conflict.

Alice, along with many of the others, was sent to Le Havre, where she boarded a liberty ship. It was an all-female ship, full of German war brides. After an easy crossing, the ship landed in

New York, and Alice was on her way home by train to Akron,
Ohio. After a visit with her family, she returned to Bad Wildun-
gen, Germany, and served GIs in the area from Wiesbaden to
Berlin.

It was a far cry from the long days and nights of wartime duty,
which Alice would remember for many, many years. And she
always would be proud of the five battle stars she was awarded
for her service in the European theater.

*Alice Niestockel stayed on in Europe, managing American Red Cross
hotels and office buildings until 1948. After a year in Los Angeles with
an oil company, she returned to Columbia University to complete her
master's degree. She then worked in the management divisions of several
firms in New York before retiring in 1984 and moving to Florida.*

PART TEN

They Also Served

Highlights of other women who served, and contributed to the book.

Many more accounts written for the author were received but limited space precludes their inclusion in this book. The author can only express regret—and many thanks.

Army Nurse Corps

Katharine Morse Dunworth served with the Michigan 298th General Hospital team, which operated in Frenchay Park, a few miles from Bristol, England, for almost two years before landing on Utah Beach, Normandy. The 298th was the first general hospital operating in France after the invasion. It later moved on to Belgium, where it set up operations in tents. Katharine served almost three years overseas before returning to the States on October 1, 1945.

Lorna McCook Fancher flew in a C-47 cargo plane to India and served as an anesthesiologist in Chinese and American operating rooms. She lived in a mat-walled *basha*, ate army K rations, and felt far removed from the war fronts. She did not come home until February 1946. After the war, she continued her nursing as a civilian.

Eleanor Wagar Gustavson joined the Army Nurse Corps in November 1942. She was trained and sent with the 69th Station Hospital to Casablanca, then to Oran, Algeria. There the hospital complex was mainly under tents set up in a former vineyard. When fraternization rules concerning officers and enlisted personnel were relaxed, Eleanor married a staff sergeant in Oran's city hall; since both could not serve at the same hospital, Eleanor moved to the 70th General, which went to Naples, Italy, then on to Pistoia, near Florence. There they set up in a Fascist parachute school. Eleanor at last was caring for the wounded men who fought in the Italian campaign.

In the spring of 1945 Eleanor was rotated back to the States. She worked at Rhodes General Hospital in Utica, New York, until her husband returned in the fall, and they were both discharged from the army.

Winifred Jacobs Walker served at Camp Luis Obispo, California, from early 1943 until a year later, when she was sent to the 76th General Hospital in Leominster, England. There she helped patch up the wounded from the Normandy landings and the advance through St. Lô. After a few months her unit landed on Utah Beach and set up a hospital near Carentan. They moved on to Liège, Belgium; at that time fighting was still raging a few miles away in Aachen and Cologne. There was a steady stream of war wounded. "So many sad cases—one young fellow, with his right side torn open, exposing the ribs, stomach, and intestines." In December, during the Battle of the Bulge, the nurses were on alert with evacuation orders. The German buzz bombs came, and one night in January 1945, the hospital had a direct hit, with twenty-five men killed. Finally with victory over Germany the hospital was closed and evacuated in July. Back in the United States Winifred married her fiancée on October 20 and received her discharge October 27, 1945.

Navy Nurse Corps

Josephine Plummer Lopatto was sworn into the Navy Nurse Corps in February 1943, and worked in U.S. navy hospitals in the States before she was sent in December to Brisbane, Australia, to work at Fleet Hospital 109. Josephine spent Christmas there, surprisingly with turkey and Christmas trees, then was sent to a new hospital in the middle of a jungle near Hollandia, Dutch New Guinea. The nurses had packed away their white uniforms and donned khakis, so were surprised to hear over shortwave radio Tokyo Rose advise them: "Those thirty-five nurses in Hollandia had better wear their prettiest dresses on Easter Sunday, for it would be the last time they would ever wear them." The nurses ignored Tokyo Rose.

Shortly after President Franklin Roosevelt died, Josephine received her orders home, since the tour of duty was for only eighteen months. When she arrived in San Francisco, she "felt like getting down and kissing the ground."

Madonna Timm Hanf enlisted in February 1942 and served in a navy hospital in California for over a year before she also was sent to Brisbane, Australia. There the hospital admitted great numbers of navy and marine casualties, sometimes at the rate of five to seven hundred each day. Madonna served there until she was transferred to Hollandia, Dutch New Guinea, in February 1945, where she worked in dermatology treating men with "jungle rot." By April, before the war in Europe was over, she received orders that her overseas duty was over. She hitchhiked home via plane and went on to nurse in the Philadelphia Navy Hospital until her discharge after the Japanese surrendered.

Women's Army Corps

Helen Rosen Ersley was part of the 149th WAAC Post Headquarters Company, which served in Algiers. Helen, along with eleven other WAACs, were called the Silent Twelve because of the secrecy of their work. They were part of Headquarters Force 141, a joint British and American effort that worked on the planning stages of Operation Husky, the invasion of Sicily.

Margaret Warren Powell served as a cook and a typist. She lived through the buzz bomb raids on England, landed on Omaha Beach, and became part of the 385th Signal Company mobile communication unit, which operated in France, Germany, and later Luxembourg. She served until her discharge in September 1945.

Mary Schisler Salm was sworn into the WAAC in February 1943 and was among the first group that was assigned to the Air Force and sent to California. It was there at the Stockton Field Army Air Force Base that the slander campaign against the WAAC was most visible. The women had a bad reputation on the West Coast long before they arrived: The civilian women who worked at the Stockton Ordinance Depot dressed in khaki, "got drunk in bars, were foul mouthed and caused fights." The townspeople believed that they were WAACs. The rumors of the low morals of the army women were widespread. "We were," Mary wrote, "in a world that originally had been the exclusive world of men, and some were angry and some thought we didn't belong in that world."

Mary went on to learn teletype and then was sent to London, assigned to the Army Airways Communication System that sent and received messages from stations all over the world. Mary worked in London through the German V-2s that came over regularly, through V-E and V-J days, until she boarded the *Queen Mary* on November 4, 1945. She became a civilian nine days later in North Carolina.

Isabel Phyllis Smith Greenhaugh lived in a wooden cabin during her service in Brisbane, Australia, and a tent in Hollandia, New Guinea. The latter area was a jungle territory where the natives greeted her with a "Merry hello" in missionary English.

Isabel worked as part of a counterintelligence corps. She celebrated V-J Day in Manila and returned home after three years in the military.

Clara Myal endured the usual WAC training—learning and marching—and was assigned to the army administrative school at Fort Leonard Wood, Missouri. She worked at post headquarters in the personnel department and met a special man who joined the Fifth Ranger Battalion before being sent overseas. Clara stayed at Fort Leonard Wood until she was discharged. She and her Ranger married after the war.

Etta Hall Johnson, at the age of 101, is the oldest living WAC veteran. She enlisted in February 1943, after taking a secretarial course to qualify for joining. She was, she said, a middle-aged lady, but she persevered, completed basic training, and was assigned to the radar training school at Victorville, California. She retired to Orlando, Florida. The city's mayor proclaimed her hundredth birthday, June 21, 1993, "Etta Johnson Day."

M. Barbara Elliott was trained at a radio and television school to learn the Morse code and how to send and receive messages. She was assigned to "a secret Monitor station in the Radio Intelligence Division of the Signal Corps." When she was stationed there, she applied for officers' training but was rejected because she had answered the question, "What are you doing now and where are you stationed?" It was secret then—and remains secret now.

Rose McCafferty Horn was a volunteer in a group to test chemically impregnated clothing (she later learned that the chemicals were mustard and lewisite gas). The women were not permitted to remove their clothes, except shoes and socks, for the entire six-day week. They were permitted to wash their face, hands, and feet daily. In one month they had four showers and four sets of clean clothing. Rose was sent to Battle Creek in November 1943 and stayed in the army until February 1946. She has suffered from skin cancers and precancerous growths, for which an appeal to the veterans authorities is pending. Yet Rose is still "proud to have served in the WAC."

Alice Killips Lonzinski served at the Rome Air Force Base in New York as a clerk-typist at a Quartermaster Corps warehouse. She fell in love with a private, and they were married in the base chapel. Pregnancy followed, and Alice was discharged with honor in March 1945.

Gertrude McSpiritt was sent to Presque Isle, Maine, and assigned to the Air Transport Command as clerk-typist in the passenger terminal office. Later she was lucky enough to be sent for further duty to Bermuda, which she called the "land of enchantment."

Barbara Boyd Bixby Hughes enlisted on her twentieth birthday; her father, an army man, was proud of her. Her mother was not. It was not the thing a "proper smart-set socialite" should do. (Her mother finally relented, but that attitude was all too common fifty years ago.) Barbara worked at breaking top-secret specs for the draftsmen at the headquarters of the Second Air Corps at Colorado Springs. She trained for overseas service and spent the next year in Calcutta, at Hastings Air Base, headquarters of the China-Burma-India theater. Technically her job was as a "statistician" in maintenance; she kept track of the status of all planes in the CBI, gathering information about the planes, the pilots, and the air crews for headquarters. Barbara found Calcutta to be a city of extremes of poverty and richness.

Most of those at the base, including Barbara, greeted the end of the war in Europe with a "that's nice" reaction, tempered by the daily reports of the casualties in their own theater. They were much more aware of the constant rivalry between the Chinese Nationalists and the Communists, and the lack of a united front against the Japanese. Then the atomic bomb was dropped. Prisoners of war started to arrive at headquarters; Barbara and the shrinking staff were busy taking inventory and disposing of aircraft and supplies. "Thousands of airplanes were unceremoniously pushed over cliffs into the sea. What a waste!" Soon Barbara took a "rough and scary flight" and eventually was home again.

Waves (U.S. Navy)

Marianna McNees Heaney was stationed at the Midshipman Training School at Northampton, Massachusetts, as a public relations officer. She later served in educational services, at the naval hospital in St. Albans, Long Island. She had married while in the service, before her husband was sent overseas. After two years' separation, her biggest worry was whether she would recognize him when he came back from Panama. She did.

Bernice Freid in WAVE formal photo.

Bernice Sains Freid served the navy in "the mundane job" of readdressing mail for the servicemen, until she appealed to her female commanding officer to use her yeoman training as a typist, a request that was granted. Bernice said that being in the WAVES made her feel rich, although all she owned fit into one suitcase. In April 1946 she was discharged. Leaving the navy was hard for Bernice—"I felt sad, kind of lost"—but her service made another dream come true. Bernice went on to college, under the GI Bill.

Mildred Friedrich Beltmann reported for storekeeper duty to her CO at the naval armory in Chicago by "saluting and reporting for duty, SIR!" The CO thereupon informed her group of WAVES that he didn't request them, didn't want them, but he'd make the best of it; if any of them stepped out of line it'd be captain's mast—a small court martial. In six months' time he requested more WAVES for Ship's Company! Mildred remembers her WAVE duty with great nostalgia. She married her fiancé after he returned from overseas in the summer of 1945, and they were both discharged from the service in September.

Ardelle Knopf Courtney, attended Hospital Corps School at Great Lakes after boot camp, and was assigned to duty at the U.S. Naval Hospital, Brooklyn, with training in neuropsychiatry. Later she was transferred to the naval hospital in Aiea, Hawaii. There she helped with patients from the Pacific theater of war and many of the survivors of the Bataan Death March. "It was war at first hand, seeing the mental anguish along with the physical pain of those young men." Mildred felt she was pioneering with the WAVES. "We were really feminists and didn't know it."

U.S. Marine Corps Women's Reserve

Josephine Smith Runnells Brown lived in a barracks with ninety-nine other women while she worked in the General Supplies Department at Marine headquarters in Washington, D.C. She was transferred to San Francisco, where she became "a very good keypunch operator" in the IBM department. She was discharged after the war was over, in October 1945. In the late 1970s she returned to Washington to show her husband and her daughter Henderson Hall, where she had lived and worked during the war. Josephine asked the guard if they could enter. He yawned, and Josephine could tell what he was thinking: Geez, another one of those old WWII broads.

Lana Marjorie Lacey Kight was sent to California after boot camp. She served as company clerk for Headquarters Company, and in public relations for a time. As she wrote, "Nothing big or dramatic occurred in my personal military life, but I felt proud to be doing my bit."

Emma Knapp Matson received her orders in August 1943. After training she was sent to Arlington, Virginia, to work in marine headquarters in the Annex to the Pentagon, in the Quartermaster Department. She applied with her best friend for service in Hawaii. When she arrived in Honolulu she discovered her friend had been killed in a jeep accident there; more disasters followed. She was "date raped" twice because she was "too trusting." In spite of these upsetting events Emma was glad that she had served. She was mustered out in January 1946. As she wrote almost fifty years later, she is, "as they say, once a marine, always a marine."

Marie Butler Bachtell enlisted in the marines in September 1943. She received twenty-one weeks of training in airplane mechanics and worked briefly at the air station in Cherry Point, North Carolina, assigned to the division testing engines. She volunteered for duty in Hawaii and was stationed at headquarters Flight Section there. She was one of ten women in the aviation branch; she was in complete charge of an advanced trainer, an SNJ-4. "It was my job to keep the plane in flying order, gassed and oiled and cleaned." She checked out the aircraft on the flight line every morning before she turned the craft over to a pilot. Later she was also put in charge of the commanding officer's plane, a dual-engine Beechcraft C-45 transport. Marie thought then that the aviation branch of the marines was more open to women in the service. "However," she remarked, "the old-time line sergeants felt the Corps was being ruined." Marie was discharged after the war was over, in December 1945.

SPARS (U.S. Coast Guard)

Emma Jean Betts Bolcar was trained in military ways and was sent to cooks and bakers school at the Biltmore Hotel in Palm Beach. She was assigned duty at the Sutter Street Hotel in San Francisco. After the war was over she remained in the service in Washington, D.C. until April 1946. "Today," she wrote, "I realize how our basic training gave us courage to face any situation in life."

Women's Airforce Service Pilots

Jane Straughan learned to fly long before the war. She and her husband, Al, who was later commissioned in an aerial mapping group, flew almost every weekend. She trained in Houston, Texas, in Jacqueline Cochran's program, and was then sent to the New Castle Air Base at Wilmington, Delaware, to participate as a WASP. Jane ended up ferrying all types of civilian and military aircraft from Piper Cubs to multiengine airplanes. She went on to the WASP Officers' Training School in Orlando and then to Palm Springs for Pursuit School. When the WASP were disbanded in December 1944, Jane was, as all the women were, sad to be leaving flying, the occupation they loved.

Alice Stevens Rohrer became "a fairly good pilot" before she was old enough to drive a car. After intensive training, she was assigned to Perrin Field, Texas, where her work consisted of maintenance testing, instrument instruction, and ferrying. Alice had only a few months "to enjoy my hard-won status as a military pilot before word of discharge came from Washington."

Betty Pettitt Nicholas learned to fly, acquired the minimum hours necessary to join the WASP, trained at Sweetwater, and then reported to Napier Field in Dothan, Alabama, where she worked as a maintenance test pilot. The CO at the base liked the WASP, and even after they were deactivated he continued to use them. Betty, who spoke Spanish, was assigned to be the instructor for the entire Mexican student officer contingent that had been sent to Napier for instrument training. On her last evening at the base, as five of those officers serenaded her outside her window, she wept sad tears. Her career as a WASP was over.

Office of War Information

Elizabeth Dorsey Rooney served with the Office of War Information in London when the buzz bombs were common. "You waited for the sound of the crash, and then went on with your life. The best way I can describe it is to cite a cartoon that appeared in *Punch.* It showed a street in London with men obviously on their way to work, but each having one ear grossly exaggerated. The caption read: 'These buzz bombs don't bother us a bit.'" Elizabeth survived all the attacks, and when the war in Europe was over, she was placed in charge of the U.S. State Department library in Brussels.

Margaret Kaveney began work for the federal government in Washington, D.C., in 1935. When the OWI was established after the war began, she transferred there, working both in Washington and San Francisco. In 1944 she went to the Honolulu office and served as confidential secretary and administration assistant to the director of psychological warfare for the Pacific Ocean area. It was from the OWI offices in Honolulu and Saipan that radio and leaflet material originated, urging the Japanese to surrender. After V-J Day Margaret was transferred to the Tokyo office. She served as a civilian employee of the federal government in both the Japanese and German occupation zones.

Office of Strategic Services

Beatrice Stevenson Latham joined the OSS in 1943. She was sent to London, where she was "loaned" out to the British Foreign MI-5 and MI-6 office. Her assignment was to register and distribute all incoming and outgoing intelligence. It was a busy time since the Allies were preparing for the D-Day landings, and contact with the French increased daily. After the landings and the armies proceeded eastward toward Germany, often the news was depressing as the OSS learned of military setbacks or that some of the Allied French collaborators had been killed. After the Battle of the Bulge in December, the V-2s landed around the clock and Beatrice had several close calls. "It was a very scary time," she wrote. Shortly after, she transferred to Secret Intelligence, where the work involved drops behind the lines and getting the individuals back to Britain for interrogation. It was at this time that Beatrice married her husband, a man she had known in Washington, then serving with the Canadian army. After their marriage he went off to Holland and Beatrice continued her work in London. She was there on V-E Day when "London went crazy." She left later that month for Wiesbaden, Germany, to OSS headquarters in the largest German champagne factory, just outside the city. After V-J Day the mission was moved to a village across the Necker River from Heidelberg and Beatrice was able to see her husband, who had been discharged from the Canadian Army and taken a position with UNRRA. When he was ordered to London, Beatrice resigned, and in October 1946 they left Germany. After a short stint in Vienna, they both returned to the United States. Beatrice had been pleased that she had adapted to foreign duty so that she was not looked upon as an "Ugly American."

Cornelia Rockwell O'Neill worked in Washington for two years after college, and in the summer of 1944 she joined the OSS. She went to London to work in the Research and Analysis division; her job was to help provide political and economic background and analysis that could be of vital importance to the Allied armies, as well as to the OSS agents and their missions.

After Paris was liberated on August 25, 1944, Cornelia was sent there the next month, one of the first women to arrive after the Nazis left. There were still snipers in the area, and the women were required to wear all their gear, including helmets. It was hard work at the OSS. The winter of 1944-1945 in Europe was very cold, and there were shortages of everything. Then there was the "scare of the Battle of the Bulge at Christmastime when rumors had the Nazis coming back to Paris through Belgium. The first joys of the liberation had worn thin with the succeeding troubles, and it seemed more important than ever that we keep trying to provide accurate information and analysis for our agents and the army."

American Red Cross

Lois White Monroe was assigned as a patient-recreation worker at the University of Michigan's 298th U.S. Army General Hospital, which was stationed at Frenchay Park near Bristol, England. She was a jack of all trades, in charge of all musical instruments, visiting the bedridden patients, helping out in the craft shop, running ping pong and pool tournaments and jam sessions. As she wrote, "One of our implied missions was also to be a living reminder of the American girls the GIs had left behind." After a year and a half, Lois followed her unit to the Continent. At a dinner dance in Cherbourg she met a tall, dark and handsome first lieutenant of the Ninth Air Force. Six months later, on April 12, 1945, they were married at the tent hospital near Liège, Belgium.

Ruth Herrmeyer Bergeson worked as a secretary at a field hospital on Kauai Island, Hawaii, writing reports, visiting patients, helping with the recreation program, and often visiting other field hospitals on the island, which had become a staging area for troops who were leaving for the Pacific battles. She was later transferred to a replacement depot on the island of Oahu, in a sugarcane field not far from Schofield Barracks. It was there that she met her future husband. They were married in July 1945, and while they were on their honeymoon on the Big Island of Hawaii, the bomb was dropped on Japan.

Mary Read La Belle was assigned to a clubmobile, first at Plymouth and then at Norwich, in England, before they crossed the Channel and landed at Calais. For a short time the women served the area around Rouen; they were then assigned to the Eighty-ninth Division, which was on its way to join Eighth Corps under General Patton's army. The clubmobile traveled with the army in convoy across France and into Germany. After the surrender they were stationed at Fulda and sent out to serve the various outposts of the occupation army. Of her service Mary Read La Belle wrote, "We hoped that we brought a little bit of what the troops believed in into focus, and that we made them smile."

Charlotte Bazeley Tuckerman was a staff assistant at a Red Cross club in Assam attached to the Forty-fourth Air Service Group which serviced the combat cargo and troop carrier planes that flew over the Hump and made air drops into Burma. It was hot and the two thousand enlisted men were bored, so Charlotte and the other Red Cross women were kept busy trying to provide as much recreation as possible—bingo, cards, music, dancing. After ten months in India, Charlotte was sent to China, first to Kunming, which was filthy, then to the more civilized Shanghai. After a four-month hiatus back in the United States, Charlotte was reassigned to Germany with the army of occupation and stayed there for two and a half years working in clubs in Bremerhaven, Bremen, Heidelberg, and Frankfort.

Chapter Notes

Introduction

This section was based on discussions with various military historians; for more up-to-date information on the military, I relied on the Women Military Aviators bulletins, the Women in the Military Service for America Memorial Foundation publications listed in the bibliography, and on the newspaper reports from 1994 also listed in the bibliography.

Army Nurse Corps

1. The material on Harriet Holmes was based on her oral history in the collection of The Center of Military History, Washington, D.C. Interview by Lt. Col. Delores Wozniak at the Retired Army Nurse Corps Association Convention in San Diego, California, on May 24, 1982; edited by Maj. Wynona Bice-Stephen and Lt. Col. Carolyn Feller; used by courtesy of Iris West, Army Nurse Corps Historian, The Center of Military History, via my good friend researcher Jake Jones of Gloucester, Virginia.

2.　The material on Edith Shacklette Haynes is also from The Center of Military History, Washington, D.C. This oral history interview was conducted by Maj. Susan McMarlin at Bolling Air Force Base, Washington, D.C., on April 9, 1983. Courtesy Iris West via Jake Jones.

3.　Susan Eaton Fox wrote a long, very vivid account of her service for the author. It is unfortunate that my limited space precludes using all of it as originally submitted.

4.　Jeanne Kahn Paul wrote up her experiences for the author, relying on her brief army nurse file for accurate dates.

5.　Emma Porteus wrote up her wartime account for the author.

6.　The material for the chapter on Signe Skott Cooper was written for the author.

7.　The story of Reba Zitella Whittle's experiences after being shot down and captured by the Germans is from an abstract by Mary E.V. Frank, "The Forgotton POW: Second Lieutenant Reba Z. Whittle, AN," an individual study project dated February 1, 1990. It is in the archives of The Center of Military History, and is used courtesy of Iris West, historian, via researcher Jake Jones.

8.　Elise Berger Hines wrote up her account for the author and supplemented it with a booklet prepared by her father, based on her letters home during the war (for more details, see the list of unpublished manuscripts in the bibliography).

NAVY NURSE CORPS

9.　Kathryn Lichty Piaskowski wrote her account for the author.

WOMEN'S ARMY CORPS

10.　Charity Adams Earley very kindly wrote up her experiences for the author for this book, although she had written a book on her wartime service, *One Woman's Army: A Black Offficer Remembers the WAC.* Material for the first paragraph of the chapter comes from the book, the rest from her account to the author.

11. Gertrude Morris wrote about her experiences in the WAC for the author.

12. Christine Shanklin Hunt wrote up her war memoirs for the author.

13. Gertrude Pearson Cassetta wrote about her experiences as a WAC for the author.

WAVES (U.S. Navy)

14. Betty Doolittle Belcher LaFontsee wrote about her service for the author and also sent many clippings and photos.

15. Dorothy Barnes Stephens and her husband, James R. Stephens, wrote up a very detailed and lengthy account for the author of Dorothy's service in the WAVES, which they stated was under copyright by them. Permission was granted the author for a one-time use in this book. The chapter was written based on this lengthy account.

16. Mary Jane Stutsman Schneider wrote up her account for the author and also enclosed material from World War II.

17. Vi Myers wrote her account of her war service about twelve years after leaving the navy. She made this material available for the author's use.

U.S. Marine Corps Women's Reserve

18. Dorothy Lloyd Hughes wrote an account of her marine service for the author.

19. Ruth Walters Ward wrote up a long account of her experiences for the author's use.

SPARS (U.S. Coast Guard)

20. Jan Thorpe Macauley was extremely helpful in contacting the other Coast Guard women, in addition to writing up her account for the author. Martha Lucinda Vaughn Butler

wrote a very lengthy account for the author. Doris McMillan Breed wrote her account originally for a SPAR booklet of memories of those veterans in the northwest area, which she made available to the author.

WOMEN'S AIRFORCE SERVICE PILOTS

21. Florene Miller Watson wrote up her account for the author and also sent a wealth of clippings.
22. Frances Roulstone Reeves had just finished writing up some anecdotes of her WASP experience for her children and grandchildren when she received my request for her story. She kindly supplemented this material with answers to my specific questions.
23. Beatrice Falk Haydu wrote up her account of her WASP service for the author and, in addition, clarified the history of the organization.
24. Geri Lamphere Nyman's chapter is based on her letters to the author.

OFFICE OF WAR INFORMATION AND OFFICE OF STRATEGIC SERVICES

Introduction. The material about Honolulu OWI activities comes from a letter to the author from Margaret Kaveney of Springfield, Illinois.

25. Grace Dolowitz Levitt wrote up her account of service with the OSS for the author.
26. Elizabeth Davey Velen had written up her experiences with the OSS, with a view to publication, shortly before her recent death. Her account was too brief for a book, but her husband, Victor Velen, kindly gave me permission to use any or all of her account in my book. This chapter contains some of that material.

AMERICAN RED CROSS

27. Marion H. Hamilton wrote up her account of service with the Red Cross for the author. Janet L. White wrote an account of her experiences some time ago, in detail, and sent a copy to the author for use in this book. Eunice Wardwell Maupin wrote up her account of Red Cross service for the author, and also enclosed a long letter written to her parents on December 27, 1944, detailing the activities in New Guinea, for the author's use. Betty Heath Oberst wrote a long account of her Red Cross work for the author. Phyllis Braidwood Dolloff wrote extensively about her experiences for her children and their progeny and kindly made a copy available to the author. She also wrote additional material for the book. Gene Sawyer wrote an account of her days with the Red Cross in China for the author.

28. Material for the chapter about Alice Niestockel was secured by twice-weekly phone conversations, over a lengthy period, with the author; in addition, Ms. Niestockel supplied maps and clippings to supplement the telephone interviews.

THEY ALSO SERVED

Most of the accounts here were based on material written especially for the author; there is one exception that must be mentioned. WAC Mary Schisler Salm had previously written up her war experiences and donated them to the Southern Historical Collection, University of North Carolina Library, Chapel Hill, which holds them as Mary Margaret Salm Papers, no. 4257. Richard A. Schrader of the university's Manuscript Department kindly gave permission to the author to publish any material contained in those papers. This brief account was written from the Salm Papers material, and from many letters to the author from Mary Salm.

BIBLIOGRAPHY

BOOKS

Department of the Navy, WAVES National. *A Pictorial History of Navy Women 1908–1988.* Washington, D.C.: Department of the Navy, 1990.

Earley, Charity Adams. *One Woman's Army: A Black Officer Remembers the WAC.* College Station: Texas A&M University Press, 1989.

Grun, Bernard. *The Timetables of History.* New York: Touchstone/Simon & Schuster, 1991.

Holm, Jeanne. *Women in the Military: An Unfinished Revolution.* Novato, Calif.: Presidio Press, 1982.

Keegan, John. *The Second World War.* New York: Viking, 1989.

Kurzman, Dan. *Day of the Bomb.* New York: McGraw-Hill, 1985.

Scharr, Adela Riek. *Sisters in the Sky.* Vol. 1, *The WAFS.* St. Louis: The Patrice Press, 1986.

———. *Sisters in the Sky.* Vol. 2, *The WASP.* St. Louis: The Patrice Press, 1988.

Seeley, Charlotte Palmer. *American Women and the U.S. Armed Forces: A Guide to the Records of Military Agencies in the National Archives Relating to American Women.* Revised by Virginia C.

Purdy and Robert Gruber. Washington, D.C.: National Archives and Records Administration, 1992.

Soderbergh, Peter A. *Women Marines: The World War II Era.* Westport, Conn.: Praeger, 1992.

Treadwell, Mattie E. *The Women's Army Corps. United States Army in World War II.* Washington, D.C.: Office of the Chief of Military History, Department of the Army, 1954.

Verges, Marianne. *On Silver Wings 1942–1944: The Women's Airforce Service Pilots of World War II.* New York: Ballantine Books, 1991.

Weatherford, Doris. *American Women and World War II.* New York: Facts on File, 1990.

Wheal, Elizabeth-Anne, Stephen Pope, and James Taylor. *Encyclopedia of the Second World War.* Secaucus, N.J.: Castle Books, 1989.

Unpublished Manuscripts

Beger, J. "Rusty in the Army: The Story of Elise Berger Hines (Known to Her Friends in the Army as Rusty)." Typescript written by her father, using excerpts from her war letters, undated.

Salm, Mary Schisler. "Duty, We're in it Heart and Soul. Victory is Our Only Goal." Mary Margaret Salm Papers, no. 4257, Southern Historical Collection, Library of the University of North Carolina at Chapel Hill.

Stephens, Dorothy B., and James R. Stephens. "Love and the U.S. Navy Versus the Empire of Japan." Typescript, 1993.

Pamphlets and Booklets

Bellafaire, Judith. *The Army Nurse Corps: A Commemoration of World War II Service.* Washington, D.C.: U.S. Army Center of Military History, undated.

Magid, Ken. *Women of Courage: The Women Airforce Service Pilots of World War II.* Lakewood, Colo.: K. M. Productions, 1993.

Meid, Pat. *Marine Corps Women's Reserve in World War II.* Washington, D.C.: Headquarters United States Marine Corps, Department of the Navy, 1968.

Monroe, Louis White. "Frenchay Revisited, 1942–1992." (American Red Cross, 298th General Hospital), undated.

Piemonte, Robert V., and Cindy Gurney, eds. *Highlights in the History of the Army Nurse Corps.* Washington, D.C.: U.S. Army Center of Military History, 1987.

Thomson, Robin J. *The Coast Guard and the Women's Reserve in World War II.* Washington, D.C.: Coast Guard Historian's Office, undated.

Williams, Betty Jane. *Women Airforce Service Pilots. World War II, 1942–1944.*

PERIODICALS, NEWSLETTERS, AND NEWSPAPERS

Douglas, Deborah G. "WASPs of War." *Aviation Heritage.*

Hasenauer, Heike. "From WAAC to Regular Army." *Soldiers,* May 1992.

Miller, Bryan. "Woman Flier Leads News Battle." *New York Times,* October 30, 1977.

Williams, Betty Jane. "Women Airforce Service Pilots, WWII." *Ninety-Nine News,* September 1990.

The Register, Summer 1994. Women in Military Service for America Memorial Foundation, Inc. newsletter.

WMA News, Spring 1994. The Women Military Aviators, Inc. newsletter.

Daily Star, Oneonta, New York, July 27, 1994.

Press and Sun Bulletin, Binghamton, New York, March 8, 1994.

New York Times, July 28, 1994.

INDEX

272